The
Word
in Play

The Word in Play

LANGUAGE, MUSIC, AND MOVEMENT IN THE CLASSROOM

SECOND EDITION

by

Susan A. Katz
Judith A. Thomas

·P·A·U·L·H·
BROOKES
PUBLISHING CO.®

Baltimore • London • Sydney

Paul H. Brookes Publishing Co.
Post Office Box 10624
Baltimore, Maryland 21285-0624

www.brookespublishing.com

Typeset by Barton Matheson Willse & Worthington, Baltimore, Maryland.
Manufactured in the United States of America by
Victor Graphics, Baltimore, Maryland.

Previous editions of this book were published by Prentice Hall and Allyn & Bacon.

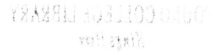

Library of Congress Cataloging-in-Publication Data
Katz, Susan A., 1939–
    The word in play: language, music, and movement in the classroom / by Susan A. Katz
and Judith A. Thomas. —2nd ed.
        p.   cm.
    Rev. ed. of: Teaching creatively by working the word. © 1992.
    Includes bibliographical references and index.
    ISBN 1-55766-616-4
        1. Language experience approach in education—United States.   2. Language arts
(Elementary)—United States.   3. School music—Instruction and study—United States.
4. Poetry—Study and teaching (Elementary)—United States.   5. Movement education—
United States.   I. Thomas, Judith A., 1937–   II. Katz, Susan A., 1939– Teaching creatively by working the word.   III. Title.

LB 1573.33 .K28 2004
372.6—dc22   2003061104

British Library Cataloguing in Publication data are available from the British Library.

CONTENTS

ABOUT THE AUTHORS

Susan A. Katz is an internationally known poet, author, and language arts specialist. Her work has received numerous awards and appeared extensively in journals such as *The American Scholar* and literary publications and anthologies, such as *When I Am an Old Woman, I Shall Wear Purple* (edited by Sandra Haldeman Martz, Papier Mache Press, 2003) and *In the West of Ireland: A Literary Celebration in Contemporary Poetry* (edited by Martin Enright, Enright House of Ireland, 1994). Her published poetry collections include *An Eye for Resemblances* (University Editions, 1991), *Two Halves of the Same Silence* (Confluence Press, 1985), and *The Separate Sides of Need* (Song Press, 1985).

Ms. Katz has served as a consultant for Disney Interactive and as a contributing editor to the Silver Burdett series *The Music Connection* (Scott N. Foresman, 2002). She has also served as Book Review Editor for *Bitterroot,* a international literary magazine. She has read her poems at colleges, universities, bookstores, and libraries, including the Donnell Library Center at the New York Public Library. She is a member of the American Psychological Association, the Academy of American Poets, the Associated Writers and Writing Programs, and the Poetry Society of America.

For more than 20 years, Ms. Katz has conducted student poetry workshops, independently and for New York State Poets in Public Service, and she has facilitated international teacher workshops based on the philosophy of integrating the arts into learning curricula. She has worked with students preschool-age through college-age and continues to work with educators and children to address timely issues through poetry intervention. She has conducted workshops sponsored by the Yale Prevention Research Center, along with Orff-Schulwerk specialist Judith A. Thomas, using poetry as a means of coping with emotions generated by the events of September 11, 2001.

Judith A. Thomas is an internationally known Orff-Schulwerk music teacher, author, and professor. She has taught and continues to teach Orff-Schulwerk certification and master classes, world music, and the integration of arts (poetry, music, and movement) to undergraduate and graduate students in the fields of music and general education, often in collaboration with her colleague Susan A. Katz.

Ms. Thomas is an honorary member of the American Orff-Schulwerk Association, having served as President and Conference Chairperson. She holds a master's degree in music in piano from the University of Illinois and a special certificate from the Orff Institute in Salzburg, Austria, where she subsequently co-directed summer workshops and taught. As well, she co-directed a course in Dartington, England, called "Theme and Variations" with Margaret Murray, Editor of the *Music for Children* volumes by Carl Orff (European American Music, 1978).

Ms. Thomas served for 37 years as Music Director and Orff-Schulwerk Specialist at the Upper Nyack Elementary School in Upper Nyack, New York, and as districtwide Arts Coordinator. She is currently conducting teacher workshops independently and for Scott N. Foresman's Silver Burdett series *Making Music* (2002). These workshops are based on the concepts of integrating the arts in education and working with teachers and children in exploring ways for them to express themselves joyfully through language, music, and movement.

FOREWORD

Even before children are born, they respond to rhythm and the tone of their mothers' voices. Kolata (1984) wrote about experiments in which babies were read *The Cat in the Hat* during the last 6.5 weeks of gestation. After birth, these babies sucked to activate a recording of their mother reading this book, rather than a recording of their mother reading *The King, the Mice, and the Cheese.* Over the ages, mothers have sung lullabies to soothe their infants and recited nursery rhymes to their toddlers. Indeed, the early vocalizations of children in the crib consist of language play. Ruth Weir, in her classic book *Language in the Crib* (1962), studied the presleep monologues of her toddler son and found that they were rich in sounds, noises, and rudimentary rhyming.

During a recent research project, we watched a group of preschoolers viewing a popular television program. They all responded to the characters' singing and dancing. The children got up, swayed, danced, and sang with much elation and spontaneity. Actually, the music and rhyming appeared to be the most enjoyable aspects of this excellent program for children, arousing the liveliest interactive participation. Simple poems appeal to very young children who are gradually becoming capable of understanding metaphors. Stella Vosniadou (1987) wrote that the pretend namings children use in play are the precursors of metaphors. The child, for example, who uses a banana as a telephone or a block as a cup is in effect rehearsing the language essentials and abstract symbolism needed for the more mature understanding of a metaphor. Psychologists have become increasingly excited about the importance of what has been called *theory of mind,* or a person's ability to understand that other people have different beliefs and thought processes. An intriguing body of research suggests that children's imaginative play and even their early games of pretending and make-believe are critical for enhancing the power of human consciousness (Harris, 2000; Leslie, 1994; Singer & Singer, 1990).

The play of words, rhythms, and music not only can enhance the fun of childhood and the beginnings of self-awareness and control of consciousness, it can also play an important role in the broader educational process, as a body of research on the utility of sociodramatic activities in the classroom has indicated (Singer & Lythcott, 2002). Beyond formal education, we propose that the kind of experiences afforded by these exercises can contribute to the richness and variety of human consciousness. Cognitive processes and ongoing thought take two forms. Jerome Bruner (1986) called these the narrative and paradigmatic modes of experience, and Seymour Epstein (1999) delineated these as the experiential and the logical-sequential thinking styles. The narrative or experiential features of consciousness involve imagery, fantasy, daydreaming and night dreaming, and the use of story-telling, metaphors, and parables to organize experience and wisdom. The paradigmatic or purely cognitive-logical style is more rare, physically more demanding, and necessary for rigorous abstract or mathematical thought.

The extensive work on "successful intelligence" carried out by Robert Sternberg and colleagues at Yale University has demonstrated that effective intellect involves more than the abstract processes tested by traditional IQ tests. It also draws on practical or street-wise intelligence and creativity, which are both reflected most often by narrative or experiential modes of thought (Sternberg & Grigorenko, 2000). Using imaginative exercises, Susan A. Katz and Judith A. Thomas open the way for children and their teachers to expand their conscious uses of the important narrative, experiential, and creative aspects of human intelligence.

We believe that all of us are capable of producing poetry, if we define poetry in its broadest sense. We can conjure up images of people we love, objects we find desirable, or scenes in nature that bring us solace or perhaps frighten us. Katz and Thomas offer a wealth of material to demonstrate how teachers can lead children step by step into the world of imagination and show them how to use thoughts and images to create a pleasing poem.

Observing a workshop that the authors carried out with teachers and other professionals, we saw the evolution of words into gems of poetry. The teachers-as-participants (TAPS) used their bodies, their voices, and their thoughts to combine stimulus words that Katz and Thomas offered and fashion brief lines, followed by stanzas, and then the final poem. All were amazed and delighted to listen to the other participants who, one by one, called out their different meanings, similes, and metaphors for the same word. *The Word in Play: Language, Music, and Movement in the Classroom* offers teachers just such an experience. Each chapter builds on the one before with many examples of words and music. The authors are fine writers who keep the reader involved and eager to try out the exercises. They have a talent for making poetry come to life through music and movement. And always the word is paramount.

Dorothy G. Singer, Senior Research Scientist
Jerome L. Singer, Professor of Psychology
Department of Psychology, Yale University

REFERENCES

Bruner, J. (1986). *Actual minds, possible worlds.* Cambridge, MA: Harvard University Press.
Epstein, S. (1999). The interpretation of dreams from the perspective of cognitive-experiential self-theory. In J.A. Singer & P. Salovey (Eds.), *At play in the fields of consciousness* (pp. 51–82). Mahwah, NJ: Lawrence Erlbaum Associates.

Harris, P. (2000). *The work of the imagination.* Oxford, UK: Blackwell Publishers.

Kolata, G. (1984). Studying learning in the womb. *Science, 225,* 302–303.

Leslie, A. (1994). Pretending and believing. *Cognition, 50,* 211–238.

Singer, D.G., & Singer, J.L. (1990). *The house of make-believe.* Cambridge, MA: Harvard University Press.

Singer, J.L., & Lythcott, M. (2002). Fostering school achievement and creativity through sociodramatic play in the classroom. *Research in the Schools, 9*(2), 41–50.

Sternberg, R., & Grigorenko, E. (2000). *Teaching for successful intelligence.* Arlington Heights, IL: Skylight Professional Development.

Vosniadou, S. (1987). Children and metaphors. *Child Development, 58,* 871.

Weir, R. (1962). *Language in the crib.* The Hague, The Netherlands: Mouton.

PREFACE

The ways in which creative elements can be incorporated into the classroom are limitless. Using language, music, and movement and all of the combinations they imply, this text offers one approach to integration of the arts by implementing the word in play. The following lessons, workshops, poems, and music extensions are designed to demonstrate the multiple rewards that may be found in the "now" of the process.

The first section of this book contains sample lessons (or scripts), many of which are reproductions of actual teacher–student classroom interactions. Annotations in the left column of the sample lessons highlight challenging situations that may arise and provide suggestions for how to handle them. The free verse poetry, music, and movement lessons in this book were developed and presented by Susan A. Katz and Judith A. Thomas from 1976 through the present. These lessons were originally geared to the fourth-grade level but can be adapted to any level by upgrading or relaxing response expectations. Edited poetry and extensions appearing in this text have evolved from original student and teacher works and reflect a wide range of creative responses. The following schools, colleges, universities, and conferences provided laboratory settings, wherein the philosophy and techniques that appear in this text were developed and continue to evolve. These venues allowed for a variety of formats: interactive settings with teachers-as-participants (TAPS), classes of students ranging in level from kindergarten to graduate school, whole-school groups in assembly settings, and national and international conferences.

Bank Street College, New York, NY

Birchwood Elementary School, Nanuet, NY

Caitlin Gabel School, Portland, OR

Edinboro University, Erie, PA

Franklin Avenue Elementary School, Bergenfield, NJ

George Mason University, Fairfax, VA

Grandview Elementary School, Monsey, NY

Hempstead Elementary School, Spring Valley, NY

Henrick Hudson High School, Chappaqua, NY

Liberty Elementary School, Valley Cottage, NY

Lime Kiln Elementary School, Suffern, NY

Mahwah Public School, Mahwah, NJ

Margetts Elementary School, Monsey, NY

Merrill Coltin Elementary School, Spring Valley, NY

New City Elementary School, New City, NY

New Haven School District, New Haven, CT

New York University, New York, NY

Suffern Junior High School, Suffern, NY

Trevor Day School, New York, NY

Tappan Zee Elementary School, Orangeburg, NY

University of Manitoba, Winnipeg, Canada

Upper Nyack Elementary School, Upper Nyack, NY

Vista Academy of Visual and Performing Arts, Vista, CA

Walker Elementary School, San Diego, CA

Wallace Middle School, Waterbury, CT

Warren Public Schools, Warren, PA

Yale University, New Haven, CT

LANGUAGE AS THE IMPETUS

The various subjects taught in the classroom as individual disciplines are fingers of the same hand. Language is the unifying element and the medium through which all subjects are taught. Therefore, it is imperative that teachers embrace the multiple inherent possibilities within the creative use of language and recognize that words are malleable and can be made ordinary or extraordinary, humdrum or holy. The process starts with a stimulus (e.g., colors, feelings, environments, fantasies) and evolves through verbal exploration of subject matter. Students and teachers-as-participants (TAPS) exchange ideas, react to one another's input, and then fashion their thoughts on paper through imagery (metaphor and simile). Experimenting with the potential power, nuance, sound, and substance of words through creative selection and juxtaposition, they commit emerging poems to paper and then share them. This sharing very often crests in a wave of excitement and enthusiasm. Some may see this as a successful ending, but for us, it heralds a new beginning.

EXTENDING THE PROCESS OF THE WORD IN PLAY

This new beginning can be further extended as a creative process into all areas of the curriculum through the complement of music and movement. Those common, everyday words, which were so painstakingly and thoughtfully selected and which proved to be uncommon (and even memorable) in the context of the poem, now become more than words. Their placement on the page, in the mouth, and within the body takes on a new dimension.

Words are found to have depth, height, weight, sound, speed, rhythm, nuance, timbre, form, melody, and texture, and they take on sensory characteristics. They whisper, scream, and smell of spring flowers or ocean spray. They burn, soothe, ooze, or melt. They are steps creaking in the night and thunder rolling over the mountains. They are the eruption of volcanoes and the softness of cumulus clouds.

Language is active and constantly in motion, refusing to recognize barriers between subjects. Together, teachers and students discover that words need not be confined to paper or even to the mouth but can be translated into a rich movement vocabulary of slashes, presses, thrusts, glides, flicks, floats, dabs, and wrings (to use Rudolph Laban's descriptions of movement qualities). Words also can be arranged into movement forms, sung, overlapped, layered, whispered, shouted, sped up, slowed down, spoken or sung canonically, or accompanied. In this manner, language skills are extended into and beyond music and movement, encouraging the weaving of individual strands of the curriculum into a cohesive, whole fabric.

SPANNING THE CURRICULUM THROUGH THE WORD IN PLAY

Progressive lessons are fashioned to engender a sense of familiarity with the unfamiliar with language as the bridge; words become user-friendly tools to understanding. This book is designed to provide opportunities for students and teachers to

- Discover the multiple layers of language: Colors, feelings, and fantasies provide doorways into the realm of poetry: metaphor, simile, sensory observation, and language experimentation.

- Realize inherent extension possibilities: Word qualities, rhythms, and tempi inspire music and movement responses.

- Envision specific focus possibilities: Poems and prose embrace the season of rebirth, growth, and renewal through word-seeding; extensions explore the sounds of words and create melodic enhancement.

- Commemorate history in the making: Poems interpret, articulate, and give personalized, in-depth meaning to events that change and redefine the world. Extension allows for personalization, internalization, reflection, and heightened expression.

- Reflect on the visual details of field trips: Poems linger over the lines of an Alexander Calder sculpture and envision the flight of birds or the menace of monsters in steel structures through imagery; movement gives impact and definition to these images.

- Reveal the limitless parameters of the natural world on site: Teachers become students of observation as poems recreate rich tidal pool environments and movement mimics tidal rhythms.

- Experience science: Poems wait to burst out of a prism, layers of rhythms reflect insect calls, and melodies sing to the emergence of monarch butterflies.

HOW TO USE THIS BOOK

This book is primarily for the classroom teacher, but others will find it very useful as well. It is helpful for the teacher who is learning to be a teacher. The curriculum specialist who teaches a special subject such as music, movement, or art will delight in the ways this book can lead him or her in working creatively with students, as will the teacher who works with students with learning disabilities or students in gifted and talented programs. The curriculum director will also benefit from using this book by finding out how to integrate learning themes across the curriculum. The techniques for enhancing self-discovery and self-awareness might successfully be used by anyone in any field dedicated to the development of a child's creative life.

Classroom Teachers

This book was written as a creative language/music/movement curriculum, revealing the interrelationship between individual basic subjects. It is meant to provide some new cross-curriculum insights that the classroom teacher can incorporate into his or her own teaching design. Although the book was written to encourage the classroom teacher to dare to try language arts as a creative departure point for music and movement extension, it does not exclude the possibility of utilizing the talents of the school's specialists. Teachers interacting with one another create a positive happening, incorporating all of the talents within the school that best serve the process. This collaboration can and should create a healthy bond between teachers in different teaching areas and foster an innovative atmosphere through "music classes and creative writing opportunities being considered core curriculum" (Levine, 2002). The text documents this approach by providing

- A teacher-scripted text for developing language arts curriculum (Section I)

- A teacher-scripted text for developing music and movement expansion lessons from existing classroom subject matter (Section I)

- An in-classroom workbook for the teacher that uses basic theory examples in language arts and in elemental movement and music (Section I and Appendix A)

- A resource book of representative teacher and student poetry and musical examples to share in the classroom and use as inspiration for students

- A departure point for designing and complementing personalized creative teaching experiences

- A flexible guide to exploring rich and varied landscapes from which to choose personal directions

- An enrichment for everyday classroom subject areas and events

- A workbook from which materials (examples, ideas, concepts, or modus operandi) can be excerpted

- A companion text for everyday teaching, with its many variables and possible pitfalls, including a chapter on troubleshooting (Chapter 6)

Teachers Learning to Be Teachers

This book, read in total, will help education students assess future classroom strengths and weaknesses and will provide good, solid examples of workable techniques. It can further be used as

- A college text for understanding the development of and reasons behind creative teaching

- A text that may be read to experience classroom pacing

- A guide to actual in-class experiences (e.g., reactions, responses, lack of responses) and ways in which these various responses may be handled (see Chapter 6)

- A guide to awareness of the scope of possibility in creative teaching and the acquisition of skills that will facilitate a multiplicity of techniques

- An inspiration to expand those areas that lend themselves to the creative classroom atmosphere

Music Specialists

This book can be used by the music specialist as

- A resource for those specialists who see music as a broad-spectrum activity, incorporating movement, improvisation, music, body percussion, small percussion, and found sounds (i.e., Orff-Schulwerk approach)

- A teaching guide for developing music concepts while using materials, ideas, events, and so forth from the general classroom and the school at large. Teaching in such an integrated style is essential for strengthening the cohesiveness of the students' day.

- A handbook for ways to draw on words as sources of inspiration for music and to evoke words that will result in substantial musical creations drawn from field trips, feelings, serendipitous class and school activities, and so forth

- An incentive for making music and movement concepts and theory an integrated and essential part of the school curriculum

Curriculum Specialists

In multiple areas, this text can be used in any of the ways mentioned previously or adapted to address student responses influenced by focus, subject area, or individual teacher goals.

PHILOSOPHY OF THIS BOOK

The philosophy of Carl Orff, music educator and composer, spanned an eclectic and broad educational landscape, encouraging and nurturing classroom play, improvisation, and exploration. Orff believed that "elementary music, words and movement, play, everything that awakens and develops the powers of the spirit, this is the 'humus' of the spirit" (1971, p. 245). Like Orff, we believe the rewards are enormous in offering students an intensified insight into their own language capabilities, with effects rippling outward to generate musical, rhythmical, and movement ideas.

In keeping with the Orff-Schulwerk philosophy, we endorse combining movement, language, music, rhythm, song, and improvisation and playing elemental instruments in order to form an amalgam that belongs in the general classroom, as well as the music specialist's room. In his autobiography, *Das Schulwerk,* Carl Orff stated that "the place where [the Schulwerk approach] can be most effective, and where there is the possibility of continuous and progressive work, and where its connections with other subjects can be explored, developed, and fully exploited... this place is in the school" (p. 245). This kind of instruction has to happen early:

> It is at the primary school age that the imagination must be stimulated, and opportunities for emotional development which contain experiences of the ability to feel, and the power to control the expression of the feeling, must also be provided. Everything that a child of this age experiences, everything in him that has been awakened and nurtured, is a determining factor for the whole of his life. (p. 246)

Curriculum Implications

We believe that this nurturing is developed through the integration of the arts and the intersection of subjects. To paraphrase part of a speech that Dr. Eliott Eisner gave at Stanford University, when science, social studies, physical education, and language arts are all well taught, they look like the arts. The aim of education is the creation of artists who can exercise creativity. We envision the artist as all teachers who explore the soaring spirit within, a spirit that when released, expands incrementally. Thus, the social studies lesson exploring medieval Europe becomes a modal melody in the music room and a poem in the language arts classroom. Word creations evolve into artwork that in turn are interpreted through movement activities in the physical education class and so forth. Happily, evidence supports that not only does this liquid learning inspire educational unity, it also greatly enhances the learning process.

Just how this integration and overlap can be accomplished has remained somewhat of a mystery, as few books address the total picture or offer techniques that specifically demonstrate how this fusion can be attained. Any number of books present the magic of children's poetry but offer only cursory insight into the process used to elicit it. Likewise, few teacher-training textbooks give in-depth, easily followed scripted language/music/movement arts templates. This book, based on more than 50 years of combined language, music, and movement in-class experience and experimentation, reveals pragmatic ways of developing crossover, evocative teaching skills. It suggests ways to consolidate activities in a cohesive manner without adding more than an introductory amount of content to already overcrowded curricula.

SUMMARY

In moving from theory to practice, it is critical that teachers believe in their abilities and realize that evocative teaching, while involving risk, opens doors to unexpected, unlimited vistas. Like all new experiences, there are moments of exhilarating success and other moments that leave us feeling somewhat lost and in over our heads. However, even in those moments when we flounder and when the process seems to have failed, the overall experience remains positive, as it fosters experimentation and, ultimately, trust in the creative process.

In our computerized, televised, push-button world, the need for artistic expression is powerful. The child who pushes a computer key needs also to be made aware of the ability to capture, internalize, and recreate everyday experiences through sensory awareness, imaginative effort, and introspective self-realization. He or she needs to be taught that ideas are the basis for all human creations—whether they are poetic, scientific, musical, or mathematical—and that ideas are conceived with words, born of language. The classroom needs to be a place of awe, in which all things are possible, and where learning delights the senses, stimulates the mind, and releases the body. This is the energized classroom, where the creative essence becomes palpable. It is our sincere hope that this book will offer teachers and their students an expectant, mutually fulfilling environment.

In a very real sense, using creative techniques to teach and teaching creative techniques are attempts to provide students and teachers with ways in which to name their world, and in naming it, expand it. Student and teacher word creations—shaped into poems and expanded into works involving movement, texture, form, melody and rhythm—flow with purpose from subject to subject. They are mini-celebrations of self, providing students and teachers with the power to unravel the mystery of themselves and the world around them.

Susan A. Katz's
Acknowledgments

I wish to acknowledge, with gratitude and love, the nourishment of my spirit by the following:

Donald I. Katz, M.D., my husband, my "pathfinder," the only love of my life for more than 40 years, and a man of infinite wisdom and gentle nature whose love for me is sustaining and whose faith in me, astounding

David L. Katz, M.D., my son; my friend; and a man of absolute honor, quiet dignity, and humbling intellect who has convinced me that "everything is possible"

Elizabeth C. Katz, Ph.D., my daughter; my confidante; a self-made, conscientious woman of amazing tenacity who does it all and does it well and who has inspired me, by example, to believe that the ultimate satisfaction in one's achievement is to be found in being able to say, "I did it my way!"

Catherine Sananes Katz, Ph.D., my daughter-in-law and daughter of the heart who can do just about anything better than just about anyone and who has the greatest capacity for love of anyone I have ever known

David Highfield, Ph.D., my son-in-law, an extraordinary father, an avid bike rider, a novice wine maker, and a man of strong convictions with whom I share the joys of friendship and laughter

My Grandchildren

Rebecca, of the "powerhouse" personality

Corinda, of the loving heart

Valerie, of the exquisite sensitivity (to whom I owe a special "thank you" for setting me straight about clouds)

Natalia, of the unshakable loyalty

Grayson, of the splendid spirit

Gabriel, of the winsome charm

Samantha, of the perennial smile

The sheer wonder of their being has expanded to infinite the horizon of my life.

Special thanks to:

Daniel Masterson, poet, professor, friend, and mentor, who taught me most of what I know about poetry and set the standard I aspired to as a teacher

Menke Katz, poet, philosopher, editor, citizen of the world, my dearly missed friend, and my unflagging champion, who never let me forget that "poets write poems. To not write is to not be."

Elaine Niefeld, Editorial Director, for her belief in this project and for providing the encouragement, intelligent insight, and constructive criticism that made *The Word in Play* possible

Amy Perkins, Assistant Editor, for her endless good humor and for never failing to return a telephone call or come up with an answer

Kimberly McColl, Book Production Editor, for keeping me on track, for sharing my enthusiasm, and for her amazing insights (into poetry in particular) and impressive wealth of knowledge, which made this final stage of production of the *The Word in Play* joyful

Jessica Reighard, Marketing Director, and all those who worked with us and behind the scenes at **Brookes Publishing,** my heartfelt and grateful thanks for making this a uniquely gratifying and rewarding experience

Thanks beyond measure to my co-author **Judith A. Thomas.** She has been, and continues to be, a source of constant delight, endless inspiration, astounding talent, and, most important, illimitable friendship.

Judith A. Thomas's Acknowledgments

I dedicate this book to my parents, teachers, teaching associates, and students who fed me good information, insights, and love throughout this art-filled life, and I do hereby give indebted acknowledgment and thanks to, in chronological order:

My parents whose vision of my education was limitless

Dean McDonald, a cousin who first drew me to music with his searing performance of the Tschaikovsky Piano Concerto in B Flat Minor before I even knew what music was

Lester Mather, whose love of piano and of sharing it with others invited me to the "feast"

The **art faculty of J. Sterling Morton High School** in Cicero, Illinois, for four invaluable years of discovering how lines can dance and colors sing and thereby providing a first understanding of the similarities between music and art

Zelah Newcomb of the Illinois Wesleyan University Preparatory Division, who gave invaluable insights into the musical capabilities of children

Dwight Drexler of the Illinois Wesleyan University Piano Department, whose kind and musical teaching lifted me to new pianistic places

Christopher Thomas, my son, who has "thought strangely" all his life in his view of art and music, as when he vocally "played" the Tappan Zee Bridge from an overlooking window in our Nyack apartment at the age of 3, and who has synthesized his abilities of acting, drawing, and composition admirably into his film scoring craft

Dr. Hermann Regner, Director Emeritus of the Orff Institute in Salzburg, for his extraordinary global vision and ability to expand graphics, music, and movement and to encourage us to do likewise, and to all of my Orff teachers, who ably promoted the philosophy that arts are "fingers on the same hand," **Barbara Haselbach** and **Verena Maschat,** to name two

My American Orff-Schulwerk associates, who have supported my work for decades and lifted everyone with their expansive musicalities, minds, good hearts and inspired teaching: **Tossi Aaron, Mary Shamrock, Danai Gagne, Doug Goodkin,**

Avon Gillespie, Jane Frazee, Arvida Steen, Judy Bond, and so many more

Long-time Nyack principals **Raymond Campbell** and **Barnett Ostrowsky** who understood the value of integrating the arts through the Orff-Schulwerk approach

My Upper Nyack Elementary School colleagues with whom I shared so many years of camaraderie, educational uplift, and music/drama activities and who reinforced the "big picture" of education: **Loretta Tito, Joanne Neibanck, Marion Anderson, Terry Dugan, Sue Plath, Pat Condello, Ruan Humphreys, Harry Sokolov** and also those teachers in the district at large: **Dal Jakobsche, Colette Tiktin, Bert Hughes, Flo Greenberg,** and more

Susan A. Katz whose drive, love of words, imagination, and rich knowledge of poetry have provided a culminating life's lesson

The students of Nyack public schools, Upper Nyack in particular, who, with their insouciance, willingness of spirit, creative sparks and intelligences, taught me the irrefutable worth of music in schools and how easily and effectively words, music, and movement can slide in and out of each other

Josef Solomon, my partner, who has consistently supplied loving interest, patience, and advice in the course of all of my book writings

I am beholden to you all, living and passed on.

INTRODUCTION TO
PLAYING WITH WORDS

THE REWARDS—TO OUR STUDENTS

You collect before us
drops of dew
on a morning rose
bright in the light
of a new day.

We know your faces
and your names
hauntingly familiar
like the image of oneself caught
beneath the surface
of a still lake.

You have moved us though
we have only met
in passing like a breeze
that turns the leaves showing
them a new view of the sun.

There is a wholeness
in this room as though
something less
than whole had just
completed itself
like a circle closing
like lips forming
circles around words
forming patterns
in the mind
poems on paper.

You have led us
time and time again
to that secret place
where children hide and poets
choose to wander
among the hills
of imagination.

Long after your tongues
have forgotten the taste
of our names we will be warming
ourselves beside the flame
we found blazing in your eyes.

—SUSAN A. KATZ

The scripts and information presented and the techniques suggested in this text can be applied by any teacher who is interested in exploring and developing integrated, overlapping, child-sensitive lessons and programs that use language as the bridge, connecting subjects that

- Draw from the essence of children's thoughts and interests

- Place a heavy emphasis on writing and vocalization

- Use a variety of learning modes (i.e., poetry, music, movement)

- Build a strong bond between teacher and student, teacher and teacher, student and student

- Provide learning tools for students, in a nurturing and wholly accepting environment

Furthermore, this book addresses the need to move freely and adeptly through the shifting landscape of the curriculum. It encourages the blurring of lines, which separate the individual territories of learning from one another, allowing for the integration of curriculum areas. It endorses the belief that there is reward in, and justification for, this type of teacher/learning unification, and it complements healthy, child-centered approaches.

ONE-TEACHER APPLICATION: PROCESS EVOLUTION

In examining the reality of a one-teacher approach to the multifaceted demands inherent in this book, the reader should know how the process came to be and how it lent itself to a one-person application. The process evolved over a period of some years and began with the introduction of a language specialist in residence on the elementary classroom level. At the beginning, the poetry workshops and the music and movement activities overlapped very little. The ineluctable problem became how to share most effectively these undeniably worthy student poetry creations beyond the borders of the individual classroom. The works were shared (in class) at the conclusion of each writing workshop, and the students' reactions to their own poetry and one another's was so intense that very often *they* posed the question: "Can we put our poems up in the hall on the bulletin board? Read them in other classes? Draw pictures to go with our poems?"

The students' need to share revealed that their creations deserved a broader showcase. At this point, the music teacher was invited to develop a 45-minute assembly focused around the poems created during the poetry workshops. Now the problem became a programmatic one: how not to bore; for no matter how vibrant the writing, the sheer numbers of students involved might make for a numbing kind of presentation. Clearly, more had to be accomplished than a marathon poetry reading.

This realization prompted the music teacher to return the students' poems to them for further consideration and reshaping. This meant reexamining them for rhythm and speech-play potential and possible music forms, for movement possibilities, and for locating those student poems that would be enhanced by melody. The subsequent reworking (by students, individually and in groups with teacher input) resulted in original poems that then were ready to move across the stage as well as be heard — to be *sung* and overlapped in canon rather than just spoken and to be *enhanced* by small percussion and body percussion accompaniment.

Now with rich word imagery, music, and movement evident within the student works, the process of creation moved in concentric circles among the language arts class, where students were editing and rewriting; the poetry workshops, where new techniques and skills were learned and honed; the homeroom, where time was given for further refinement and brainstorming; and the music room, where extended developments were created.

The resulting assembly delighted the senses. It captured the imagination and held the attention of those presenting and their audience. In analyzing the success of the presentation, we were struck by the diversity of input, and we concluded that curriculum layering enhanced the individual effort and made for an enriching experience. At that time it was not apparent that this experience was memorable for the students themselves in the language arts and music areas; skills and techniques resurfaced in positive ways, year after year. Of equal merit was that poetic techniques and skills were now appearing in daily classroom and music room work. Metaphors and similes were being used routinely in student writing, and movement and music exploration took on a new depth and richness. Having had the experience of applying these techniques to their works, students were now able to also use them to analyze masterwork poetry.

Another unexpected dividend was the discovery that the language arts specialist was using movement and music layering in the poetry workshops both to enhance and inspire student work. The music teacher was helping students create original, free verse poetry complementing sculpture graphics (see Section II, Chapter 8), and classroom teachers were using students' newly learned skills to increase enthusiasm for the extension process. Metaphors and similes that had been taught to enhance poetic imagery became devices to describe science experiments, current events, environmental issues, and so forth; a nature study of leaves became an impetus for movement lessons; and fall became the inspiration for reflective poems and musical modes that paralleled them. And so the process went.

Administrative and parental enthusiasm and encouragement developed for this kind of teaching, which produced outstanding creative results (e.g., poetry anthologies; poetry/movement/music assembly showcases; poetry/art ongoing bulletin board themes; enriched writing skills, cutting across the curriculum; cooperative, all-school writing focuses; classroom/school/community poetry publications; poetry collections created for fund raising). At this stage, much of the inspiration for themes and focuses began to come from the classroom teachers (see Section II, Chapter 13), and these teachers did much of the work within the framework of their own curriculum. The result was increased flow of ideas and interaction from student to student, class to class, teacher to teacher, and subject to subject. The evocative process strengthened teacher investment and fostered a sense of ownership. And so it is today as we present this book, confident from our experiences that a one-teacher application is indeed both possible and educationally sound.

HOW TO USE SAMPLE LESSONS

Scripting, in any text, is simply a way to illustrate interaction in a format that may guide others in creating their own lessons. No one can plan ahead (or script) the actual lesson or predict the infinite number of student responses, but studying scripting can build confidence in the lesson orchestration.

Sample lessons may be used as outlines for in-class presentations: Teachers and student teachers may wish to practice possible classroom scenarios by using sample scripts to create scripts of their own design, tailored to their specific classroom needs. As well, these scripts may be studied to build troubleshooting skills. Lines of questioning and commentary may be lifted from scripts for application in appropriate classroom settings. Finally, scripts may be used as maps to chart directions and ultimate destinations of lessons.

CONCLUSION

This book is mainly—but not exclusively—for the classroom teacher. The *music teacher* will find the level of music easy and applicable and may benefit from experimenting with the less familiar poetry skills. The *student teacher* in a college classroom or in the field will find the book useful as a projected vision of actual classroom interactions and as an introduction to the evocative process of creative teaching. An experienced teacher may wish to use this text in addition to ideas and applications of his or her own, or he or she may simply wish to experiment with materials and formats presented in this book. The *teacher of gifted and talented students* may use this book selectively to spark ideas or to develop new and extended projects with his or her students. In the special case of the completely *nonmusical teacher,* the book may still be effectively used by enriching the classroom through creative language aspects. The *language specialist* will find application of creative techniques valuable in enhancing skills and promoting enthusiasm for language development. The *art specialist* will find rich art resources in the words and movements of student creations. Furthermore, if teachers work together, they can create teaching teams that help children reach their creative potential!

THE COLOR POEM

Often, teaching poetry in the classroom is achieved successfully through imagery. This introductory lesson provides students with an insight into their own creative depths, helping to establish their "eye for resemblances."[1] Furthermore, it helps create the sense of language as a visual medium. Defining a relationship between the *image* and the *art* is the key to explaining how everyday words can be patterned to create memorable language experiences (e.g., poetry). Poems do not begin with ideas so much as they begin with words that are developed into language patterns that *create* imagery.

FROM A WORD OR TWO AGAINST RHYME

Give the word the fresh scent of ripe corn
swaying in the wind of a hopeful field,
tasty as the rare bread of my hungry childhood.
Oh let the word ride endlessly, fantastic
speak face to face, heart to heart
with your neighbor of the farthest century.

—MENKE KATZ

In poetry, each word has monumental importance. The goal is to create the most potent sensory image possible. Out of imagery is born the poem and a new understanding of and delight in language. This experience leads to a new insight into one's own possibilities. Like fingerprints, the unique images each individual is capable of creating encapsulate personality, psyche, memory, and experience: *self.* This first lesson introduces imagery using color and the five senses.

SAMPLE LESSON: POETRY

Teacher: Today we are going to be talking about poetry. Who knows something about poetry?

---

[1]Aristotle's *Poetics*: "The greatest thing by far is to have command of metaphor. This alone cannot be imparted to another; it is the mark of genius, for to make good metaphors implies an eye for resemblances."

Student: Poetry uses rhyming words.

T: Always? Does a poem always have to rhyme?

S: No, not always. But most of the time it does.

T: It's true that most of the poetry, limericks, and nursery rhymes that we study and read in class do rhyme. However, most poetry that is being written today, and much that has been written in the recent past by those we call *contemporary poets,* does not rhyme.[2] It may have a rhyme inside the poem, and we call that *internal rhyme,* or it may have a line or two that rhymes, but the poem overall is written in what we call *free verse.* Free verse allows us, among other things, not to rhyme. We'll be getting quite familiar with free verse once we begin to write our poems. Does anybody else want to tell us what poetry is?

S: Poetry tells a story.

T: Sometimes. But again, not always true and, in fact, the type of poetry that tells a story has a very specific name. It's called a *narrative poem.* Has anybody ever heard the word *narrator?*

S: Yes.

T: What does a narrator in a movie or on television do?

S: Tells the story of what's happening.

In this particular form of questioning, the intent was to give the students

T: Right. So a poem that is a narrative is the kind of poem we would want to write if we wanted our poem to tell a story. The kind of poetry we are

[2]For example, Theodore Roethke's poem "Orchids," from *The Collected Poems of Theodore Roethke* (1975), doesn't rhyme:

They lean over the path
Adder-mouthed,
Swaying close to the face,
Coming out, soft and deceptive,
Limp and damp, delicate as a young bird's tongue;
Their fluttery fledgling lips
Move slowly,
Drawing in the warm air.

And at night,
The faint moon falling through whitewashed glass,
The heat going down
So their musky smell comes even stronger,
Drifting down from their mossy cradles:
So many luminescent fingers,
Lips neither dead nor alive,
Loose ghostly mouths
Breathing.

something familiar with which to name the less familiar subject, poetry. The technique of linking familiar to unfamiliar is extremely helpful when introducing new ideas or new subjects.

The teacher is attempting to build a foundation of ideas that will clarify the terminology to be used and, in this case, illuminate in understandable language the essence of poetry. As in all of the scripting, the emphasis is on repetitive reinforcement of newly presented ideas and increasing vocabulary.

By encouraging students to draw on their own views of the world, the teacher provides them with a means of personalizing their feelings through poetry.

This encouragement is also a way of subtly reassuring them that their responses are neither right nor wrong but rather a projection of their creative use of words, flavored by their experiences. The teacher is therefore constantly creating this accepting environment, which will allow for the greatest freedom of ideas. Note also that the teacher presents image examples (modeling).

going to be writing today is not going to be narrative. Today we are going to be most concerned with the words themselves. In poetry, words are often *more* important than the idea. Let's explore poetry a bit by trying to define what makes a poem a poem. If we were going to bake a cake, for example, what ingredients would we need?

S: Flour, sugar, milk, eggs.

T: Right. And we might also want to add a bit of salt, some butter, and maybe top it all off with some chocolate icing. Now, if we want to make a poem, we need to know what ingredients go into the poem. The first and most important ingredient, like the flour in our cake recipe, is a small word. It comes from the larger word *imagination*. The small word we are looking for is the word *image*. An image in poetry is what we call a *word picture*. We will explore how word pictures work in a few moments. The second ingredient is almost as important. Without it, there is no poetry. I'll give you a clue: We laugh or we cry, we yell or pout or kiss and hug, depending on how we —

S: Feel.

T: Yes, feel. *Feelings* are the second ingredient in our poetry recipe—how we feel about what we are writing. We need to put ourselves into our poems. We need to try to make the reader understand our emotions and feelings so that when they read our poems they will be able to feel and understand what we felt when we wrote them. Our goal, in poetry, is to capture our own personal energy and to project our very own personal feelings. How do we know how we feel about something? From where do feelings come?

S: The heart.

S: The brain.

T: Yes, but how do we know, for example, that we like chocolate cake but dislike spinach (or like spinach and dislike chocolate cake)?

S: Because we've tasted them, and chocolate cake tastes better than spinach.

T: True for most, and this tasting is what we call *experience*. Drawing on this experience is what we call *memory*. So, feelings can be said to come from experiences and memories. When you are writing a poem and are looking for an image or word picture to describe the beach, let's say, and you, Barbara, went to the beach once and found a shell with a pearl inside—and you, Neal, fell asleep in the sun and got a terrible sunburn, do you think you would use the same images or word pictures or put in the same feelings when writing your beach poem?

S: No.

T: No, of course not. One image might be: A day at the beach is as shiny and pink as the inside of a shell and white and brilliant as a newly formed pearl. The other image (or word picture) might be: A day at the beach is red and hot and painful as a blister. Both images convey the visual impact of a word picture, and both draw on memory and experience. Each image is a very personal statement, and each image tells us something about the poet who wrote it. Are you beginning to see how images and feelings work in poetry?

S: Yes, but how do you really know what a day at the beach is like?

Inventing the poetry recipe through class discussion.

T: A day at the beach is like the poet who writes about it. If we chose today to write about the beach, there would be as many different views of the beach as there are students writing, and that's what makes writing poetry so exciting. It gives us each a chance to be who and what we are through our poems and to explore our own very personal feelings about things.

Let's move on now to the final major ingredient. This ingredient, like the eggs and the salt in our cake, completes the main part of our poetry recipe, and it is the subject: what we are writing about. Most people think that the subject is the most important ingredient, and if we were writing a book report or term paper, it would be. But in poetry we are concerned with language, words, what we can do with them, and what we can make them do for us. So far, then, this is what our poetry recipe looks like:

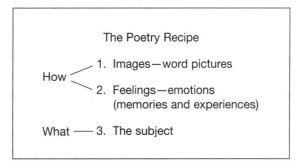

The Poetry Recipe

How
1. Images—word pictures
2. Feelings—emotions (memories and experiences)

What — 3. The subject

T: The image and the feelings are what we call the *how* of poetry. How do we put words together to form pictures? How do we shape those pictures by using feelings and emotions? And the subject is the *what* of poetry. What are we writing about? Now we have a basic understanding of what goes into making a poem. There is still one more thing we need to include if our poem is going to come to life. It's something you have five of, and it isn't your fingers and it isn't your toes. What else do you have five of?

S: The five senses?

T: You're right. The five senses. Let's list them on the board.

See—how things *look*
Hear—how things *sound*
Taste—how things *taste*
Touch—how things *feel*
Smell—how things *smell*

Emotions—how things make us *feel* inside

You'll notice that I added an additional sense—emotions. It's not a physical sense, but it is important in writing the poem. Now that we have all of these ingredients, let me give you an example of how they work. Suppose I wanted to describe the color of my blouse without ever using the color word in my poem. I might write something like this:

My blouse is the color
of midnight, of bats that flap
their wings on Halloween, of the
sleek limousine that cruises
down the street. My blouse is
a color that smells like smoke
drifting up from a campfire in
the woods and the rich, dark
smell of chocolate melting

Learning about
the sense of touch.

Poet/teacher
collects sensory words.

Learning about the sense of feeling.

in a pot. My blouse is a color
that tastes like licorice
and burned marshmallows and steak
cooked on a grill. My blouse
is a color that feels bumpy
and rough like coal or sticky
and bubbly like tar on a summer
day. My blouse is a color
that is frightening like stairs
that creak in the middle of the
night. It is a lonely color
like a sky without stars or a
room without lights.

Learning about the sense of smell.

T: What color was I describing?

S: Black.

T: Did you see the word pictures? Could you have drawn pictures of the images I used? Bats on Halloween? Smoke drifting up from a campfire? A sky without stars?

S: Yes.

T: Did you hear the five senses in the poem? Can you give me an example of one of the five senses?

S: You can smell smoke.

S: You can see a limousine on the street.

S: You can feel sticky tar.

S: You can taste chocolate.

T: Good. What about an emotion? Did I use an emotion to describe the color black?

S: Yes, you said it was frightening.

S: And lonely.

T: I can tell you were thinking and listening very well. So now we begin to see how images—word pictures—work, and also how we use our five senses to create images. It's important to remember that this was *my* black poem. Your black poem would have been different because you would have had entirely different memories and experiences to draw on. Let's work on a poem together before we try individual poems. Let's use the color red and try to describe it, through poetry, using all we now know about poetry: images, word pictures, feelings, the subject (red), and emotions; and let's try to bring our own personal memories and experiences into our images. Now. What does the color red look like?

S: An apple.

This illustrates the process of creating an image, and extending it through the use of adjectives. The teacher extracts ideas by using a technique of quick, insistent questioning. This type of lesson needs to move quickly, and the teacher should be

T: I can see that. An apple. Let's take that a bit further to find the word picture. Where is the apple? Is it in a bowl or on a tree?

S: On a tree.

T: On a tree. What time of year is it?

S: It's fall.

T: I see. Is the apple ripe?

S: Yes.

constantly aware of pacing. Note also how the teacher adds weight to the student response by thoughtfully and reflectively repeating it, indicating to the class that he or she is a truly attentive and involved listener. In doing this, the teacher is modeling the listener role, so important to any class dynamic.

T: Tell me more about it. Describe this apple, this particular apple on this particular tree on this particular fall day. Describe it.

S: It's shiny.

S: It's round.

S: It's juicy.

T: Those are fine descriptive words that tell us something about the apple. Let's put them all together and see what we have:

Red is a ripe, juicy, shiny,
round apple on a tree
in fall.

What else does red look like?

S: A fire engine.

T: Ah ha! A fire engine. Describe it.

S: It's long.

S: It's fast.

S: It's sleek.

T: Where is the fire engine? What is it doing?

S: Racing to a fire.

T: *Racing* is a good word choice. All right, let's put it together:

Red is a long, fast,
sleek fire engine racing
down the street to a fire.

What does red sound like? Is it loud or soft? Does it scream or whisper?

S: Red sounds like the siren on a fire engine.

T: I can almost hear it. What does the siren on a fire engine sound like? Find a word or combination of words that describes that very particular sound.

S: It's very loud.

S: It's also a very long sound. It goes on and on.

T: Good. What time of day do you think the siren sounds the loudest? Day or night?

S: It sounds loudest at night when everything else is quiet.

T: That's good, and that tells me you've listened to the sound of fire engines. Then our image or word picture for the sound of the color red might be:

Red is the loud, long sound
of a fire engine siren
at night.

A good device you can use to help yourself come up with images is to list words that go along with the five senses and emotions. List *see* words or *sound* words or *touch* words. How about the feel of the color red? Let's start out by listing *feel* words.

S: *Hot* is a feel word.

S: Cold.

S: Sharp.

S: Sticky.

S: Bumpy.

T: Good words. Which ones, or perhaps others we haven't mentioned yet, might best describe the feel of the color red?

S: Hot. Red is definitely a hot color.

T: Hot as what?

S: Hot as a fire.

S: Hot as an oven.

S: Hot as a fire in the woods on a cold winter's night.

T: Now we're beginning to see how to extend the image. Make it more visual, a better word picture. So then we might say that

Red feels hot as a fire
in the woods
on a cold
winter night.

How about some more feel images?

S: Red is hard as a rock.

T: What kind of a rock?

S: A volcanic rock.

T: Interesting! What else might red feel like?

S: It might be dry.

T: Dry as what?

S: Dry as a desert sun.

T: Yes! Good image! What does red smell like? What is the scent, the fragrance, the aroma of the color red?

S: Red smells like a rose.

T: Where is this particular rose? Your particular rose? In a vase by the window? In the garden? Where?

S: In the garden.

T: What time of year is it?

S: Springtime.

T: What time of day is it?

S: Morning.

T: Now put it all together and tell me what we have.

S: Red smells like a rose in the garden in the morning in the springtime.

T: It works! What else might red smell like?

S: Smoke.

S: Perfume.

T: Fine. Let's take these one at a time and make them into word pictures. Let's do the perfume first. Tell me about it. Whose perfume is it? What does it smell like? What does the fragrance remind you of?

S: It's my mother's perfume, and it smells like flowers.

T: Red is the flowery smell of my mother's perfume. Good. Now, what about the smoke?

S: Red is the smell of smoke from a campfire in the woods on a snowy night.

T: Very effective string of words. That's putting it together! What does red taste like?

S: It tastes hot.

T: Hot as in temperature or spicy hot?

S: Spicy hot.

T: Like what?

S: Pizza.

S: Hot peppers.

S: Spaghetti sauce.

T: Put it together.

S: Red tastes spicy hot like pizza and hot peppers and spaghetti sauce.

T: What emotion does red make us feel? Happy? Sad? Lonely? Excited?

S: Red is brave.

T: Brave as what?

S: Brave as a soldier in war.

T: What else?

S: Happy. Red is happy as a birthday party or a clown.

T: That's really good imagery, and it's a good place to end our red poem. Let's go over it and see what we have:

RED

TO SEE

Red is a ripe, juicy
shiny, round apple
on a tree
in fall.

Red is a long, fast
sleek fire engine racing
down the street
to a fire.

TO HEAR

Red is the loud,
long sound
of a fire engine siren
at night.

TO FEEL

Red feels hot
as a fire
in the wood
on a cold
winter night.

TO SMELL

Red smells like a rose
in the garden
in the morning
in the springtime.

Red is the flowery smell
of my mother's perfume and the smell
of smoke from a campfire in the woods
on a snowy night.

TO TASTE	Red tastes spicy hot like pizza and hot peppers and spaghetti sauce.
EMOTION	Red is brave as a soldier in war and happy as a birthday party or a clown.

T: Good poem. Let's see if we can put together everything we know and everything we've experimented with today and write our own color poems. I want each one of you to choose a color (the subject) and using images and feelings and the five senses (plus emotion), describe that color for me through free verse poetry.

STUDENT POEMS

WHITE

White feels like two people
getting married.
White smells like peppermint
candy getting ready
to be eaten.

White looks like fluffy
clouds in the blue sky,
feels like roses growing
in a garden, white tastes like vanilla ice
    cream cones.

White feels comfortable.

—THIRD GRADE

PINK

I sound like
a meek voice in the distance,
a little baby crying at night.
I sound like
anything young or a cat's meow.

I smell fresh but not crisp
calm, like
talcum powder
and a clear river
seen at the harbor.

I look small,
pale, and from a distance
I look light but not bouncy.
I'm calm.

I feel smooth like
a baby's skin
soft as a new pillow made
from light colored fabric.

I taste almost like
nothing, an old piece of paper,
dried meat
seltzer with the fizz all gone.

I taste calm.

—SIXTH GRADE

PEACH

Peach reminds me of cool summer
    mornings,
It's shaped long, bold and curvy.
It is like a sculpture of an Oriental
    woman
warming peach juice for her baby.
It smells natural,
sounds like fur brushing a new leaf,
relaxing,
peach cobbler,
a child
with a freckle on her nose
sleeping under a mother's smile.

—FIFTH GRADE

GREEN

I smell like lemons and limes and juicy
    leaves
and grass and ripe peaches.

I taste like bananas when they're not
    ripe
and grapes and grass and papaya, salad
    and peas.
I am soft as cotton and comfortable as
    playing
in the leaves, cold as ice, squishy as
    peas.
I am the color of the Hulk
and leaves in the spring and grass in
    the summer,
dinosaurs, apples, caterpillars.
My voice is the sound of grass swishing
    in the air,
wind blowing very hard through the
    trees.

—CLASS POEM, THIRD GRADE

SUMMARY: POETRY

In this introductory poetry lesson, we provide some simple writing tools for our students. These tools enable them to explore new language possibilities. By asking them to enter an arena that had no definitive borders, no hard-and-fast rules for right and wrong, we asked them to take risks. Praise, encouragement, and emphasis on the positive were essential.

Each group of students (on any given day) generates its own unique energy. It is this energy, this spontaneity and sense of sharing, that cannot be captured in print. What is lacking is the giggles, the laughter, the delight in students' eyes when confronted with the wonder of words (their own and others'). The exhilaration, exuberance, and sense of accomplishment that comes from the metamorphosis of *red* into *an apple, an apple* into *a bloody moon,* and the *moon* into an *angel's pillow* are memorable. Each creative strand becomes part of a fabric that is woven of words, conceived joyously one at a time. But the real moment of truth is the time of sharing. The poem, personal and personified, is given as a gift and more often than not, accepted in the same spirit. The enthusiasm with which the poems are read and greeted readies the group for further word/music/movement exploration.

MOVEMENT

Although imagery seems to lead naturally to a richer vocabulary and lends itself to the creation of the poem, movement also provides a natural starting place, both for the teacher and the students. Because movement does not have to be learned, it is a good way to extend the poem beyond the page. Student poems often undergo additional editing, with the poets' permission, as they are recreated through the extension process of movement and music.

Analyzing some of the preceding poems with the kind of vision mentioned previously, we first find the common denominator, color. The names of colors, in and of themselves, provide a possible impetus for group movement exploration and a necessary flexing of movement imagination, giving students confidence and skills with which to apply their ideas. The word *pink* creates a light, quick sound in the mouth that might be equated in movement with the flick of the hand or the toss of the head. In its brevity, it requires quickness and lightness. Two of the three possible elements of movement are already evident:

Time—how long a movement takes

Weight—the light or heavy quality of that movement

Space—where in space the movement happens: high, low, behind, under, through, around, in opposition

As another example, *red* might be perceived as a word in transit—powerful, bright, possibly increasing in speed as it goes, ending with an explosion. *Brown* suggests a dark quality and thus might call for a heavy, ponderous accompanying movement. *White* has air in it and glides in the mouth as it would in space, except for the little catch at the word's end, which brings it to a delicate stop. All these sounds and thousands of others can become the source for first explorations in movement.

Although the sounds of the color words determine the time and weight of the movement, the teacher should suggest to beginning explorers which body parts to use and where to place the movements in space. One approach that works well is to start the group exploring any movement from seated positions (floor or chairs), moving gradually to an upright position, and finally involving forward movement (locomotion). This sequence gives the student a greater sense of security in what may feel like a new experience and also gives the teacher time to isolate the task, making refinement possible. When choreographed, these simple movements can lead to surprising artistic results.

SAMPLE LESSON: MOVEMENT

Introducing new concepts in ways that demand involvement and thought by students is always desirable. Here, it becomes a guessing game of how to link the abstract movement with the sound of a color. The teacher had the particular color red in mind but accepted the related colors offered as possibilities.

T: You've recently created some wonderful color poems. Let's explore these colors in yet another way. In a moment I'm going to communicate to you in the language I would like us to use. I'll say the name of a color in this new language. See if you can guess the color *and* the new language. [The teacher makes strong, upward motions, first with one fist, then the other.] First, can anyone guess the language?

S: Movement.

T: Right—a language we use to communicate with much of the time, right along with words and facial expressions. Anyone know the color I was moving?

Modeling first, asking the class to try the demonstrated movement, then moving to students' own ideas provides a sure and comfortable framework. Asking students to model other student ideas is another technique for showcasing originality and giving weight and credence to student input.

Starting a movement from a stationary spot provides students with a comfortably restricted area. The inexperienced or overly exuberant student is more likely to stay on task and not take the lesson in an unwanted direction. More difficult to control and to accomplish with merit is movement that moves into the room (i.e., loco-motion), and thus it should follow those movement tasks that are static.

The insistence for concentration comes first when working with all levels of children. If the task does not involve vocal sound, the movements should be done in concentrated silence. Recognition of those children who can accomplish a task with a kind of single-mindedness and unawareness of the group is one way of reinforcing these goals and ensuring a more interesting resulting movement.

S: Probably yellow.

S: I think orange.

T: You were both on the right track with your bright colors. I was thinking of red. From your seats, would you all make my motions as you say the word *red?* Say the *r* very strongly. Right. Thrust up and outward. Do it as often as you wish but say the word with each motion. Stop when you feel your red piece is ended. Is there any other way we could move the word *red?*

S: You could sort of twist your body and bring your arms around.

T: Would you stand and show us what you mean? Could everyone stand and copy Neal's motion when I say *begin?* Each time you say the word *red,* you are going to accompany it with a strong twisting motion. Begin. Now we have two ways to move *red.* Could anyone think of a way to move *red* that would take us into the room, moving forward?

S: You could take a slow step and raise your knee on the *r,* then on the end of the word, stamp your leg down.

T: Demonstrate it, please. We'll watch. Class, was this a strong or a weak motion? Yes. It almost had a pressing quality and had great weight behind its slowness. Try pressing the word *red* with your arms outward this time. Upward. [The teacher says the word each time.] A harder one—press your back into space and stop. I liked your concentration. You've all moved red in three ways—thrusting, twisting, and pressing it in all directions. Could you now combine these three versions into one movement piece called "Red," accompanying your own movements with your voice throughout? Let's let half the room demonstrate while the other half observes. Observers be ready to tell us who had good concentration, who had motions with the greatest variety, who used their space in an interesting way (high, low, or middle), who connected the movements into a convincing whole. Performing group, begin, and freeze when you are finished.

T: Who saw someone whose movement they liked?

S: Neal looked good. I liked his concentration.

T: That's very important in being convincing in movement. What else?

S: I liked the way Betty went from one version to the next and sort of connected it into one idea. I liked when she kneeled down.

T: Good. A movement can start from any position: standing, sitting, kneeling.

S: I liked the way Bob said the word as he moved. He really looked in "movement" like his color "sounded."

T: Your comments will help the next group! Switch roles, please. [Other half of the group explores and is critiqued in a positive way by peers.]

The teacher sums up what has been observed in the student movements and labels them using movement vocabulary. These words now become a handle for both student and teacher, for future movement use and analysis.

In the situation of peer evaluation, the teacher defines the parameters wherein the discussion will take place (exhibiting a strong teacher presence). These margins delineate the goals of the exercise and suggest what qualities the observing group should be looking for. This tactic can suc-

T: Before we try another color, let's see what we've learned so far: Movement can begin with any part of the body, from any position, and happen in any part of space possible. The word *red* called for a heavy, pressing kind of movement quality and was slow. All movement has three qualities: time, weight, and length (or duration). With that information, let's explore another color: pink. Sit down, please. As I say the color randomly, think how the word makes you feel like moving, only move mentally. Now from your seats, will you show me what you imagined, as I say the word? If I'm silent, don't move. If my voice is high, show me in space where that would be.

Pink — pinkpink / pink \ pink / pinkpinkpink \ pink

cessfully sidestep any negative comment tendencies of the group or individuals and again make the experimental zone a safe haven for trying.

The summation of any task in effect headlines for students the salient bits that the students should remember and hopefully reapply.

I enjoyed watching your responses! I saw quite different movements this time: flicks, quick light motions. Antoinette, you moved your shoulders quickly. Rob, you moved disjointedly, like a robot. All of your movements reflected the weight and time of the word *pink*. Good. Everyone, please stand and let's practice this quick flicking with all parts of the body. Let's see you flick with your nose. Flick with your hips, one knee, one foot, your hands, a shoulder. [The teacher pauses for student movement after saying each body part.] Flick with your hands *and* your head! That's interesting! Instead of saying the word *pink* this time, I wonder if we could find a sound in this classroom which sounds light and pink. [The teacher taps metal cabinet with her ruler.] Pink sound?

S: How about this? [The student runs a pencil up the spiral of a notebook.]

S: I have a better one—the bell on your desk!

T: [The teacher plays the bell.] Do the rest of you like that sound for pink? Then that's the way it will be. As I play the bell, I'll suggest body parts and places in space in which to move.

Flick fingers - high space:

Flick fingers - high and low space:

Flick shoulders and knees while turning:

This lesson is geared toward building experiences in actual movement and in labeling what is being done for later, more sophisticated application within the color poetry itself. It is, if you will, a playing with the elements of an idea before putting it into a more complex structure. To have started with the color poem might have invited shallow and tentative results because that task could

This time, can you make up—*improvise*—a flick piece with any body parts of your choice—but always look in the direction of your movement. (Your eyes are like a flashlight that illuminates your movement.) Excellent. That little trick of looking in the direction you are moving makes your improvisation look very convincing. It made me want to look at you. Shall we divide up the class again and watch each other? Which student would like to play the bell? Remember, this time the bell is the leader of your movement, so you will have to listen carefully to know when to move. Be ready to say what you liked!

♩ = bell sound

have been overwhelming. It is helpful for students first to isolate elements, regardless of what they are, before fixing them into a more involved form.

Pink got us into movement qualities that are light and fast. These are named *flick* and *dab.* Let's try the word *brown,* and this time I would like you to choose movement qualities from this list that you think best express brown:[3] slash, press, punch, glide, wring, float, flick, or dab.

S: I think *brown* has to have a slower movement, so I choose *glide.*

S: I think *glide* is too light for brown. I pick a slow, heavy one: *press.*

T: Other ideas?

S: Well, it's definitely not flick. What about *wring?* Is that like *twist?*

T: Exactly—imagine your whole body is a large, wet towel that you are wringing out—takes a heavy, weighted movement and lots of time to get the water out. Then, most of you agree with press, wring, and possibly glide? Fine. Will you divide into two groups, five people each of pink and five brown—pinks over by the windows, browns near the door. I have a picture I would like you to move. Can you tell what will happen as you study this drawing?

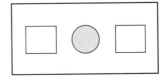

Which shape do you feel represents pink best? Then this means the pink group will begin, followed by the brown group, resuming (and concluding) with the pinks. Will the groups ever be moving at the same time?

---

[3]For more information about movement qualities, see Rudolph Laban's book *Modern Educational Dance* (MacDonald & Evans, 1963).

Who would like to play the bell sound for the pink group? Browns, yours will be a vocal sound—let me hear you say BROWWWNNNNN, and make it sound like the color it is. Fine. Harry, you are the leader of the brown group—when Harry starts, pinks stop. Ready to do a color movement piece in ABA form? Begin. [The teacher gives critiques about having concentration, interacting in groups, letting eyes move in the direction of the gesture, using space in a varied and interesting way, and using parts of the body in a varied way.]

This next color will take us to the poem called "White" (p. 17). Say the word *white* and feel it in your mouth. It has air at the front end, and a *t* stop sign at the end, and in the middle? Show me the middle. Yes, a long glide motion does nicely. We may then need to combine some movement qualities to meet the needs of *white.* Try dab, glide, and flick. Repeat this and on the glide, move forward in the room. Nicely done. Find a new starting position for the word *white.* Yes, it could certainly be twisted with arms extended, and I see you want to start the word from low space. All of these ideas are equally good. You've shown me a good beginning vocabulary of movement, so I think we are ready to try the poem. Read it to yourself from the board. May I hear some ideas about how we might move the first two lines, "White feels like two people getting married"?

S: We could have a few people move the word *white* and let others say the part about getting married.

T: Yes, and you're controlling your giggles very well. How many people do you think should be in each group?

S: Let everybody except two people do *white* and freeze their last movement, while the two getting married say and move their part.

T: Volunteers for the couple? Volunteer for the *white* leader who will breathe just before beginning? The class will watch and listen for that breath and thus know when to start. Will you lead, Joe? Breathe a beginning for us and see if the group can come in wordlessly with you. Nice leading—your group came in beautifully! Can the two people getting married invent a movement that suggests they like each other? No? Anyone suggest something for them?

S: They only have a short line and not much time, so maybe they could just raise their arms into an arch.

T: Good point. Please try it so far. Look to your breathing leader to know when to start, speak as you move, ready? [The group tries first line.] That was the idea. Let's go on further. There's another *white* at the next line: "White smells like peppermint candy getting ready to be eaten." Should the larger group do this? Divide off? Have a solo? What do you suggest?

S: I think the whole group should do *white* again and have a solo on the candy.

T: Right. Volunteer for the solo? Perhaps you can think of the shape of a peppermint candy in a state of readiness, and use that as your movement when you say your line. Let's all try it from the beginning. Married couple ready? Candy? Listen for the breath from your leader. Well done. Going on "White feels like clouds in the sky." Any movement ideas for that line?

S: We could have some separate clouds like we had the candy and the couple.

T: If we do that, what movement quality do you recommend? Is it the same glide for *white* or is it a press or float or dab? What does the key word *cloud* suggest to you, and where should the movement take place?

S: I think the movement should be a light one. A float maybe. And since it's sky, we should use high space.

T: Would you all try this idea of the larger group again saying *white,* then completing the line with a float on "looks like clouds in the sky?" Begin. It's looking nice. Let's continue. What are the key words in the next line, "And white feels like white roses growing in a garden"?

S: Roses.

T: Another?

S: Growing.

T: Would you all try to move a "growing rose" please. Where will you begin in space? Right, low, so you have somewhere to grow. Be aware of how you are moving, sensing in your muscles the feeling of this movement. Begin. Most of you floated slowly, upward. Some of you also pressed your flower open, which was effective. Will the whole *white* group perform this?

S: I think three people should be roses.

T: Three volunteers please? Let's now get the couple, the candy, and the rose people placed in a way that makes the visual arrangement of our movement piece look interesting. Any suggestions?

S: The solo people should be off to the side.

T: Agreed? Let's then try to go from the beginning. Give me a piece of quiet, and when the sound paper is blank, your leader will breathe the lead breath. It's beginning to look convincing, and we're almost through. Ready? [The students perform the movements.] That was good so far. Our movements have been mostly slow and light, but here comes "vanilla ice cream cones" and those words speak something different. Can the whole group find a way to move "white ice cream cone" as a floor pattern, making the shape of the object on the floor as you move it in space? I saw some people moved forward, a few to the side, one person moved very lightly side to side, hopscotching the cone shape. I especially liked that because it changed the speed of our movements and added contrast. Variety is good. Consider now the last line of the poem: "White feels comfortable." Ideas please?

S: I think only a few people should do the ice cream part so we can all do the last line.

S: I do, too.

T: Okay. Let's try it. Three volunteers for the side-to-side ice cream cone movers. What, then, will the whole group do to look comfortable?

S: Lie down.

T: I know you were being funny—but that's really not such a bad idea. What if we didn't go clear to the floor, but got into comfortable low shapes? Everyone, show me a comfortable shape. I see people with their elbows up on each other's shoulders, leaning, slouching. Okay, we'll try these, but can you get to these positions in a slow-motion float? As you say "white feels" from this point on, move as slowly as you can until you come to the word *comfortable* and be ready to hold your final pose. You should relate to each other as if a photographer placed you for this final picture.

S: Can I end up kneeling?

T: Certainly. In fact, why don't we have about three of you end up in a kneeling position—levels are always more interesting than everyone being the same height. Can you end with your elbow on your knee and fist on your chin? And would one of you end up in a delicious stretch, using your high space? This variety should look good. Hold the final picture for three slow counts. Let's just practice the ending. Remember—everyone is doing the last line. Ready?

Speak the words of the last line very slowly and relax. Bravo. Shall we take it from the top? Erin, we are honored to be celebrating your choice poem in movement, and we will try to do it as beautifully as you wrote it!

S: If it's good, can we do it for the class across the hall?

SUMMARY: MOVEMENT

Successful movement lessons have some givens:

- A room or space big enough for movement exploration

- Clearly defined movement tasks for exploration with time for trial and mutual reflection

- Clear signals on how to begin and end movement efforts

- Reinforcement of the need for concentration on the task at hand

- A trusting, accepting class atmosphere consciously nurtured by the teacher in which risk is comfortable and criticism is always positive by both students and teacher

- A teacher willing to model movements occasionally and explore along with students

- A nonthreatening lesson progression for the inexperienced that moves from small movements at the lesson's beginning and later spirals to more complex tasks that use the whole body, space, and locomotion

- A process that is accomplished by a combination of the students' improvised ideas and suggestions, joined with light additions and gentle shaping by the teacher

- Movement lessons accomplished either with provided sound, self-sound, or in silence *but always without conversation.*

Any introductory movement lesson serves as an invaluable tool for subsequent movement involvement with poetry. Whatever time is taken isolating qualities and playing with the ideas of time, weight, and space will pay enormous dividends in helping children adapt movement to their own poetry. This kind of specific movement focus is not limited to older children—in shorter spurts, young children benefit just as much from analyzing movement qualities, along with the less abstract kinds of movement more commonly associated with the young.

Movement can be an important keystone to all your creative word works. Its sources are many: vocal sounds, the sounds of words, word meanings, musical instruments or "found sounds" (see Chapter 4), along with the whole area of visual motivation that is not covered in this book: graphics, paintings, children's art works, or combinations of aural and visual stimuli. Movement helps bring "shape to joy . . . and release to tension."[4]

---

[4]Ginott, H.G. (1972). *Teacher and child: A book for parents and teachers.* New York: Macmillan.

THE FEELING POEM

Poetry speaks of our lives, of the holy and humdrum aspects of our lives. And although some poems may elude the reader, there are those that make us gasp with recognition, that make us say, "Yes, that's who I am. Yes, oh, yes, that's how it feels. Yes, that's the way it happened."

> For poetry knows our empty places
> and the deep rush of unrestricted joy
> and the shattered heart that is inconsolably broken
> and how that heart, through love,
> might somehow be restored.
>
> —SUSAN A. KATZ

After exploring poetic expression through sensory perception and imagery, students will be ready to evoke emotional input through the feeling poem. During this lesson, students are asked to identify feelings and internalize them for the sake of the poem. Because feelings cause people to react with intensity, students may need something in addition to words to express themselves. This lesson, therefore, provides a comfortable opening for the introduction of poetic concepts such as *alliteration* and *onomatopoeia*. By using sounds of words and series of sounds to help intensify and dramatize the poetic impact of the feeling, students achieve a greater understanding of the relationship between the poem and its emotional effect (on their classmates). The search for sound words (onomatopoeia) also helps them to identify more clearly exactly what it is they are trying to express. By asking them, as well, to call on their own memories and experiences (the source of feelings) for their images, the teacher affords them the opportunity to deal honestly and intimately with their own emotions.

SAMPLE LESSON: POETRY

In this example, the teacher is relying on the repetition of ideas and concepts to make them familiar to the students

Teacher: In our first poetry lesson, we learned how to create images (or word pictures). We used our five senses when writing a poem. In fact, if you remember, we put together a "poetry recipe" and discussed the ingredients that go into making a poem.

and easily accessible as resources. This repetitive beginning to the lesson acts, as well, as a basis from which to reach for the next plateau in the sequence of poetry exploration. Sequential teaching has the advantage of nurturing itself and expanding the learning process in a natural and ever-widening spiral.

Would someone like to remind us what those ingredients are?

S: Images and word pictures are the first ingredients, and feelings are the second, and the subject is the third.

T: That's right. So we know that if we want to write a poem, we need to use images or word pictures. We practiced using word pictures by writing what kind of a poem?

S: A color poem.

T: That's right. A color poem. And along with our images, what else did we use in writing that poem?

S: The five senses.

T: Yes, the five senses. How things look to us, sound to us, taste to us, smell to us, feel to us. And what "sense" did we add to the five senses—does anyone remember?

S: Our emotions. How we feel inside about things.

T: That's correct, and I'm especially glad that you remembered because today's poem is going to be dealing with that subject. Feelings are the subject of today's poem. What exactly are feelings?

S: Feelings are stuff going on inside you.

T: What kind of stuff?

S: Good stuff, bad stuff. That kind of stuff.

T: I guess *stuff* is a vague word. Not much of a word picture. Let's see if we can zero in on *stuff* and come up with some examples. What are some feeling words?

S: *Happy* is a feeling word. So is *sad*.

T: That's the idea. Let's see how many feeling words we can come up with, and let's list them on the board. More feeling words, please.

S: Excited.

S: Angry.

S: Furious.

S: Lonely.

S: Scared.

S: Brave.

S: Proud.

S: Bored.

The teacher needs to know when to jump in and take control by saying, in essence, "Enough is enough." To allow the students to continue offering feeling words would threaten the pacing of the lesson and thereby weaken the structure.

T: I think it's becoming obvious to us that there are many feeling words, and we could probably go on thinking them up all day. In our first lesson, we talked about the fact that feelings come from memories and experiences. Do you remember the example we used?

S: We talked about two people who go to the beach, and each one has a very different experience. One person has a good experience, and one has a bad experience.

By setting up a concrete example through imagery (using memories and experiences), the teacher is demonstrating how to internalize the subject that will ultimately become the poem. Although the teacher example is an invention, it suggests that the students should reach within themselves for a personal response, while the teacher gives them a form to follow and helps them to articulate their own memories and experiences through imagery.

T: That's right, and what did we say that would mean in terms of the kind of poem they would write about the beach? What kinds of images would their poems have?

S: The person with the good experience would have happy images, and the person with the bad experience would have unhappy images.

T: That's exactly right. Therefore, when we write our feeling poems today and we draw on our own memories and experiences, those memories and experiences will really decide for us whether our images will be joyful, sad, moody, or humorous. So it is especially important today for us to get in touch with our feelings and with specific feelings about specific moments in our lives. From those very personal memories, we will be creating poems that are uniquely our own, in much the same way that our fingerprints are uniquely our own. No one has the same set of fingerprints that you have, and no one has the same sets of memories and experiences that you have. So when you honestly put your own memories and experiences, through imagery and word pictures, into your poem, you create something that no one but you could have created. You also give us—your classmates and those people you choose to share your poem with—a very real and a very meaningful insight into the person you are.

Let's talk a little bit about a couple of devices that we use in poetry to make our poems more dramatic, to enhance not only the imagery but also the meaning. They also, happily, add a rhythmic and musical quality to our poems. The two devices I'm talking about are alliteration and (a long, funny-sounding word) onomatopoeia. Has anybody ever heard either one of those words before?

S: No.

We have examples again of teacher modeling and reinforcement of student responses by providing immediate, positive feedback. This kind of enthusiastic teacher response encourages students to vocalize in the discussion and makes learning playful, giving students an opportunity to feel good about their contributions.

T: I think if you had heard onomatopoeia before, you probably would have remembered it. It means, simply, words that sound like or are imitations of the sounds they are describing, words like *buzz, hum, crackle, roar, rage, boom.* Do you get the idea? Could you give me some examples of onomatopoeia?

S: How about chuckle?

T: Yes, indeed. I think that's a great one. Some more, please.

S: Screech.

S: Scratch.

S: Gurgle.

S: Burp.

S: Groan.

At this point in the lesson, the teacher is simultaneously attempting to broaden the pleasure of words and to give students another source for selecting words that will enhance and enrich their poems.

T: Those are all marvelous words, and I wonder if we say them again, this time trying to make them sound like what they are describing, we won't get an even better idea of what onomatopoeia is all about. Let's say the words again and try to be dramatic about it. Okay. Let's go.

Class: Screeeeeeeeech. Scraatch. Guuuuuuurgle. Buuuurp. Groooan.

T: That's the idea. These words feel good in your mouth. Don't you agree? They enable us to create very strong and very meaningful images. The other word or device that I mentioned was alliteration. Alliteration is simply the repetition of the same initial sound or beginning letter. For example, the silent sun set slowly. How about giving me an example of alliteration?

S: The gray ghost gurgled gleefully.

T: A special pat on the back for using what? What did Evan just use along with alliteration?

S: He used *gurgled,* which is an example of onomatopoeia.

T: Right! And for that he deserves a bonus. How about letting Evan be the first to share his feeling poem today? Now see if we can, using everything we now know about poetry, do a group feeling poem. Let's do a happy poem. What does happiness look like? (Remember, please, to use alliteration, onomatopoeia, and word picture images, and certainly we want to put feelings into our feeling poem.)

S: Happiness looks like a big, beautiful, breathtaking butterfly.

Although these are examples of teacher modeling, more importantly they are examples of a teacher getting involved in the process on the same level as the students. This is done subtly, without calling attention to the fact that the teacher has chosen to participate in the exercise, and in the process of doing this, the teacher takes risks and becomes vulnerable along with the student. There is also a lessening of the usual distance that separates teacher from student.

T: Wonderful. What else does it look like?

S: Happiness looks like a fragile flower fluttering in the wispy wind.

T: You are all exceedingly expert example givers. What does happiness sound like?

S: Happiness sounds like the chittering, chirping, and chuckling of birds in the summer time.

S: Happiness sounds like big, booming bells.

T: Fantastic. What does it smell like? And remember, let's try to personalize our images. Remember to draw on your own memories and experiences. The smell of happiness is—?

S: Christmas candy canes.

S: My mother's marvelous muffins.

T: Those are wonderfully, workable images. What does happiness taste like?

S: Sunday supper.

S: Tasty turkey on the Thanksgiving table.

T: More marvelous images. What does happiness feel like?

S: Happiness is as soft as my baby sister's skin.

In this exchange, the teacher relinquishes some of the decision making to the class, relying on leaders to point the way but leaving the matter undecided. This acts as further reinforcement for the concept that there will be no judgment here. The teacher becomes a filter for ideas, letting them flow

T: I love that one. How about another?

S: Happiness feels fluffy as a kitten's fur. Is *fluffy* an example of onomatopoeia?

T: What do you all think? Let's say the word aloud together and let's say it in a dramatic sort of way. Together now.

Class: Fluffffffy.

T: What do you think?

S: I think it does, because it sounds like something soft.

through him or her, back to the group. Students are allowed to have some control over the direction the lesson will take.

S: I don't think so, because it doesn't sound as much like what it's describing as the word *gurgle* sounds like gurgling.

T: It's good to have a difference of opinion. It points out that poetry is not set in stone, something that is either right or wrong, but rather a poem is something that is creative and personal and, by its very definition, has a strong emotional impact on the reader. It also points out to us that any single poem may mean different things to different people because the reader brings something of himself or herself to the poem and that's the way it should be. Let's remain undecided about *fluffy*, and look at our happy poem.

HAPPINESS IS

This poem is a compilation of individual responses (thus becoming a group poem). The creation of this poem represents the immediate coalescing of individual ideas into a finished product. This is an important end result because it is a model for what the students are about to be asked to do by themselves; it gives added meaning to what they have been doing by collecting the disparate images and turning them into a finished product; and it is simply good teaching to demonstrate how a variety of ideas can be fashioned into a complete and excellent piece of work.

Happiness looks like a big, beautiful butterfly and like a fragile flower fluttering in the wispy wind.

Happiness sounds like the chittering, chirping, and chuckling of birds in the summer time and like big, booming bells.

Happiness smells like Christmas candy canes and my mother's marvelous muffins.

Happiness tastes like Sunday supper and tasty turkey on the Thanksgiving table.

Happiness is as soft as my baby sister's skin and feels fluffy as a kitten's fur.

—GROUP POEM

T: That is really a fine poem! It contains all of the elements that we have been talking about and gives a very clear picture of what happiness is to us, in this class, on this day. Finally, I would like to finish with an image that deals with the emotion itself. For example, happiness is my birthday party or a huge hug from my marvelous mom or the song we sing softly in summer. What I want is something personal, something that expresses your very own definition of the feeling happiness. Someone, please?

S: Happiness is the hard, high home run I hit in my Little League game.

T: That's the idea. Another one, please.

S: Happiness is the soft, slippery, sweet-smelling sheets on my bed when I crawl into it on a stormy, snowy, winter night.

S: Happiness is the feeling of finding no F on your report card.

T: Those are exactly what I was looking for. I think we're ready to move on to today's assignment. I want you to choose a feeling, one of the ones we've listed on the board or one of your own, and write a poem using all that you know about poetry: images and word pictures, feelings (putting yourself into the poem through memories and experiences), the five senses, and onomatopoeia and alliteration when you feel it will contribute to the intensity and emotional impact of your poem. If there are no questions, let's begin writing.

STUDENT POEMS

TRAPPED

When I go to school I feel
trapped, like a frightened fish
gasping,
I'm always thinking
of running, leaving my
worries behind, like a baby bird
in flight, winging over vast fields,
looking for places to fly to.

When the bell rings, I
feel like someone opens
the door and I fly free.

—FOURTH GRADE

HAPPY

Happy like a rose from a bush.
like someone smiling
singing a song.

Two people talking,
a band playing,

me roller skating, swimming
at my aunt's house.

Happy tastes sweet
like candy hearts,
fresh like pancakes,
maple syrup and
sweet plums.

—THIRD GRADE

CLOSING IN

I feel like a bird in a
dark forest, my path
leading to a black bottomless pit.

Arrows point in
different directions, I run,
I walk, I bump into walls.
I'm living in a box with not
enough air.

—SIXTH GRADE

HAPPINESS

I am children playing in an open field,
and dogs and cats
licking people's hands and faces
and when you go on a trip to
see old friends
and when you go to the beach.

Children laughing, eating candy
and sweet things,
and like beautiful butterflies landing on
stumps of trees,
Birds chirp, flying over tree tops,
Sweet, sticky taffy stretches,
People have fun at the park

Animals at the zoo,
Popcorn and butter,
Kites on cool days.

Flying in a balloon over clouds,
roses, hot pretzels, cotton candy.
luscious lollipops in your mouth,
and sweet sticky bubble gum crackling
as you blow bubbles,
steak and candy apples,
and melted butter with pancakes
and sweet candies.

—FIFTH GRADE

ANGER

You hear people
Yelling at you
Running at you
With mad faces,
With weapons.

It tastes bitter
Like a bad lime,
Rough as red dirt
Like smoke and gas
From an exhaust.

—THIRD GRADE

THE NAG

A coyote howling
A knife at somebody's back
Your hands frostbitten,
A real estate salesman,
A bull running rampant in the city.

A whip being slashed on a horse,
An ice storm.

—FIFTH GRADE

SUMMARY: POETRY

Not all of the students' poems use the entire range of elements that have been discussed. Still, they use something of great importance—honest, introspective reflection. There is a sense of self in the poems that goes beneath the surface to illuminate unexplored depths. Within the safe yet limitless boundaries of the poem, students explore anger, fear, frustration, death, and loneliness, and they linger with a dawning sense of wonder over the delights of love, friendship, and happiness. Without being directed, they seem naturally to move themselves into the feelings that will be the most satisfying for them to explore poetically.

At the conclusion of the lesson and the first presentation of their poems to their classmates, the teacher can generally ask, "When is a good time to write a poem? What is a good emotion to write about?" In most cases, having experienced the cathartic effects of exploring their own emotions, students respond enthusiastically, "All the time! All emotions!"

SPEECH AND RHYTHM: THE FEELING POEM

Chapter 1 focused on movement, and the students' word choices prompted a variety of physical responses. This chapter analyzes some of the students' poems for speech and rhythm-play possibilities. Speech and rhythm are as natural and elemental as movement. Rhythmic repetition of words and body movement are common and comfortable for children, and they feel at home exploring them. A simple foundation can be laid using only the sounds and words that can be created with mouths and bodies—claps, leg slaps, finger clicks, stamps, facial taps—called *body percussion.* When the teacher adds the idea of a pulse or heartbeat, countless variations can be built.

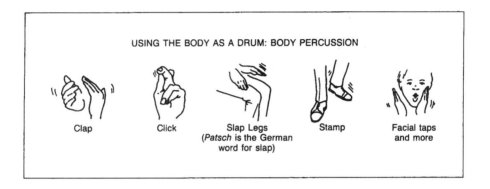

USING THE BODY AS A DRUM: BODY PERCUSSION

Clap   Click   Slap Legs (*Patsch* is the German word for slap)   Stamp   Facial taps and more

The pulse, sometimes called the heartbeat, is a constant beat. It can be felt most easily in examples of poetry that have been written in a particular meter, such as follows. You might want to try speaking them as you patsch the beat on your legs:

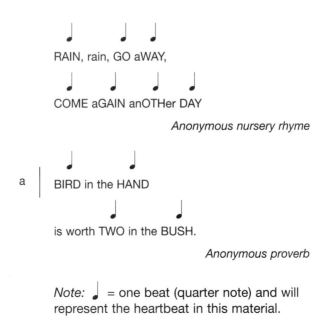

RAIN, rain, GO aWAY,

COME aGAIN anOTHer DAY

Anonymous nursery rhyme

a | BIRD in the HAND

is worth TWO in the BUSH.

Anonymous proverb

Note: ♩ = one beat (quarter note) and will represent the heartbeat in this material.

Both of these examples clearly demonstrate beat, and this particular feeling—straight, march-like—can be counted off in twos or fours. This type of metrical feeling is called *duple meter*. Student examples are included later that call for a different kind of rhythm or meter.

Notice, too, that though both examples used duple meter in their straightforward rhythm, one started on the beat, and one started *before* the beat. Music or a word that starts before the heavy downbeat is called an *upbeat* or *anacrusis*:

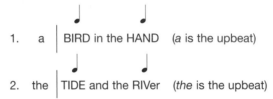

Upbeat (anacrusis) examples:

1.   a │ BIRD in the HAND   (*a* is the upbeat)

2.   the │ TIDE and the RIVer   (*the* is the upbeat)

On-the-beat (downbeat) examples:

3.   IF at FIRST you DON'T sucCEED

4.   GATHer OUT of EARTH DUST

When you are analyzing poetry for speech and rhythm possibilities, it is often important to know whether you are dealing with an upbeat or a downbeat, as it can affect the naturalness with which you treat words; for example, without allowing for the upbeat in the second upbeat example, you get THE tide AND the RIVer. The poetry assignments that have been used for the previous lessons did not impose meter requirements, primarily because we are working in free verse, which is the least restrictive poetic form; but the reality is that all writing contains elements of meter. Words themselves are rhythmic and metered, as follows:

(*upbeat*)   I FEEL like a BIRD   FLYing in a DARK   FORest

Thus, pulse can be imposed on essentially nonmeasured verse. Rap sometimes contains good examples of rhythmical treatment of nonmetered speech.

How then does one identify the type of student-written poem that will lend itself to rhythmic treatment? You first look for poems that have a bounding, driving quality about them and that, because of the mood or subject matter, might be enhanced by shaping them into frameworks with a heartbeat—poems that lend themselves to something ongoing and constant. The exploration that will uncover this type of poem can be done by the teacher alone or jointly by students and teacher.

The poem "Happy" (p. 35) falls into a rhythmical category: The word content is joyful, and the mood invites rhythmical interpretation. One way of approaching heartbeat exploration with students is to suggest that the beat should fall on the most important syllables, here shown in caps, with the beat appearing as quarter notes.

SAMPLE LESSON: SPEECH AND RHYTHM

T: Class, can you keep a "heartbeat" going with both hands on your legs while I read the first stanza of a student's poem? Remember, the beat, once established, will be constant and unchanging.

Notice that sometimes you have a heartbeat going by, which falls where it is not comfortable to have words.

How about taking the poem "Anger" and seeing if we can put a pulse under the important words? Howie, would you try, please? We'll all keep the beat going, and you read it, making the strong words fall on the beat where you think it sounds best. [The student experiments.]

Adding Speech Ostinati to Create
Texture and Complementary Rhythms

At the onset of this lesson, many examples of reading a poem within the framework of a heartbeat were

T: Right now this poem is linear—one line happening at a time. I wonder what it would sound like if the piece had more than one thing happening, if we thickened the texture by adding words to the orig-

given by the teacher, and time was given for students to practice. At this point, the teacher needs to have some concrete ideas about how to enhance that linear presentation:

1. *Reading the poem, but thickening the texture by adding something such as little pieces of the lines repeated (i.e., ostinati) or silences (i.e., rests).*

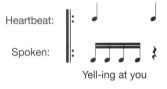

2. *Using a variety of word rhythms (words spoken quickly or slowly)*

Trial and error becomes an important technique in sampling ideas volunteered by students, and verbal traffic management definitely comes into play. Explore different ways of determining the final choices: teacher's say, class vote, or a combination; most important is that the ideas, in their student forms, be tried.

inal poem. It might be interesting. Would you like to try? Please read the poem once more to yourself, and find some words which could be repeated effectively. Tanya?

S: Anger [pause] anger.

T: Fine. Some others?

S: Yelling at you.

T: Both ideas would work. When you repeat that phrase, wouldn't you agree, it's fairly hard to say continuously and perhaps not terribly interesting either? What would happen if we put three rests or silences after each outburst, like this:

When a pattern repeats itself, it's called an *ostinato*, and the plural form is *ostinati*. Your "yelling at you" created an interesting speech ostinato. I especially liked that the speed (or tempo) of the ostinato is faster than in the original poem. When this happens, we say the rhythm ostinato complements, or improves, the original text rhythm. It enhances the original by being different. Later, we might try adding a second complementary ostinato. Tell me how you all liked the sound of the three beats of silence (rests) following the ostinato.

S: I thought it was okay.

S: I felt like something should be happening.

T: Silence can be very effective, but you also have the option of filling those silences with sound. What might we use?

S: Claps—or better, stamps. The words kind of make me want to stamp.

T: Can you demonstrate, please?

S:

T: I like it. Can we try putting the first ostinato pattern with the first stanza? Both the group doing the ostinato and the poem group should keep the heartbeat going as you speak. Ready? Begin.

Both Groups Speaking Simultaneously

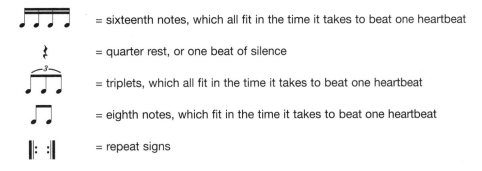

T: How many of you heard both parts going on? It was good!

For those readers less experienced in what music looks like on the page, the following symbols have been used thus far:

= sixteenth notes, which all fit in the time it takes to beat one heartbeat

= quarter rest, or one beat of silence

= triplets, which all fit in the time it takes to beat one heartbeat

= eighth notes, which fit in the time it takes to beat one heartbeat

= repeat signs

SAMPLE LESSON: CONTINUED

The teacher is as much a part of the warp and weave of this fabric as the students and should an idea occur to him or her, the teacher should express it. The class has a reciprocal responsibility to try the teacher's idea. Other possibilities to facilitate this multifaceted creative process are:

T: I remember another word someone said earlier as a possible ostinato—*anger!* Just how did you say that, Ben?

S: Anger [pause] anger.

T: As if you're taking a breath—or a rest—in between. Can you all do it with Ben?

Class chanting:

ANger   ANger

1. *An awareness of the need for contrast. This means that word rhythms that may be happening at the same time as the original poem will be different and thus enhance the original and not cover it. The term for this is to complement.*

2. *An awareness of the variety of dynamics to suggest to students: loud, soft, gradually getting louder, grad-*

Let's see how that fits with the first ostinato—this half of the room, you're "anger"—the other half, "yelling at you"—all groups feel the heartbeat first. Ready? Begin. [The class performs the combination.] Interesting! Can anyone think of another word or combination to try?

S: What would happen if we did one pattern of "yelling at you," followed by the "anger" pattern?

T: We'll try it. First, tell me what happens to the rests after "anger."

S: This time let's clap on the three beats following "yelling at you" and stamp on the rests in between "anger."

T: Let's try it:

Yell-ing at you (clap) (clap) (clap)   AN - ger (stamp) AN - ger (stamp)

ually getting softer, suddenly louder (f, p, cres., dim., subito).

T: You've made an even more interesting ostinato that has more variety, less predictability, and gives more contrast to the ear. Can you suggest how you imagine the loudness or softness—or the *dynamics*, using musical term?

S: I think it should all be fairly loud.

T: Forte it is then. Is everyone ready to try it with the first line?

It is always the combined artistic discretion of both student and teacher that determines when something should stay the way it is or change. It is the teacher and students who decide together if another part is to be added or if the creation seems right as it is. Sometimes a vote clears the question. If the group could handle a third complementary part, it could add one with dramatic dynamics that start softly and gradually get louder (i.e., crescendo). (It is always helpful to start with the heartbeat to help stabilize the pattern.)

Heartbeat:
New complementary pattern:

YELL-ing   RUN-ning   YELL-ing   RUN-ning   AN - ger

Crescendo (gradually getting louder)

Other musical terms for dynamics:

Forte (*f*): Loud

Piano (*p*): Soft

Pianissimo (*pp*): Very soft

Fortissimo (*ff*): Very loud

Mezzo (*m*): Medium

Crescendo: Gradually getting louder

Decrescendo: Gradually getting softer

Were you to see the original poem plus the two ostinati plus the heartbeat happening at the same time in score form, it would look like this:

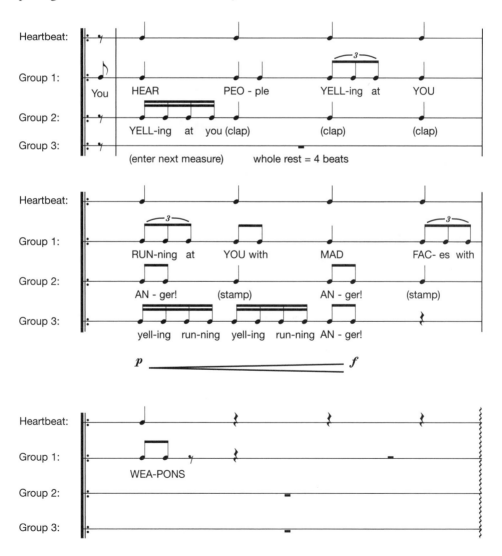

SAMPLE LESSON: CONTINUED

Introductions and Codas

A piece can be expanded by the addition of an introduction and a coda or by students improvising rhythms in interlude sections.

T: Sometimes a piece wants something to happen before the main event, something that relates to the original but introduces the listener to what is about to happen. This is called an *introduction*. As with the ostinato, excerpting phrases and ideas from the poem is a good way to find material for an introduction. In "Anger," Group 3's part might become an introduction if spoken twice before the original work began. Try it.

YELL-ing RUN-ning YELL-ing RUN-ning   AN - GER

We are beginning to build a form. You can tell from the picture I've drawn on the board which is the introduction and which is the main body; thus, the form is as follows:

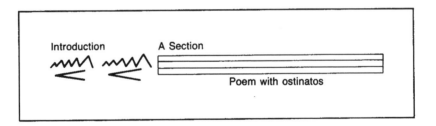

If the following is added, what do you think has happened to the form?

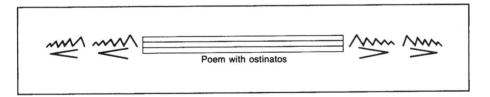

[Students respond.] You're observant. The material used in the introduction appears to have made it to the end, but now it is called a *coda*, which means a final, finishing section, a rounding out of ideas coming to a final point. But is it exactly like the introduction?

S: The crescendo mark is going the other way.

T: Right! Which means, just as it looks, we're getting softer, or decrescendoing. Class, please say the coda with me and see if you can decrescendo. [Class responds.]

Working for Contrast

T: Another important element in manipulating speech and rhythm is *contrast,* the art of creating the unexpected. Contrast of sounds, rhythms, and texture keeps the participant and the observer interested. Contrast can also occur through varied dynamics, as well as in the number of voices involved (sometimes many, sometimes few, sometimes one) and in the form of the piece. In the middle section of "Anger," there is an opportunity to savor the different vocal timbres, or qualities of voices if the lines are assigned like this:

Student 1: "Anger tastes like lime."

Student 2: "It feels rough as red dirt."

Student 3: "Like smoke and gas from an exhaust."

Anger's form would now look like this [putting the graphic on the board]. Shall we try the whole thing?

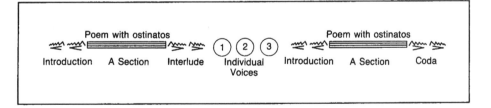

The life of this work has been extended through *repetition.* Student poems are often too short and need this kind of extension. The possibilities are literally endless. In this short poem, only a handful of ideas have emerged through layering one group texture over another, each complementing the other, one a heartbeat with the original poem text, the others contrasting rhythmic ostinati. The musical elements have added up, as teacher and students have expressed and put into practice dynamics, form, ostinati, increased texture, and body percussion to complement the original work. While maintaining the integrity of the student's work, the class has had the fun and excitement of seeing a new work emerge, one in which they all have shared the joy of creation and performance.

The Process Applied to a Poem in Compound Meter

All of the poems in the sample lesson have had a duple-meter feel. This poem's choice of words is more naturally spoken and played with in a new feeling meter called *compound.* Say the first lines of "Humpty Dumpty sat on a wall," and you will immediately be in this meter. It is a rhythm that has hidden rhythms within it, because its beats can be felt in two groups of three:

(in this case a two beat is felt) or three groups of two:

SAMPLE LESSON: CONTINUED

T: Let's work through one more poem, applying the ideas of layering speech with body percussion ostinati. "Happiness" rollicks along and is a good choice for rhythmic treatment. As before, could one person volunteer to read his or her version over the heartbeat the group will provide?

S:

T: A fine interpretation. [Note that again you will have beats going by without words, which helps the poem feel more natural.] Next, as with the previous poem "Anger," let's add a complementary rhythm pattern. To help get the feel of this pattern, which has a different rhythmic feel than the "Anger" poem, say these words after me:

‖: HUMPTY DUMPTY FELL   :‖

In the same rhythm, say these excerpted words from "Happiness":

‖: DOGS AND CATS AND FRIENDS   :‖

This new meter is called 6/8, and it is very familiar to you from many children's poems and nursery rhymes. Try clapping it as you say the words.

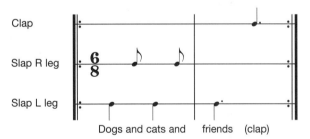

DOGS AND CATS AND   FRIENDS

Rather than just being clapped, it might be transferred to different places on the body for a variety of sound colors. Who could make a body percussion out of this clapped rhythm, perhaps even using two or more sounds?

S: Pattern 1

Dogs and cats and   friends   (clap)

T: That feels very comfortable. Let's call that pattern number 1. Can half of the room pat the heartbeat while saying the poem, while the other half does pattern 1, "dogs and cats and friends?" If we hear both parts clearly, we can invent another complementary layer for further interest. Ready? Here's the heartbeat. Begin. [Students try two parts together.] Fine. Would anyone like to excerpt another idea from the poem to add as another rhythmic pattern? Eric, why don't you try it?

S: How about "when you go to the beach?"

T: I liked the way you kept the heartbeat under your reading. Can everyone say those words in the rhythm Eric used? Who can invent a way of putting them on the body with a body percussion?

S:

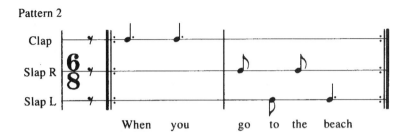

T: Try that one, class. Is it the same as "dogs and cats and friends" rhythmically, or different? Dante? You're right. It is different and therefore complements the original set of words and the first pattern. Let's divide into three groups and try the text with the two additional patterns and see how it sounds:

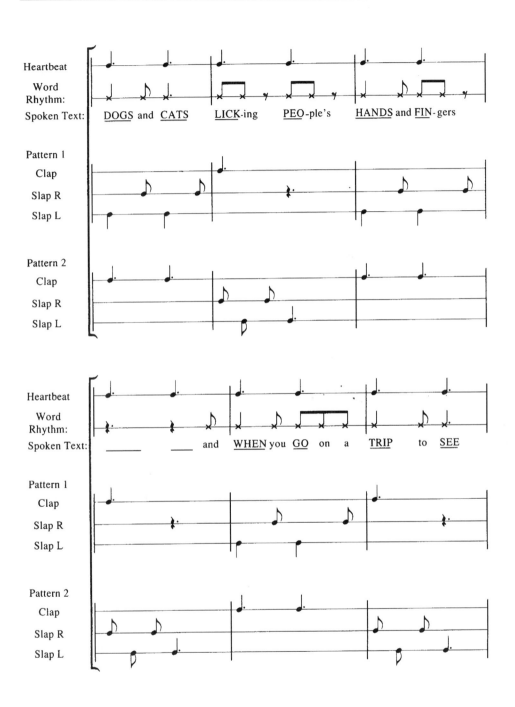

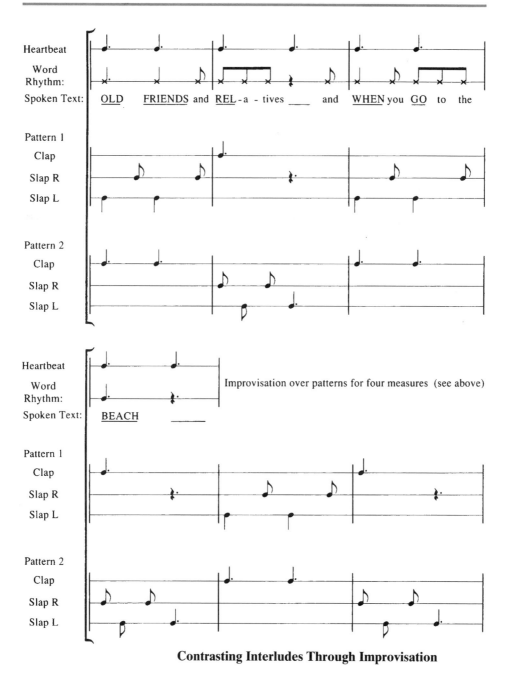

Contrasting Interludes Through Improvisation

T: Rather than going immediately on to the second
    stanza of the poem "Happiness," something hap-
    pening next could provide a contrasting interlude.
    The two ostinato patterns could continue under an
    improvised clapping section. An *improvisation* is
    something made up spontaneously. It is not at all
    planned and is new and different every time. It de-

pends entirely on the inspiration of the moment. The only aspect the improviser has to take into consideration is where the heartbeat is, so that the speed (tempo) and rhythms relate to that heartbeat, making the solo effective. Improvisations can be measured in length (as in "so many beats of improvisation") or unmeasured, where the soloist goes until finished and in some way signals the end. Let's get our improvisation rhythms warmed up through this echo game. I'll clap some made-up patterns the length it would take you to say, "Humpty Dumpty sat on a wall" (two measures, twelve beats).

May we have a student volunteer to lead some more patterns with this compound-meter feel? [Students volunteer.] We're almost ready to use these ideas in the poem. One more rhythm game. This time, instead of copying my rhythm or echoing me exactly, will you all make up your own pattern, which will answer mine? I will clap you the question, and you invent the rhythm answer. Here's the question:

[Variations to this game: Have one student be the question and another the answer, or have one person be both question *and* answer.]

T: I think you will have some good ideas when we come to the improvisation interlude in the poem. Here's what the form looks like so far:

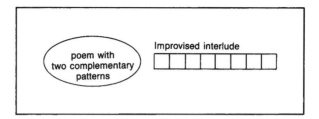

CANON

The second stanza of the poem has such nice word–rhythm contrast, that it would work well in canon.

> Children laughing and eating candy and sweet things,
> and like beautiful butterflies landing on
> stumps of trees,
> birds chirp flying over tree tops,
> sweet sticky taffy stretches,
> and people have fun at the park

Canon is a technique of overlapping that can be used to enhance a poem, and it is related to a round: One group begins a rhythm or song, a second group enters later with the same rhythm or song, and a new rhythmic or tonal complexity results, and a new texture as well. Canon can be applied to speech, song, movement, instrumental rhythms, or body percussion. Visually, a two-part canon might look like this:

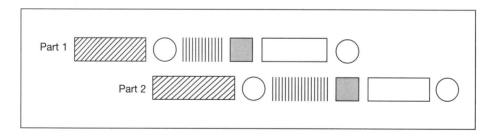

After exploring and agreeing on a way to read the second stanza consistently, again making the important words fall on the heartbeat, the group could be divided in order to decide where the second part would enter. A possible entry would be at the second measure, that is,

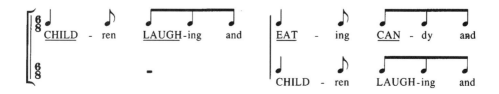

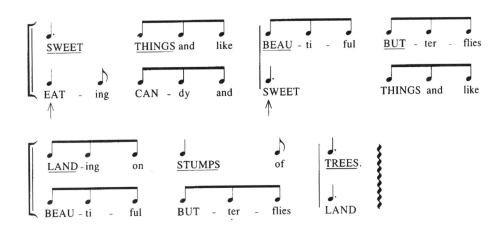

The arrows show where the contrast is the best in this canon. Where measures are the same, there is doubling and thus no contrast. The canon should create two separate, distinctive rhythms when it is at its best. If it is not possible to write out a canon to see this distinction, you will hear it on performing the canon aloud. Were a canon to be used in the poem, a change of ostinato running under it would be good for contrast. The alliteration of "beautiful butterflies" might sound effective fluttering under this canon but in a two-measure form. (Were you to repeat the pattern without stopping, it would be too relentless and too difficult to sustain with both the body percussion and the spoken poem.)

The form of happiness now looks like this:

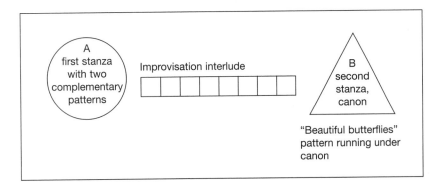

Repetition of sections or recurrence of patterns helps solidify the form of any piece. It would therefore be appropriate to bring back the improvisation interlude once more, over the original complementary patterns 1 and 2:

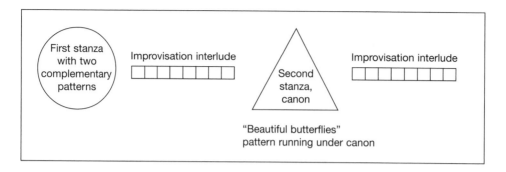

The form is beginning to resemble a *rondo,* which is as follows: same, different, same, still different, same, or:

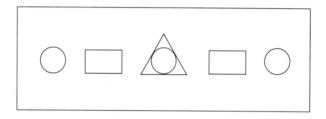

The circles refer to the poem's verses, the rectangles to the improvisation. A literal rondo form would look like this:

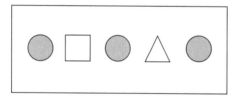

(ABACA form, or rondo form). The poem is one example of a fairly lengthy and complex work. If a poem happens to be of this type, it might benefit by excerpting. In "Happiness," skipping to the last stanza would result in a finished and satisfying completion of form.

> Luscious lollipops in your mouth and
> sweet sticky bubble gum crackling
> as you blow bubbles.
> Steak and candy apples and
> melted butter with pancakes and
> sweet candies!

Because we have used a rhythmical treatment so far in this poem, the contrast of letting students read at their own unmeasured speeds would be welcomed. Nowhere in the poem have we had the singular sound of one voice speaking, to appreciate the individual timbres and colors of voices, so this would be an appropriate way to go.

Student 1:   Luscious lollypops in your mouth.

Student 2:   And sweet sticky bubble gum crackling as you blowwww bubbles.

Student 3:   Steak!

Student 4:   And candy apples.

Student 5:   And melted butter with pancakes.

Student 6:   And sweet candies!

THE CODA: AN ENDING

Now the piece needs to return to something familiar to pull it all together and make it feel cohesive. We need to feel the earlier heartbeat and hear the earlier patterns:

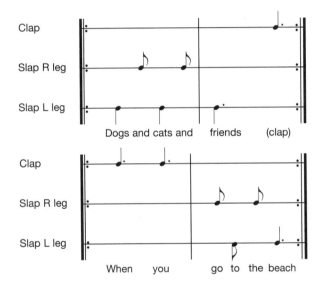

SAMPLE LESSON: CONTINUED

T: If we came in with those familiar rhythms immediately after Amy says, "and sweet candies," can anyone think of a word or phrase that might slim up the poem for use in a coda?

S: What about the title "Happiness"?

T: Fine. When should it happen, and how loud do you want it to be?

S: Three times, getting louder.

T: Three times with a crescendo. Okay. Let's try it at the beginning of each pattern. Here's the heartbeat [demonstrates]. Group 1, begin your pattern:

S: Dogs and cats and friends [claps].

T: Keep it going. Group 2, now add yours.

S: When you go to the beach.

T: Both groups, now add the word *happiness* at the beginning of each pattern, every two measures. Here's the beat. Now begin.

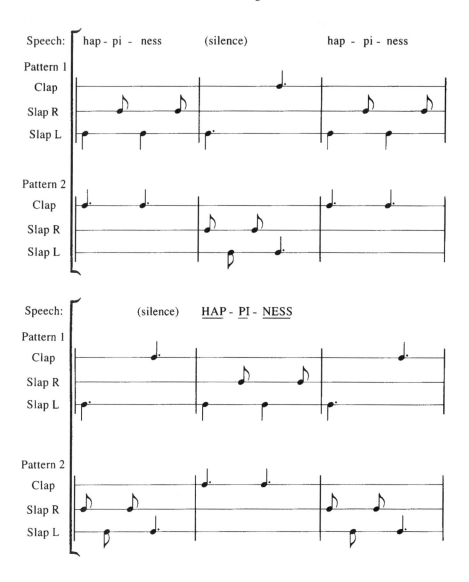

T: A very effective coda. Let's put the whole piece together now. We'll need two small groups for pattern 1 and pattern 2. In the second stanza, these same people can do the accompaniment for "beautiful butterflies." May I have six solo volunteers for the third section of our piece? Look at the final form I've drawn on the board. Here's what the poem has been transformed into:

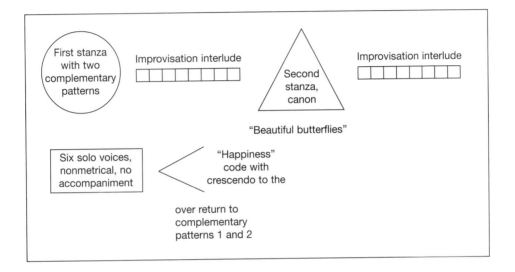

SUMMARY: SPEECH AND RHYTHM

Although it's probably obvious, it still should be pointed out that this process does not happen at one session. Time permitting, it is desirable to savor and revise the experience in installments. The pieces when finished become part of the group repertoire, along with the songs students may share or poetry they have memorized; they can be reviewed with immense pleasure by students and teachers throughout the school year.

In Chapter 2, patterns, repeated ostinati, dynamics, form, word coloring, timbre, duple and compound meter, heartbeat, and canon have been explored and applied to children's poetic works. We've seen how ideas can come from excerpting the student work, and we've observed the need for contrast between complementary patterns for maximum interest. During the process, equality and an ongoing creative dialogue have been established between student and teacher by each empathizing with the intuitive reactions and spontaneous input of the other.

METAPHOR, SIMILE, AND USE OF ADJECTIVES
The Daydream/Wish/Fantasy Poem

Poetry implies an adventure beyond formats, beyond limits, beyond restrictions. It offers students the exhilaration of creative flight. It says, "Give in to inspiration; fly with your ideas; be willing to be outrageous." Because everyone wants to be right and dislikes being wrong, teachers need to find ways to make limitless more desirable than limit and outrageous more fun than safe, thereby eliminating the concept of right or wrong. One way to accomplish this is to initiate an assignment that will be accepted in the spirit of fun. The daydream/wish/fantasy poem[1] provides this kind of creative abandon. We can (and do) daydream or wish for anything, and our fantasies are, after all, supposed to be farfetched and beyond the realm of possibility.

The element of personal investment in the poem still needs to be stressed. Simply because you are wishing and fantasizing does not mean you are entitled to forget or forgo the need for self-involvement. These are your daydreams, your wishes, and your fantasies, and although they may be absurd, you need to approach them seriously and explore what you would wish for if wishes came true and where you would let your fantasies take you if you had access to a flying carpet.

The image, even in a daydream, wish, or fantasy, begins with an original point of inspiration and then blooms, through comparison and the use of adjectives, into something extended and enhanced. If you fantasize a tree, it's just a tree until you imagine it as something else: a soldier, for example. Through the use of adjectives (*tall* and *proud*), you extend the image further into the visual dimension. "The tree stood tall and proud as a soldier." You offer a view of your tree, as you see it, leaving room for the reader to do some creative interpreting on his or her own. The process of choosing the comparison and the adjectives that will make it work is a highly selective one. It needs to reflect individual perceptions and personalities and mark the poem with the poet's signature.

In the preceding chapters, students developed an awareness of the basics of poetry writing. We introduced students to the ingredients that go into making a poem. We investigated the importance of the image and the use of the five senses. We explored, as well, the need for emotional input and the need to stamp individual identities on the poem through the use of personal memories and experiences.

---

[1]For more about dream/wish/fantasy poems, see Kenneth Koch's book *Wishes, Lies, and Dreams* (Vintage Books, 1970).

In this chapter, we define the types of images and establish a process for selecting adjectives. At no time is it more appropriate to be crafting visual comparisons (word pictures) that help bind the unfamiliar to the familiar than when writers journey to the farthest corners of imagination. If you wish for gold, is it a pile bright as sunlight, high as the far side of clouds, shiny as a full moon, heavy as Santa's sack? If you fantasize a journey to the stars, is the way as long as an endless tunnel, as frightening as walking blindfolded into a damp cave, a miracle of lights like birthday candles on a cake? The image becomes the anchor, a point of reference, that transforms the unimaginable (through metaphor and simile) into the imaginable.

SAMPLE LESSON: POETRY

T: In our previous two poetry sessions, we learned how to write poetry using our five senses, imagery, feelings, onomatopoeia, and alliteration. Today we are going to expand our poetic experience by writing poems that stretch our imagination to its limit. How many of you are good at daydreaming? Ah, lots of hands are up. I think daydreaming is something we all spend a lot of time doing, sometimes when we should be doing something else. But there are good times to daydream, and one of those times is when we are writing poetry. What kinds of daydreams do you have? Will someone share a daydream with us? John, how about you?

S: I like to daydream about sports.

T: In what way?

S: I don't know, different kinds of things. Hitting a home run in the World Series. Winning an Olympic Gold Medal. That kind of thing.

T: Interesting. Anyone else want to share a daydream with us? Betsy?

S: I daydream about being a rock star and making a video and singing on MTV.

T: Sounds exciting. What is another word for daydreaming? Can anyone think of a word that really explains what daydreams are or where they come from?

S: Imagination.

T: Absolutely. Daydreams are our imagination at work. Another word to explain that function of our imagination might be *wishing*. Wishing is a big part of daydreams. Daydreams are perhaps our wishes in a moving-picture form and fantasy, perhaps, when we wish for something that doesn't really have much chance of coming true or happening, but we see it in our imagination as if it were real. "I see myself crossing the finish line first at the Olympic marathon. I see myself being the first poet in space. I see myself sliding like a cloud across a summer sky." Daydreams born of wishes? Like moving pictures, they travel across our mind and become a part of our private fantasy world.

How many of you wish for things or fantasize the impossible in your imagination? Good. All of the hands are up and waving. Daydreams, wishes, and fantasies are the subject of today's poem. But before we begin exploring this subject on the page, I'd like to help you stretch your imagination to its absolute limit as you reach for those secret places in your mind. In a moment, I'm going to speak two lines very slowly. Listen very, very carefully. At first, they may sound very much alike, but there is a difference between them. Listen for that difference. "The soft, white snow was like a sheet settling over the land. The soft, white snow was a sheet settling over the land." Jenny, did you hear the difference between the two versions of that image?

S: Yes, I think so. In the first image you said the snow was like a sheet settling over the land. In the second image you didn't use the word *like*.

The teacher is layering ideas and poetic concepts in an attempt to establish a firm foundation of skills from which students may draw when writing their poems.

T: Good for you. You caught the difference. In the first image I said, "The soft, white snow was *like* a sheet settling over the land." That is what we call a simile. I compared one thing to another using the word *like*. I could also compose a simile using the word *as*. I might have said, "The snow was as soft as a sheet settling over the land." That would still have been a simile. The second image, "The soft, white snow *was* a sheet settling over the land," is what we call a metaphor. It compares one thing to another by saying one thing is another. In the second version of the simile, I could change it into a metaphor by saying, "The snow was a soft sheet settling over the land." I hope everyone is beginning to see the difference between the metaphor and the simile. Just to make sure, let's do some more examples. "The trees stood still as soldiers." Metaphor or simile?

S: Simile.

T: Why?

By reviewing terms and ideas previously learned, the teacher is also subtly saying that learning is an additive process and that he or she expects students to remember and call on what was learned in the preceding lessons. In the classroom jargon, this is called student accountability. The only way that a teacher can ensure that these skills (or any skills) become a part of the students' intellectual persona is to consciously and repeatedly provide a framework in which these skills may be used.

S: Because you used the word *as*.

T: Right. By the way, I used something else you should recognize. Listen to the sound of that simile. "The trees stood still as soldiers." Did you hear it? What is the poetic term that describes the choice of words in that simile?

S: Alliteration?

T: Exactly. I'm delighted you remembered. It's important for us to understand that we are *adding* new ideas and increasing our poetry skills, not replacing one with the other. So, "The trees stood still as soldiers" is a simile *and* it uses alliteration. Would someone try and turn that into a metaphor? Gary?

S: The trees stood—

T: Let me write the image on the board.

> The trees stood still as soldiers.

Study it a moment and then decide what word or words may need to be taken out or changed for this simile to become a metaphor.

S: The trees were soldiers?

T: Yes. You transformed the simile into a metaphor. Does anyone else see another way of doing it?

Learning to create
metaphors and similes

S: The trees were still soldiers.

T: Well done. Let's try another.

The sun is as bright as a giant eye.

Metaphor or simile?

S: It's a simile.

T: Why?

S: Because you used the word *as*. You used it twice.

T: So I did. Who would like to try and change our simile into a metaphor?

S: The sun is bright— The sun is a giant eye?

T: Absolutely. Someone else see another way it might work? What word was left out that might be included?

S: Bright?

T: Yes. Would you like to try creating the metaphor and include the word *bright?*

S: The sun is a bright, giant eye.

T: Nicely done. One more example. Metaphor or simile?

Her eyes shone like stars
out of the pale moon of her face.

Please study this one carefully. Let's say it aloud. Now, metaphor or simile?

S: I think it's a simile because you used the word *like*.

T: Is Ray right or wrong? I see we have a difference of opinion. Erika, why do you think Ray is wrong?

S: Because you said her face is a pale moon. So I think it must be a metaphor.

T [speaking to a third student]:   Do you agree or disagree with Erika?

S: I think they are both right.

T: Could you explain?

S: Well, because half of the image is a metaphor and half of it is a simile.

T: You're absolutely right. We have a simile and a metaphor happily snuggled up together. Let's look at it again. "Her eyes shone like stars out of the pale moon of her face." Do you all hear it now? Let's diagram it on the board.

| Her eyes shone like stars | Simile (eyes *like* stars) |
| Out of the pale moon of her face | Metaphor (face *is* pale moon) |

Someone please give me a metaphor for the sun.

S: The sun is a yellow balloon.

T: I like that. Another one?

S: The sun is a burning ball of fire.

The reminder of fact steers the student back toward a more viable vantage point and also says, "It was okay to miss the target—but try again." Occasionally, the teacher must point out a more poetic way in order to clarify what is sought.

T: We can picture that. However, scientifically, the sun is a burning ball of fire. It's actually more like stating a fact than creating a metaphor or simile. Do you want to try another?

S: The sun is a gold coin?

T: That's a very nice image. How about a simile for the moon?

S: The moon is like a clean plate.

S: The moon is as pale as milk.

S: The moon is like a buttermilk pancake.

T: Those are extremely effective, and they used, consciously or unconsciously, some of the five senses. I'd like for us to remember the other skills we've learned—alliteration and onomatopoeia. Remember, alliteration is the repetition of beginning sounds of letters and onomatopoeia is a word that sounds like what it is. So we want a metaphor or simile, using the five senses, alliteration, and onomatopoeia. That, I think, requires some time for thought. Please take a few moments, and when you're ready jot your image down on paper. Ready? Liz?

S: The moon is yellow as melting mozzarella cheese on a sizzling meaty hamburger.

The teacher reinforces use of sensory imagery by responding to the student's image with the word tasty. The students are given the opportunity to demonstrate their listening skills by being asked to analyze and evaluate the qualities of the student image.

T: What a tasty image. Did Liz use all the required elements?

S: Yes, I think she did.

T: Would you explain, please?

S: She created a simile by saying "the moon is yellow *as.*" She used the letter *M* to create alliteration, and she used the sense of taste. Also, *sizzling* sounds a lot like what it is.

T: You did a very fine job with that. And the image itself was wonderfully done. While we are creating our images, our metaphors and similes, we need to think about adjectives as well. Adjectives are those picturesque words that describe things, making them real for us. We've already learned that poetry needs to say as much as possible while still using words sparingly and with great care. When we choose an adjective for our image, it needs to be just the right adjective (or adjectives). The adjective must add something positive to the image. I think of adjectives as adding color to our poems, so I've come up with something I call my rainbow of images. Let me give you an example on the board. Let's use the sun as our subject. Now, what shall we compare the sun to?

SUN ———————

S: A red balloon.

SUN ——————— RED BALLOON

T: I would like for you to now think about what the sun and a red balloon have in common. What is it about the sun (our subject) that made us think of a red balloon (our comparison)?

S: They're both round.

T: Good.

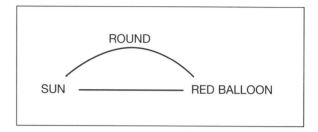

T: What else do they have in common?

S: They both are bright.

T: Yes. I'll add that to our growing rainbow.

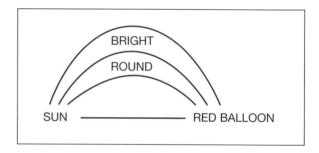

Can you think of more words that describe the sun and a red balloon?

S: Shiny.

S: Hot.

S: Sparkling.

T: Those are all fine descriptive words, and we are in the process of building a beautiful word rainbow.

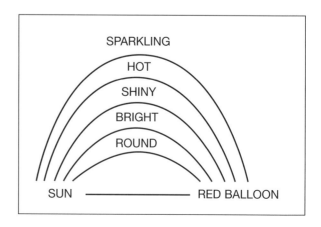

This is an exercise in selectivity, the lesson being that more is not necessarily better. The teacher hopes to show in the resulting responses to this assignment that there are many workable images possible, and that poetry is an individual, creative effort and reflects the responsive "I" soul of the poet.

Now, we need to be selective. Remembering that we are poets, we need to choose the best possible adjective or adjectives to make powerful personal metaphors or similes. Lisa, would you like to be the first to select the word or words for your metaphor or simile?

S: The sun is a shiny, bright red balloon.

T: Good selecting. Lewis, is that a metaphor or a simile?

S: A metaphor. But I would rather use the word *round* because then you are using alliteration, too.

T: Let's hear your image for the sun, using the word *round*.

S: The sun is like a round, red balloon.

T: Metaphor or simile?

Class: Simile!

T: You've convinced me you know the difference between the metaphor and the simile. Let's work a bit more on building adjective rainbows. Begin this time with clouds as the subject. What shall we compare them to?

CLOUDS ─────────

S: How about cotton balls?

T: That works. I'll diagram it on the board.

CLOUDS ───────── COTTON BALLS

T: How high can we build our word rainbow? Descriptive words, please. Words that tell us what clouds and cotton balls have in common.

S: They're both soft.

S: They're white.

S: Fluffy.

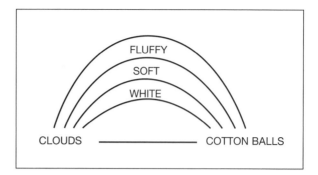

T: Reach inside yourselves for those words that others may not think of. When creating an image, strive to make it unique, to make it yours. More words, please.

S: How about *feathery?*

T: That's a playful one.

S: *Gentle.* Or how about *weightless?*

T: Excellent. Let's see what we have.

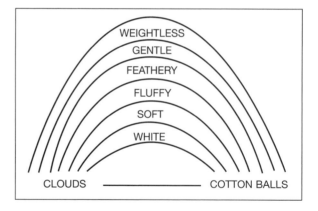

T: Please take a moment to study the rainbow on the board. Think about the words—what they mean, how they relate clouds to cotton balls. Close your eyes and picture the clouds—your clouds—now see them as cotton balls. Place the picture firmly in your mind. Then carefully, thoughtfully, creatively craft your metaphor or simile. Who's ready to try? Karen?

S: The soft, white clouds are fluffy and feathery as cotton balls.

T: Very nice. You chose to describe your clouds twice. First, as soft and white and then as fluffy and feathery. It really worked for me. Anyone else?

S: The clouds are gentle cotton balls.

T: You chose to be very selective, but the image works. It's interesting to see how many different ways there are to describe clouds. Let's try one more.

S: Clouds are white, weightless cotton balls.

T: I like that one, too. You chose the two *w* words and added a bit of alliteration, and it worked very well as a metaphor for clouds. Those *w* words almost feel like clouds in your mouth. Everyone together, slowly, savoring the sound, say the image aloud.

Class [slowly, articulating each sound]:   Clouds are white, weightless cotton balls.

T: It sounds and feels soft on your tongue. Poetry should feel good in the mouth when you speak it aloud. I think we are quite comfortable with the selection of adjectives and the creation of metaphors and similes. What I'd like for us to do now is start thinking about our daydream/wish/fantasy poem. When we are doing our writing today, we will be trying to bring together all of the elements of poetry we have been learning. For now, let's see what kinds of imagery express our daydreams, wishes, and fantasies. A wish image, please.

S: I wish I were rich.

T: Is that an image?

S: No.

T: I don't think so, either. Is there some way we can help John turn his wish into an image?

S: I wish I were rich as a king.

T: Yes, that's better. You chose to turn John's wish into a simile. Is there anyone else who would share a wish or fantasy with us? How about something in the realm of a fantasy journey you might take or a place you might like to visit? Anyone?

S: I am swimming beneath the ocean in a dark, dreary, drab, wet world.

T: That's an excellent one. Good use of alliteration. Someone else.

S: I wish I were a long lightning bolt booming across the sky.

T: What elements of poetry does that image contain?

S: Alliteration.

T: Yes, it most certainly did. Did it contain anything else? Poetry needs to be written very carefully. It also needs to be read and listened to very carefully because every word is so important. Please speak your image again.

S: I wish I were a long lightning bolt booming across the sky.

T: Did you hear it this time? A word that sounds like its meaning?

S: Booming?

T: Would you all agree that boooooming sounds a lot like what it describes?

S: Yes. How about *bolt?*

T: Good question. What does everyone think? Does the word *bolt*—everyone say it out loud, *bolt,* again, *bolt*—sound like what it is? Raise your hand if you think it does. Well, everyone seems to think so, so let's include *bolt* in our praise of the poet's use of onomatopoeia. More wishes or fantasies or daydreams?

S: I wish I were the sound of silence in the sleepy summer night.

T: Very nice. It's fun to experiment with alliteration and we are aware, I hope, that your very complete image included the sense to hear. How about a scent image?

S: I wish I were the smell of smoke rising slowly in the starry sky.

T: A simply sensational image. You certainly used your imagination and lots of alliteration. How about a tasty wish or fantasy?

S: I am the pretty pink roses on a chocolate-covered birthday cake.

T: That tells us something about you. That you like chocolate cake and pink roses, perhaps. How about one that uses the sense to feel?

S: Moonbeams are smooth ladders I climb to reach the stars.

T: What a lovely image. Let's take what we've created thus far and put it into a group poem. While we're doing that, let's also remember that we don't always use all of the poetry ingredients all of the time. Some of the time we will be using alliteration, some of the time onomatopoeia, but most of the time we will be creating powerful metaphors and similes. This is, after all, where the poem happens. As I write the poem on the board, I want you to study it. Read it line by line, remembering all we now know about poetry. Is there a spot, for example, where we can make a comparison, create a metaphor or simile, select an additional or more effective adjective, use alliteration or onomatopoeia?

I WISH I WERE RICH AS A KING

I wish I were rich
as a king.
I am swimming beneath
the ocean in a dark
dreary drab
wet world.
I wish I were a long
lightning bolt booming
across the summer sky.
I wish I were the sounds
of silence in the sleepy
summer night.
I wish I were the smell
of smoke rising slowly into
the starry sky.
I am the pretty pink
roses on a chocolate
covered birthday cake.
Moonbeams are smooth
ladders I climb
to reach the stars.

—GROUP POEM

T: Suggestions, please, to improve our poem.

S: How about swimming like a mermaid?

T: Fine. We'll add that to our poem. Other ideas?

S: Booming like a jet plane.

T: Great. Another one?

S: The smoke was rising like a shadow.

T: That works very nicely. By adding those few word comparisons, we've created some very powerful word pictures. Let's look at the poem again, with the additions.

I WISH I WERE RICH AS A KING, REVISED

I wish I were rich
as a king.
I am swimming like
a mermaid beneath
the ocean in a dark
dreary drab wet world.
I wish I were a long
lightning bolt booming
like a jet plane
across the summer sky.
I wish I were the sounds
of silence in
the sleepy summer night.
I wish I were the smell
of smoke rising like a shadow
into the starry sky.
I am the pretty pink
roses on a chocolate
covered birthday cake.
Moonbeams are smooth
ladders I climb to reach
the stars.

—GROUP POEM

T: I am delighted with the reach of your imaginations. Remember when you are writing your personal poems today, the only limit you must face is that of your own imagination. You have the words (the poet's tool). Take out paper and begin, please.

STUDENT POEMS

My Ultimate Fantasy

When I sleep
I become as rich as
a king and as powerful
as an emperor.

I drown in
power and riches.

I have everything
I wish to have.

In the red hot
summer I have
a cool refreshing
swimming pond.

In the clear cold
winter I have a warm palace
away from all the
frost and snow.

I have a limousine
that takes me
everywhere I want to go.

But then my
palace suddenly
tumbles.

All my riches
are stolen.
Everything I had now gone.
Everything I owned or was
given is now gone, gone until . . .

—Fifth grade

I Wish

I wish I was a feather
flying freely on the wind.
I wish I were a bird
sliding through

the sky.
I wish I was a tree
gently shaking
in the wind.
But I am me.

—Fourth grade

Fantasy

When I dream, I am a
hawk flying over mountain peaks
and sloping hills. I fly
over hot deserts, and
cold snow fields.

I dream I am perched on a
tree, flapping my wings.
Sweet smell of wind,
darkness of night go by,
I am the strongest bird
and rule the sky. I
fly proud.
I am supreme, all
being like me,

When I dream.

—Sixth grade

I Wish

I wish I could be
as beautiful
as a rose
and as smooth as a
frozen pond.

I wish I could fly as high
as the birds swirling
high and low.

—Second grade

SUMMARY: POETRY

It is often the case that the lines spoken aloud in class exhibit a greater scope of imagination, freedom, and adventure than when poems are committed to the page. In writing a poem, the student claims permanent responsibility and feels the need to be more cautious. On occasion, the desire to create the image results in lines that have little or no logical meaning. In these early stages of creative experimentation, the emphasis should be on positive verbal rewards for exciting, innovative, successful imagery. It is helpful, however, to suggest that the students return to their work and assess it for clarity of idea and meaning.

The sample poems in this section use metaphors and similes, adjectives, alliteration, and onomatopoeia sparsely, but are nonetheless stunning in their spirit and zest. There is a burgeoning pleasure in the limitless possibilities of language. Students may have some difficulty in sustaining poetic form, but they are attempting it and their poems display a gleeful spontaneity and inventiveness, as in the following example:

WONDER

Waterfall in a garden
with a tulip
in my mouth.

the feel of fingers running
through my hair.

hoofs
banging like
an exploding
earthquake.

feather flying
freely in the
wind.

clouds raining
as if they're
crying.

quiet like a
forest after a hard rain.

as beautiful
as a rose.

as smooth
as a piece of glass.

they jump out at me
like thousands of grasshoppers
jumping through the grass.

crickets are playing like an
orchestra of violins.

stars are falling out of the sky like
snowflakes.

the night is whispering a tune like a
happy bird.

—GROUP POEM

Language has become something more than individual words strung casually together. It has evolved into word combinations, patterns that create images so real they can be seen, smelled, tasted, touched, heard, and felt. Words that seemed flat and lifeless on the page have suddenly taken on shape and become lively and animated, and the poems themselves are malleable material ready to be re-created through movement and music. In the ongoing lesson, the emphasis is on making the words sing.

MELODY: THE FEELING POEM

As with most activities, the greater the initial preparation and stirring of ideas is, the richer the response. To request suddenly that a student try singing one of his or her poem lines would probably not produce a satisfying result. Thus, these next lessons back into the idea of melody, starting with the basis of inflection and nuance. The lessons work toward melody through

- Word interpretation

- Phrase interpretation

- Melodies that are sung as conversation

- Spontaneous melodies using limited pitches (improvisation using simple five-tone pentatonic scales)

- Melodic shapes observed as they occur in common examples, which influence meaning (i.e., melodic contour)

- More advanced concepts of combining melodies, creating melodic texture or harmony

- Melodic canon

Creating good melody deserves the exploration of these types of musical experiences. With younger children, it may be appropriate to go only as far as nuance and recitative in this sequence. The following lesson covers this aspect, and then goes even further, as would be appropriate for older students.

SAMPLE LESSON: MELODY

Inflection, Nuance, and Accent

In this reflection over past explorations, the teacher is pointing out to the students that (as with language) musical extensions also are layered and that there is a sequence of anticipated difficulty. This sequence is one for the reader to note as well when using this text: Movement exploration is perhaps the most imminent and readily available aspect in the classroom. It requires only space (which can be created logistically) and students, and so it is a workable departure point. Sounds that bodies can tap, slap, clap, stamp, and shout are also born of the body. The texture, becoming more complicated, now includes complementary rhythms, form, and combined ostinati, deepening the musical observation while keeping the level of complexity operable. Melody involves more specificity both for teacher and student, and so is a realistic additional layer at this point for both.

T: Looking back over our work, we have applied movement to your poems, letting the words take us into space. We have added word patterns, created forms, added body percussions, and experimented with canon. Let's now involve our voices, not just in speech but also in song. Let's see how we can develop ideas toward setting the lines of poetry you have written into melody and observe what that involves. You are singing, slightly, even when you are talking! If you listen, your voice has high and low sounds in it as you speak or as I am speaking now. This singing sound that enters your speech, even when you are not actually singing, is called *inflection* or *nuance* of speech. Try this: Read the following words out loud and try not to put any changes in your voice at all, no rise or fall of inflection:

---

grasshopper . . . snowflakes . . . feather . . .
beautiful . . . waterfall

T: You sounded somewhat like mechanical people. Now read them like you would normally say them and be aware of the rise and fall of your voices, the nuance and inflection:

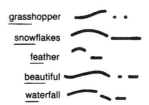

Generally, where a word is accented is where the rise of the voice comes, as in

con – sti – TU – tion   ▬ ▬ ⌢ ▬

Try graphing some words of your own choosing. Who has a suggestion? [Children can notate their inflections on the board.] To take those words one step toward song, you simply have to hold onto the vowels a little longer:

becomes

Waaaaa teeeeer faaaaaaaaall

Try singing this while moving your hand high and low with the inflection. You should be able to hear a little melody. When people write for the voice, they consider a word's natural nuance and where the accent or stress falls naturally on a word. For fun, try saying, then singing, *waterfall* putting the stress on fall:

wa ter FALL

or sung:

waaaa ter FAAALL

It felt wrong, didn't it? It wouldn't work because the natural inflection of the word is changed or distorted. Let's take some words from the poem "I Wish I Were Rich as a King," created by the group. Try the word *swimming:*

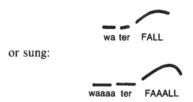

Natural word stress: SWIM ming

Unnatural word stress: swim MING

If we were to sing *swimming* and observe its natural inflection, *swim* would be higher in pitch than *ing.* The same is true of *mermaid, ocean, lightning, summer, shadow, starry, pretty,* and *moonbeams* within this poem as well.

Sung Conversation: Two-Note Recitative Style

With nonrhyming verse, it is especially effective to sing lines using only two pitches, saving the higher sound for the nuance that needs emphasis and the lower for those word parts that are not stressed. This technique has been used for thousands of years, dating as far back as the Greek tragedies. Operas call this style of sung dialogue *recitative.*

SAMPLE LESSON: CONTINUED

How does the teacher find those pitches, or a related shape as notated above? One way is to have an elemental, portable instrument such as a glockenspiel in the general classroom with letters on the keys. Another is to sing the universal teasing chant heard around the world. The first two notes are the minor third needed.

Na   na   na   na   na

Whenever the extended task involves melody, the most critical point of the lesson is the beginning where the students must hear, repeatedly, whatever sets of pitches (la pentatonic, do pentatonic) will be the sounds used in the melody (or improvisation). The extent to which the student's response is self-conscious is in direct proportion to the amount of time and clarity with which the teacher is willing to sing/speak using those tones.

Because wishing is so important in this poem, try isolating the "I wish" part, letting the group all sing that particular thought together, in between solo voices in the recitative style.

T: I'm singing two sounds:

Higher sound
Lower sound

G   E

If I were singing the first line in recitative, I might do it like this:

High sound		WISH		RICH
Lower sound	I		I were as	as a king.

If I wanted more stress on *rich* and *king*, I might do it like this:

High sound			RICH	KING
Lower sound	I wish I were as		as a	

So depending on where you choose to put the higher sound as an emphasis, you can affect the interpretation of a line. Here is where the poet really has to say what his or her intent is and to choose the way that best fits those intentions. Putting the importance of the rising sound on *wish* and *rich as a,* it would look like this in music:

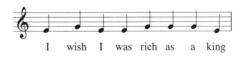

I   wish   I   was   rich   as   a   king

Going on with the poem, the next phrase might be sung like this, giving importance to *swimming, mermaid,* and *world:*

*fermata: Hold the note as long as you wish.

The final expansion of this poem, using recitative and the idea of the rising and falling inflection as it relates to words and their accents, might look like this from the students' ideas:

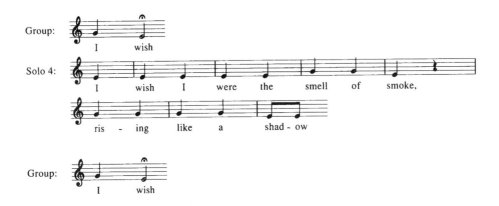

The variety resulting from children's individual vocal timbres (qualities), coupled with the group sound, while very simple, can still be extremely effective. Music thus adds leaves to the winter tree, making it still the tree but new.

Three- or Four-Note Recitative Style

Let's move toward a slightly more complex melody by adding tones. You've been working with children and the idea of a two-tone recitative, using the two tones just presented (named *minor third* or *falling third* because of the downward movement and the particular space, or interval, between the tones). Another space, or interval, which is commonly used for recitative, is five notes apart and is thus called a *fifth*. You can find it by singing

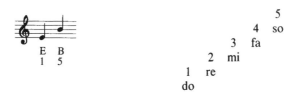

Adding the lower tone below the fifth, we now have three sounds that work well in a recitative style as before:

With these three tones, the reciting tone will mostly be the fifth, using the lowest tone (1) almost as one uses a period in a sentence. Nothing substitutes for modeling by the teacher. Thus, edging into these three tones in a recitative style, "My Ultimate Fantasy" might begin like this.

SAMPLE LESSON: CONTINUED

T: I'm going to play [or sing] three sounds to explore for a melody setting of "My Ultimate Fantasy." Listen to these three sounds [plays or sings: 1, 4, 5]. I'm going to start on tone 5 and make up a melody for "When I sleep, I become as rich as a king." I will use tone 4 and 1 as well. See if you can tell which tone I end on:

[Teacher invents.]

Did anyone notice which tone I ended on for *king:* 1, 4, or 5?

S: 1.

The acceptance of many ideas on the same phrase gives credence to the fact that within the structure, there are many right ways.

T: Good ears. And ending that way was intentional. Perhaps you could hear how it made *king* sound final. The first tone of any scale has that characteristic. If you want to sound final, you end on tone 1. Would anyone else try making up a three-tone melody for that phrase using [teacher sings or plays again] 1, 4, 5, 1?

S:

T: Another good possibility.

Melodic Ostinato

In the previous poem, the idea of wishing was heightened by having the group sing the recurring "I wish." The same kind of returning to group thought works well in this poem with the phrase "rich as a king."

Rich as a King

By repeating this, you are creating a melodic ostinato much like you did earlier with rhythm. Putting the two parts together, you have a very simple harmony. In notation, with the group and the solo singing at the same time, it would look like this:

An easy addition of tone is accomplished by going to the leading tone to 1, which is called 7. In this case it would be

7   1
D   E

A variation of the melodic ostinato could then be

1   7 7   1
Rich as a King

Have a soloist try another improvisation over the class's new ostinato variation.

Five-Tone Pentatonic Melodies (la)

The addition of the G in the D, E, A, B series gives further opportunity for melodic interest. It increases the tones in use to five, which is called a *pentatonic scale* or *mode.* This particular flavor of pentatonic is called *la* because it is based on the sixth tone of the scale: do, re, mi, fa, so, la, ti, do. The scale now looks like this, with E still being 1, or the home tone:

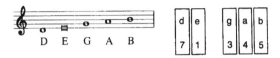

Although this set of tones can sound cheerful given a fast tempo, it lends itself especially well for regal, pensive, lonely, mystical moods and thus is good for "My Ultimate Fantasy." Again, one of the best ways to get into any set of tones is by the teacher modeling these sounds in recitative style. If the goal is to get a student to improvise in la pentatonic in a recitative style, just the sounds of those tones sung or played by the teacher is a start or an echo game in which the class echo sings what the teacher is singing.

SAMPLE LESSON: CONTINUED

T: [Plays on an elemental instrument, such as a recorder or glockenspiel, E G A B D B A G E D E, then sings in recitative style using those tones.]

Does anyone recognize his or her poem?

S: That was the first part of "My Ultimate Fantasy!"

T: Yes! And wouldn't it be the ultimate if we could turn your poem into a sung/spoken piece! We've experimented with word nuance and turned it into two-note songs. We've explored different words and their natural inflections and turned them into mini-melodies. Now we have a new scale today, which will get us even closer to what you generally call melody. But this is not anything you have to remember or write down because every time you perform it, you will spontaneously create a new melody for the words. This is what improvisation is all about. The sounds will be the same five tones [plays five sounds again], but the way you arrange them will differ every time you improvise. Let's use the idea of melodic ostinato as we did earlier. Could this group over here keep the ostinato going that I'm about to sing? Echo me, please.

[Group echos "when I sleep."]

When   I   sleep

Fine. Now can we keep this going while Alice improvises using the words? [Class tries.] Lovely. Will another student try improvising using the la pentatonic and the words? [Class begins ostinato, and soloist improvises over.] Looking through the poem, is there any place where it might be more effective to stop this ostinato?

S: Where the mood changes, down at "but then my palace suddenly crumbles."

T: The mood is definitely shattered there. Perhaps at that spot, the soothing repetition of "when I sleep" should stop. Let's try it again, eliminating the ostinato at that point. Andrew has volunteered to be the soloist this time, and he will be using all he has learned so far about the rise and fall of words, of natural word nuance; and the new idea he is trying to use is keeping those five tones in his recitative. [Teacher again reinforces E, G, A, B, D, B, A, G, E and restarts the ostinato group.] Here is the hypothetical improvisation, riding under the group's melodic ostinato:

The following silences (rests) are used:

➖ = four beats of silence, whole rest
➖ = two beats of silence, half rest
𝄽 = one beat of silence, quarter rest

Still using the la pentatonic set of tones, another student, another day, might give yet another interpretation of this poem, improvising a new melody above the group-sung ostinato. Such pieces are simpler to do than to notate. They tend to look more complex on paper in notation form than they are in actual practice. Even a teacher with a limited background in music should not fear this type of exploration. The rewards are great.

Touching on Form in Melody

When students repeat phrases in their improvisations, using similar melodies for different phrases, this presents a good opportunity to talk about form in melody. The main distinction between recitative and song is form. The latter often purposely repeats phrases, creating a predictable and purposeful kind of framework for a melody. The best melodies have not only a good melodic form but also are shaped to best serve the nuance of the word and phrase, thus enhancing the song's meaning. Notice the improvised phrase in the previous example, "in the red hot summer,

I have" "and in the ice cold winter, I have." The student sensed the parallel nature of the text and automatically sang these two phrases in a similar way, creating a repetition that hinted of form.

Older students may enjoy analyzing familiar songs to get a feeling for like, unlike, and similar phrases. Drawing these forms is a helpful way to visualize what is heard. This kind of observation of folk songs and familiar simple melodies strengthens understanding of how repetition creates structure in songs. For example,

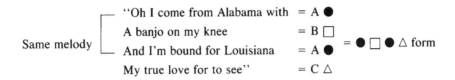

The same form is found in the first part of Beethoven's "Ode to Joy" from the Ninth Symphony.

There are many other song forms, and although it is not important to go into these in detail, refining the task to emphasize form may be helpful for older students. This understanding might allow the poet to hear her two stanzas in a similar way, thus creating a form of ABAC for her poem (still using la pentatonic):

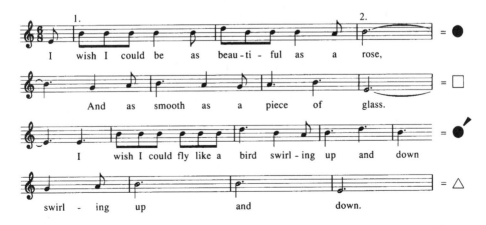

The A sections are not exactly the same, so this form would be ABA'C.

Melodic Canon

The pentatonic scale is very functional as a musical tool because of its simplicity and absence of half-steps, which can cause notes coming together to sound wrong. With the half-steps missing, the scale's tones are spread more evenly over the eight-note span (or octave); therefore, one of the other good features is that the notes blend. This makes the pentatonic scale useful when creating canons. Many pentatonic melodies work as canons, such as the preceding melody. Try it with two groups entering at points 1 and 2, for a two-part canon.

When a child constructs a melody with a form, one to be remembered, the tape recorder becomes essential to the mildly musical teacher who would not be expected to notate it. The repetition afforded by the tape recorder makes hanging onto melodies, such as the preceding one, possible in the regular classroom.

The "Shapes" of Melodies (Melodic Contour) and Relation of Sound Duration and Choice of Interval to Word Meaning

It can be interesting to observe the shape of a melody as an indication of its worth. Notice in "The River Is Wide" how the melody actually widens with a long-held note and on a higher pitch, then how it descends with the thought of "not being able to get across it." Notice the beautifully shaped arch that the outline of the melody creates with a gentle ascent and descent:

American Folk

The riv-er is wide   and I can't get o'er

In "Swing Low, Sweet Chariot," notice how *low* moves literally to a lower pitch, and how the phrase then soars upward to the high point of the idea, "home." Also observe the varied contour created from the melody outline:

Spiritual

Swing low, sweet char - i - ot   Com-ing for to car-ry me home

In the example "This Land Is Your Land," notice how the word *your* is emphasized by the placement of notes and of *my* in the next phrase. Notice the phrases that are the same in melody, thus creating another example of the ABAC form shown earlier.

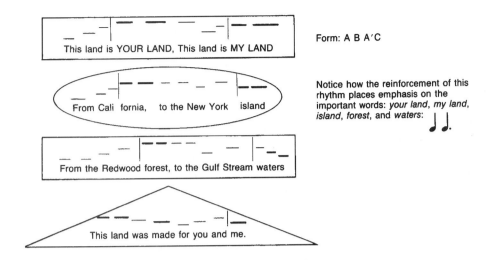

Form: A B A'C

Notice how the reinforcement of this rhythm places emphasis on the important words: *your land, my land, island, forest,* and *waters:*

In "America the Beautiful," notice how the attention is turned to the words *beautiful* and *spacious* by the contour of the melody as well as attention to the nuance of the word:

In the American folk song, "Cindy," note how the word *wish* jumps out because of the high melodic placement:

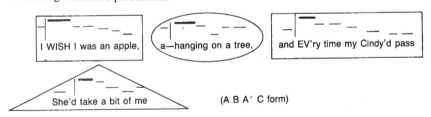

(A B A' C form)

Taking songs common to a group of older students and letting them observe the ups and downs, nuances, and contours of these melodies strengthens their awareness for their own creations.

Using Do Pentatonic, the Major Five-Tone Scale

There is another five-tone elemental scale useful for setting student poems into melodic pieces: *do pentatonic,* so named because it starts on do of the scale. Written on C, it looks as follows:

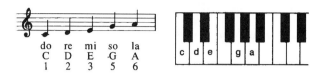

Because of the way the tones are arranged, this mode creates a brighter mood owing to the interval between C and E, called a major third. This mode is thus called a major pentatonic, unlike la, which is minor and darker in sound. A way for the less experienced reader to hear that scale is to sing the first two phrases of "Oh, Susanna," which outlines it perfectly:

Getting the sounds of that mode into the students' ears becomes the task before asking them to create in that scale. Again, teacher-sung conversation, using these notes, will help prepare them.

SAMPLE LESSON: CONTINUED

T: Class, as you read the first line of this poem, will you make a gesture with your arm that looks like her words sound? [They read: "I wish I was a feather flying freely in the wind" and gesture.] Your arms rose and fell, much like the feather in her line. Thank you, Grace, for letting us use your poem. Who will try to sing me what your arms moved using Grace's words?

[A relaxed pause here is essential for the melodic ideas to happen in the students' minds. The teacher's body language and relaxed manner wordlessly say, "There is no doubt that someone will come up with something." If the pause is inordinate, the teacher can sing encouragement, "Can someone help with only the first two words, 'I wish?'" If class courage is low that day, the teacher can start the "I wish" and ask for someone to go from there.]

S:

T: Can everyone sing that line as I tape it? I like the way your melody makes *feather* important and also helps ensure the natural word accent: FEATHer. Who can continue that phrase? Everyone sing their ideas at once and use your arm movement again to give you melodic ideas. Begin. [Whole group explores.] Will one person share his or her idea? I'll sing the first part, and you raise your hand if you would like to sing your continuation. [T sings: "I wish I was a feather."]

S:

fly - ing   free - ly   in   the   wind

S: Could the whole group echo that after the solo sings it?

T: Try it. Grace, would you sing the solo?

S:

[Solo] I   wish   I   were   a   feath-er   fly - ing   free-ly   in   the

wind .   [group] Fly - ing   free - ly   in   the   wind

T: That was a good idea—it sounded fine. Perhaps the other lines would lend themselves to that kind of echo. Will someone please sing an idea for the next line?

S:

I   wish I   were   a   bird,   fly - ing through the   sky

Here the teacher empha-sizes a form that was cre-ated when the student sang the second line almost like the first. The observation of the student's slowing of

T: I like the way you began the second line like the first. You've started a feeling of melodic form. I also liked the way you slowed down on "through the sky," which gave the bird time to fly. Nice. Can we sing the song so far, starting with "I wish I were a feather," with the group echoing the last part of

the rhythm pointed out the appropriateness of time to word meaning and spoke to the sensitivity of the student who instinctively did the artistic thing. It is important to be able to reflect along the (creative) way, alerting students to their own inner perceptions and sharing these strengths with their peers.

the line? [Group sings.] There is one more thought in this poem: "I wish I was a tree swiftly shaking in the wind." Are there any ideas for a melody?

S: Why don't we do the third line like the other two?

T: Can you sing your idea?

S: No, but I like starting "I wish" from low to high like you did before.

T: Like this?

S: That's it.

T: Can someone complete this idea?

S:

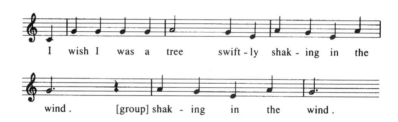

Rather than let students inadvertently drift into less than satisfactory musical experiences, the teacher should feel free to alert them to a better solution, in this case, the need for contrast so the form will be interesting and convincing.

T: So far our form has been AA'A"—the first three phrases have been very similar. This is fine. It would be good to have the last line contrast these three lines by being different, however, making our form AA'A"B, another possible song form. There are different possibilities for the last note of this piece: If you want it to sound final, the ending note should be C, or 1, or do. If you want an unfinished feeling, you can end on the third tone or the fifth (E or G) and make your music walk off into the sunset, so to speak. Grace, do you prefer a wispy or final-sounding ending?

Grace: Wispy.

T: Then will someone volunteer a melody for the words "But I am me" and not end on C? Will the class be ready to echo the line?

S:

But   I   am   me [Group echos]

T: Get ready to try the whole poem while I find some blank space on this tape. As we are taping your performance, consider anything else you might imagine doing with this work, and be ready to share your ideas with the class. [Entire poem with melody and group echo is taped.]

S: In my mind I saw movement, on the words *feather, bird,* and *tree shaking.*

S: I heard other sounds, like the mark tree Jason made from house keys that jingle during the part where the tree is shaking.

S: I heard just one sound being blown on a bottle throughout the whole poem—maybe C—or two people on bottles so you could breathe and not have it heard.

T: All very good ideas. I would like you to divide up into three groups—sound effects, movement, and bottle sounds—and take 5 minutes to polish your ideas. Your group will share its ideas with the class, and from these we will decide on a final version of this poem. Shaniqua, will you be the leader of the movement group over there, bottles to that corner, and sound effects stay here. Walk to the group in which you are most interested and we'll come back together in 5 minutes.

SUMMARY: MELODY

Here, we've considered melody from its simplest level: that of vocal inflection and nuance, moving into more complex melody through sustained vowels, through sung conversation (i.e., recitative style), and through elemental four- and five-note scales. We looked at melodic form and contour, and we touched on melodic canons.

The ideas offered are appropriate for students of all ages and provide many levels of experimentation for teachers with much or minimum experience. It is hoped that the suggestions will encourage boldness in an area that can bring music to the students' poems and to the general classroom.

POETIC FORM
AND REVISION TECHNIQUES
The When-I-Fall-Asleep Poem

The aim in these introductory poetry sessions has been to initiate experimentation with language. In an uninhibited, nonjudgmental environment, the lessons explore individual creative responses to a variety of subjects. The emphasis has been on language skills and word play rather than poetic form. However, at this point, having inspired students to be creatively adventurous, the teacher needs to map the boundaries of their adventure by defining the structure of free verse poetry. How does a poem look on the page? In what ways does it differ from the story? What is a line? A stanza? In what ways do lines and stanzas differ from sentences and paragraphs? Many students in the sample lessons are already aware that the poem differs from the story and that what they have been writing is, in fact, different from most routine classroom assignments.

Using, once again, a fantasy-inspired writing task, the teacher introduces editing techniques, requiring that each student approach the poem with an eye toward tightening and enhancing it. By providing some simple guidelines that help to clarify the intent of poetry, the teacher also provide the tools each student will need to critique his or her own work and identify those elements that are essential to poetry and those that are superfluous. Because students tend to overwrite, much of their editing will take the form of shortening. This shortening or tightening process emphasizes the fundamental goals of poetry: to be compact and have sensory impact, or more simply stated, to say the most in the best possible way, using the least amount of words. The precision of poetry is the most beneficial to the student in all aspects of language application. By learning to choose between what is important and what is not, students learn to be selective. They learn, as well, to think in terms of the impression their words have on their audience. The students begin to understand the importance of weighing the meaning of words and their dramatic effect. Ultimately, in this writing, rewriting, and editing process, they learn to take responsibility for what they have written and to accept that their words are an extension of themselves.

A poem rich in imagery, "Hands," was selected for use in the poetry sample lesson. This poem provides fertile soil for the students' imagination, allowing them to reach daringly beyond themselves for the unique and extraordinary.

SAMPLE LESSON: POETRY

Teacher: I'd like to begin today's lesson by reading a
           poem. The poem deals with a fantasy experience.
           Listen very carefully to what the poem says and for
           those poetic tools we've been learning to use.

           HANDS

           I
           When I fall asleep
           my hands leave me.

           They pick up pens
           and draw creatures
           with five feathers
           on each wing.

           The creatures multiply.
           They say, "We are large
           like your father's
           hands."

           They say, "We have
           your mother's knuckles."

           I speak to them:
           "If you are hands,
           why don't you touch?"

           And the wings beat
           the air, clapping.
           They fly
           high above elbows and wrists.
           They open windows
           and leave.

           They perch in treetops
           and hide under bushes
           biting
           their nails. "Hands,"
           I call them.
           But it is fall

           and all creatures
           with wings prepare to fly
           South.

           II
           When I sleep
           the shadows of my hands
           come to me.

They are softer than feathers
and warm as creatures
who have been close
to the sun.

They say, "We are the giver,"
and tell of oranges
growing on trees.

They say, "We are the vessel,"
and tell of journeys
through water.

They say, "We are the cup."

And I stir in my sleep.
Hands pull triggers
and cut trees. But

the shadows of my hands
tuck their heads
under wings

waiting for
morning,
when I will wake
braiding three strands of hair
into one.

—SIV CEDERING FOX[1]

T: That masterwork poem was filled with some lovely images. Would someone tell us a little about one of the images they particularly liked? Barbara?

S: I liked the way the poet compared hands to birds.

T: I liked that, too. Why is that an effective image?

S: Because hands are a little bit like birds.

T: In what way?

S: Sometimes they move like birds do.

T: How do birds move?

S: Slowly.

S: Gracefully.

S: Birds don't move slowly. They move a lot and very quickly.

---

[1]from *Cup of Cold Water*, 1973; reprinted by permission of the author.

T: What's a good word for the quick movements that birds and hands make?

S: Fluttering?

T: Excellent. Can anyone think of another?

S: Darting?

T: That also works very well and describes perfectly the movement of birds and hands. Anybody else have an image or a line from the poem that they particularly liked?

S: I liked the way the poet said that the hands bit their nails. It's silly, but I liked it.

T: It does bring an amusing picture to mind: hands biting their own nails. Perhaps this tells us that the poet has a sense of humor. Another image or line that you liked? John?

S: The poet compared hands to vessels and cups. I liked that.

The teacher is directing the students (through pointed questions and responses) toward deeper understanding of the masterwork poem, while encouraging them to create their own imagery. She offers a great deal of affirmative input and keeps the discussion propelled in the direction of a pre-planned goal—student understanding of and appreciation for the masterwork poem and discovering inspiration within the masterwork poem that will initiate written student work.

T: I see those images work for you. Good. Are you able to picture them?

S: Yes. I think so.

T: Explain how you see them in your imagination.

S: Well, hands can hold things just like a cup. I guess that's the way I see them.

T: What did the poet mean by *vessel?*

S: I think *vessel* meant a boat because the *vessel* tells of a journey through water.

T: You were really listening very carefully. Does the image work for you? Can you picture it?

S: I can, but it doesn't seem to be as good an image as hands being cups. I liked that one better because it's easier to picture. But hands can swim through water.

T: You thought that through very well. Some other images, please. Perhaps some that will let us know that the poet was using the five senses.

S: The poem talks about water and oranges.

S: The poet also says that the hands are softer than feathers and that they are warm.

T: That's the way to listen to a poem. And, by the way, you've chosen some of my favorite lines from the poem. "They are softer than feathers / and warm as creatures / who have been close / to the sun." Does anyone else have a favorite line or lines?

S: The poem says the hands tuck their heads beneath their wings. I really liked that.

The line between what is real and what is not becomes blurred in the context of the masterwork poem. The teacher (acting as a director) is letting the students discover for themselves the extent of the fantasy and the extent to which the poet is able to make the unreal seem real and believable. This helps to enforce the concept that language used with the skill of a poet is capable of great accomplishments. Furthermore, the teacher-led discussion is drawing a parallel between the skills being learned in the classroom and their actual application in a published poem by a master poet. The work ends with an image that is real—and revealing about the poet—once again reinforcing the power of putting oneself into one's poem.

T: It's interesting, isn't it, that we can accept these fantasy images so easily? Somehow, we can picture hands becoming birds tucking their heads beneath their wings. It requires a leap of imagination, but we all seem to be able to do it. Poetry gives us the freedom to be outrageous, to paint an impossible picture with words and make it seem possible. Why do you think poetry can do that?

S: Because everyone knows that poems don't have to be real.

S: Also, because it's your imagination and you can imagine anything you want.

T: That's true. What makes us believe the unbelievable? What makes it so real that we can see it, hear it, taste it, touch it, smell it?

S: Using the five senses.

T: Absolutely. What else?

S: Using adjectives and images.

T: Using adjectives and images effectively. The poem works when we use language that makes it work. How does the poet end the poem?

S: By saying, "I will wake up."

T: Does that bring us back to reality?

S: Yes.

T: What is the very real thing that the poet's hands do upon waking?

S: Braid hair.

T: Exactly. A very real and even ordinary thing to be doing. Not a fantasy thing at all. And because it ends the fantasy, it becomes even more meaningful. Perhaps it even tells us something personal about the poet.

S: That the poet has long hair.

T: Yes, and she wears it braided. Remember, we've talked often about the importance of putting ourselves into our poems. The poem needs to belong to you. Like your signature or your fingerprint, it needs to identify you even if the subject is a fantasy. Let's try to come up with some images for a when-I-fall-asleep fantasy poem. It doesn't have to be about your hands. Let's try to come up with images that tell us what your feet or eyes or voice or all of you may do when you fall asleep. An image, please.

S: When I fall asleep, my eyes roll out of my body like stones.

T: Excellent. Can you take it a bit farther and tell us what those stones do?

S: They roll down a mountain and fall into a lake.

T: Nicely done and easy to picture, I think. Another image, please.

S: When I fall asleep, my bed becomes a river and I become a mermaid and swim my way to morning.

T: I love that one, Jessica. Someone else?

S: My feet become frogs and hop all over the place.

T: Tell me a little about those frogs. Color, size — are they muddy?

S: They are fat, squishy, bright green frogs.

T: That's the way to use adjectives. Another image, please.

S: My voice becomes thunder and crashes down on sleeping cities.

T: You have the beginnings of alliteration there. Sleeping cities — hear the same sound? Expand on that, please. Give us some more alliteration for that line.

S: Sad, sleeping cities.

T: More.

S: Sad, silent, shadowy, sleeping cities.

T: Well done. It's fun to try and come up with words that have the same sound and still add meaning to our poems. May I hear another image for our poem?

S: When I fall asleep, my body rolls into a ball and bounces down Broadway.

T: That's a fun one. Let's have one that deals with the sense of taste.

S: When I fall asleep, I become a pepperoni pizza at a party.

S: When I fall asleep, my fingers twist into pretzels.

T: How about one for the sense of smell?

S: When I fall asleep, my ears blossom into fragrant flowers.

T: Ears do have a flowery look to them, so I'm really able to picture that quite clearly. An image for the sense of touch?

S: My skin turns hard and brown as the bark on trees.

T: Excellent. I remember that we already have an image for the sense of hearing. Does anyone remember what it was?

S: The one about thunder.

At this point in the lesson, the teacher gives cues to the students to help them fashion their responses. Even if levity was not the direction the teacher had planned, the students have, in exuberant fashion, taken control by providing humorous (but nonetheless well developed) imagery. The teacher now follows their lead, praising the richness of their images and going with the flow.

T: Right. I think we now have an image for each of the five senses. How about an image that has to do with an emotion? Is anyone able to think of one?

S: That's a lot harder.

T: Perhaps it is. Let's see if we can come up with something together. When we fall asleep, might something turn into laughter or tears?

S: How about my eyelashes turning into tears?

T: That works. Remember, we decided that in poetry it's all right to be outrageous.

S: When I fall asleep, my hair starts to giggle.

S: And my eyebrows become caterpillars and tickle me till I laugh out loud and wake myself up.

T: Delightful, happy images. Let's take all the images that I've written on the board and look at them as a whole when-I-fall-asleep group fantasy poem.

WHEN-I-FALL-ASLEEP GROUP FANTASY
POEM

When I fall asleep, my eyes roll out of my body
like stones and roll down a mountain and fall
into a lake. When I fall asleep, my bed becomes a river and I become a mermaid and
swim my way to morning. My feet become fat,
bright, green, squishy frogs and hop all over
the place. My voice becomes thunder and
crashes down on sad, silent, shadowy, sleeping
cities. When I fall asleep, my body rolls into a
ball and bounces down Broadway. When I fall
asleep, I become a pepperoni pizza at a party.
When I fall asleep, my fingers twist into pretzels. When I fall asleep, my ears blossom
into fragrant flowers. My skin turns hard and
brown as the bark on trees. My eyelashes turn
into tears. When I fall asleep, my hair starts
to giggle. My eyebrows become caterpillars
and tickle me until I laugh out loud and wake
myself up.

The teacher is now prepar-ing to superimpose form over the group student poem. Using their own (group) creation as the clay, together with class input, she begins to mold the unwieldy imagery through editing techniques, into the precisely elegant language of poetry. The teacher is also using a sim-ple visual device to rein-force the definition of po-etic form. Whenever possible, appealing to stu-dents on more than one sensory level is a helpful and memorable teaching technique.

T: Do you like your poem? Do you like your images?

Class: Yes!

T: I like it, too. But I'm wondering if your poem looks and sounds like a poem. What do you think?

S: It doesn't look like one the way you've written it on the board.

T: No, it doesn't. Why not?

S: Poems look shorter and they don't go all the way across the page.

T: True. Poems do have a shorter look to them and the words do not usually go all the way across the page the way they do in a story. Can you point out some other differences you've noticed between a poem and a story?

S: Poems don't always have periods at the end of a sentence.

S: Sometimes the first letter in each line is not capital-ized.

T: In certain types of poetry, that is quite true. I think we all agree that poems really don't look much at all like stories. They tend to be shorter. They don't usually stretch across the page from margin to margin, and sometimes the punctuation seems a bit creative. The truth is that poems are really very different from stories. They are meant to be. If you will all look at my hands [raises hands over head extending wide the fingers on one hand and tightening the other hand into a fist], you will notice that one of my hands is wide open while the other is curled into a fist. If one of my hands represents a poem and one a story, which hand do you think is the poem?

S: I think the hand curled into a fist is the poem because poems look shorter than stories and use less words.

T: You are absolutely right. A poem is meant to be tight, compact, and powerful, just like this fist. A story, which can be told in a leisurely fashion, is represented by my relaxed, wide-open hand. Stories take their time. Let me give you an example. First, I will describe, in story form, a walk in the woods on a summer day. [The teacher writes a story on the board.]

It was a beautiful day. The sun was shining overhead in the clear, blue sky. Many birds were singing in the trees. There were robins and blue jays and sparrows and other birds I did not know by name. There were flowers everywhere: daffodils, jonquils, lilies, daisies, and wild roses. Those lovely, colorful flowers filled the air with the most wonderful and delicate fragrance.

Look at the story written on the board. I think we can all agree that we are very comfortable with its form. We see that form in books and write in that form ourselves all the time. It's familiar to us. Let's take this story and turn it into poetry. [The teacher writes a poem on the board next to the story.]

> The sun shone
> like a giant eye, out
> of the cloudless depths
> of a summer sky. The air
> was filled with a chorus
> of birds. There was
> a rainbow at my feet and the air was
> perfume sweet.

There are some very obvious differences between the sound and the look of these two versions of the same walk in the woods on a summer day. Let's go back over the poem and find some of the things left out and some of the changes that were made. Begin, John, by finding some missing words.

S: You left out the names of the different kinds of birds and the names of the different kinds of flowers. And you also had a rhyme.

T: Yes, true enough. Actually, the poem has a couple of rhymes. Even though we are not writing rhyming poetry, we are, in free verse, free to use rhyme on occasion if we feel it will enhance the poem or the flow of words—the rhythm.

T: What other differences are there between the poem and the story?

S: You used words like *chorus* and *rainbow* and *perfume* instead of saying that the birds were singing or that there were lots of different kinds of flowers and that they had a great smell.

T: Good for you for noticing all that. You hit on the key to writing poetry: always to look for the one word or combination of words that will create the image rather than give a lengthy explanation. I want to point out to you, at this time, that we are dealing (in poetry) with lines and stanzas, not sentences and paragraphs. It is the line, in particular, that I want to emphasize. Unlike the sentence, which begins and concludes a thought, the line may want to leave the thought unfinished and in so doing create a moment of drama or suspense. Where a line (or lines) ends may drastically change the meaning of the poem. Where a line ends is often of vital importance to the musical flow and dramatic effect of the poem. Leaving an unanswered question at the end of a line will serve to coax the reader's eye on to the next line. Let's look at our summer walk again, line by line, and see if we can figure out why the lines ended where they did and how they affect the meaning and flow of the poem. First line, "The sun shone"—is there an unanswered question there?

S: Yes, I think so. How did the sun shine, or maybe, where did the sun shine?

T: Right. Next line, "Like a giant eye, out."

S: Out of what?

T: Next line "Of the cloudless depths"

S: Depths of what?

T: "Of a summer sky, the breeze"

S: The breeze what?

T: "Was filled with a chorus"

S: A chorus of what?

T: "Of birds. There was"

S: There was what?

T: "A rainbow"

S: Where?

T: "At my feet and the air was"

S: Was what?

T: "Perfume sweet." In this instance, each line did end with a question. We don't always have to do that. Sometimes we will end a line where we would naturally take a breath if we were speaking the lines out loud. Sometimes we want to make a line seem more important, and we can do this by leaving a key word or image all by itself on the line, and sometimes we end (or break) a line for the visual impact it will have on the reader. In any event, we now understand clearly that the poem does not look or sound at all like our story. The story combines sentences into paragraphs. Each sentence offers us a complete thought, and each paragraph offers us those sentences that have something in common. We end a paragraph and begin a new one when there is a break in the idea or a move to a new idea. In free verse poetry, we deal with lines and stanzas (instead of sentences and paragraphs). We've already done some experimenting with poetic line. The poetic stanza (in free verse) may contain one line or twenty or more. We end the stanza when we choose to create a break or a pause in the flow of our poem. Some poems have no stanza breaks and some have many.

Let's work now with our group poem. We have agreed that it does not look like a poem, and if it does not look like a poem, it will not read (or sound) like one. Using what we now know about lines and stanzas, let's rewrite and diagram (on the board) our when-I-fall-asleep group poem.

WHEN-I-FALL-ASLEEP GROUP POEM
REVISION PROCESS

remove/capitalize M   *remove*
When I fall asleep | my eyes roll out of my body / like stones, | and | roll / down a
                                                    line break   *line break*

---

            remove   *comma, remove*   *remove*
mountain, | and | fall / into a lake⊙ When I fall asleep | my bed becomes / a river, | and |
                  line break   *line break*

---

                    remove   *new stanza*
I / become a mermaid / | and | swim my way / to morning. / | My feet become fat, /
line break   *line break*   *line break*   *line break*

---

                                        comma, small m m
bright green, squishy / frogs and hop all / over the place⊙ My voice becomes /
                line break   *line break*   *line break*

---

        remove, add comma   *remove*   *new stanza, remove*
thunder⊙ and | crashes down / on | sad | silent, shadowy, / sleeping cities. / | When |
                line break   *line break*

---

        remove,   M *capitalize*
I fall asleep | my body rolls into / a ball and bounces down / Broadway. When I
                        line break   *line break*

---

remove   *comma, remove*
fall asleep | I become / a pepperoni pizza / at a party⊙ When I fall asleep | my
                line break   *line break*

---

                comma, remove
fingers twist / into pretzels⊙ When I fall asleep | my ears / blossom into
        line break   *line break*

---

comma, small m m   *stanza break*
fragrant flowers⊙ My skin turns / hard and brown as / the bark on trees. / | My
        line break   *line break*   *line break*

---

            comma   *remove*   *comma, small m* m
eyelashes turn / into tears⊙ When I fall asleep | my hair / starts to giggle⊙ My
                line break   *line break*

---

eyebrows / become caterpillars and tickle / me till I laugh out loud and wake /
        line break   *line break*   *line break*

---

myself up.

T: The title of our poem, "When I Fall Asleep," tells the reader what the poem is going to be about. It is, therefore, unnecessary to use that line in our poem. You will notice, from the diagram, that we have removed it each time it appeared. This tightens our poem and heightens and intensifies the rhythm of the poem. We can also tighten our poem by removing words like *and* and *sad*. We remove *and* because it doesn't add anything to the meaning or flow of the poem. We remove *sad* because although alliteration is an effective poetic device, we don't want to overuse it. I chose to remove the word *sad*. You might have chosen to edit out a different *s* word. Removing a word or words from a poem gives us the opportunity to exercise value judgments about which words express our ideas most clearly and add to the drama of the piece. We discover that we can end or break a line in odd and unusual places; right in the very middle of the idea. We can often remove a period and put in a comma instead. This exchange provides an interesting pause but does not interfere with the flow of the lines. We can choose to end a stanza and begin another at a point we feel will add to the impact of the poem. By ending a stanza, we give additional dramatic weight to both the stanza that has just ended and the one about to begin. It is as though we are advising the reader that he or she has come to a corner and is about to turn in a slightly (or dramatically) different direction.

[*Note:* The following changes and revisions should be accomplished through group discussion and experimentation. There is more than one way for the poem to happen. During the revision process, the teacher and the students should read the lines aloud repeatedly noting how different people place the emphasis on different words and breath phrasing. Let each student decide for him- or herself which phrasing works best, which seems to capture the rhythmic and musical flow of words into poetry. How a poem sounds should be a significant factor in how the words, lines, and stanzas ultimately arrange themselves on the page.]

WHEN I FALL ASLEEP

My eyes roll out of my body
like stones, roll
down a mountain, fall
into a lake, my bed becomes
a river, I
become a mermaid

swim my way
to morning.

My feet become fat
bright green, squishy
frogs and hop all
over the place, my voice becomes
thunder, crashes down
on silent, shadowy
sleeping cities.

My body rolls into
a ball and bounces down
Broadway, I become
a pepperoni pizza
at a party, my fingers twist
into pretzels, my ears
blossom into fragrant
flowers, my skin turns
hard and brown as
the bark on trees.

My eyelashes turn
into tears, my hair
starts to giggle, my eyebrows
become caterpillars and tickle
me till I laugh out loud and wake
myself up.

—GROUP POEM

T: Does the poem look and sound more like a poem now?

S: Yes. A lot more. But sometimes the lines look and sound funny.

T: Give me an example of a line, in our group poem, that you think looks or sounds funny.

S: When the poem says: "roll down a mountain, fall into a lake." I think it would sound better if you left in the word *and*.

T: I see what you mean. I also understand why it sounds strange to you. We have to get used to the idea that we are not writing stories. Poems have different requirements and as we have already mentioned, are shaped by different rhythmical considerations. You could use the word *and* but you don't have to. It's a choice that, as a poet, each one of you has to make privately during the editing process. You may choose to leave the word in, but if you do, you need to have a good reason. It needs to add to the poem in some important way. If it doesn't, then it probably needs to be edited out. Sometimes, when we are rewriting our poems, we will choose to change a word because we find a better, more emphatic, way of saying something. In editing our group poem today, most of our editing took the form of removing words and groups of words, but we might just as easily have been called on to add words or change words. Each revision that you do is unique and will place different demands on you as a poet. With all this in mind, I'd like for each of you to begin writing a first draft of a poem entitled, "When I Fall Asleep." *First draft* means that I will expect you to revise, or edit, your poems at a later time.

[*Note:* Some of the following revisions were done with the help and advice of the teacher. Some were done by the teacher to use as classroom examples, and some were done primarily by students with little or no help.]

STUDENT POEMS

MY FANTASY (FIRST DRAFT)

When I am asleep my spirit leaves me.
   It
travels far over land and over the sea
   until
it comes to the Nile where the
   pyramids used
to be. I plunge deep into the river and
   then travel
back through time to the time of the
   Pharaohs. I
become an Egyptian Queen and rule
   over all
the lands. I wake to join my body.

MY FANTASY (REVISED VERSION)

In sleep my spirit
leaves me, it travels

over land and sea and comes
to the Nile where pyramids
used to be. I plunge deep
into the rivers
traveling back through time.
I wake
to join my body in my bed.

—SIXTH GRADE

WHAT HAPPENS TO ME OVERNIGHT (FIRST DRAFT)

When I fall asleep I feel myself
   beginning
to change. I am
growing and I am shrinking.
You can hear my raging voice
I sound like this: RRRR

You can see me turning different
shapes and different sizes.
I am growing and I am shrinking.
I can even stretch.

WHAT HAPPENS TO ME OVERNIGHT
(REVISED VERSION)

I grow
I shrink
my voice bellows
I sound like
this, RRRR
I turn all shapes
all sizes
I grow
I shrink
I stretch.

—FOURTH GRADE

MY FANTASY (FIRST DRAFT)

When I am asleep I think of my
feet. My feet do lots of work.
They can always run as fast
as a locomotive and they are as strong
as a huge football player's legs.

And I feel the hot sand
when I walk on the beach and
when I go swimming
I feel the freezing cold water
on my feet.
This is my dream.

MY FANTASY (REVISED VERSION)

When I am asleep I think
of my feet, they do
a lot of work.
They run swift
as a locomotive, are strong
as a big football player's
legs.
I feel the hot
soft sand as I
walk down the beach, when
I swim, I feel
the cold water
on my feet.
This
is
my
dream.

—THIRD GRADE

SUMMARY: POETRY

These revised poems represent the students' attempt to critique their own work. In an effort to explore the rhythms and responsibilities of poetry, they have tried to experiment with the unknown. Often, their own poems sound strange to their ears. The lines seem somehow incomplete without the *ands* and *buts* and *therefores*. The students are, however, beginning to acknowledge that language is workable and, like stone or clay, merely awaits the artist's hand to mold it into form and shape it into meaning. In today's lesson, students have begun to realize that creative writing (poetry) is a form of word art, and the material they have to work with is the rich ore of their own vocabularies and imaginations.

DISCOVERING FOUND SOUNDS
IN THE CLASSROOM: THE WHEN-I-FALL-ASLEEP POEM

Thus far, those sounds used as a backdrop for poetry have largely come from the body: the voice (in vocalization, sound effect, and melody), finger clicks, stamps, claps, and patsches. In addition, the classroom offers a repository of imaginative and useful sounds with which to play as poem enhancements. Locating and categorizing these sounds for use throughout the year is a delightful lesson unto itself.

In general, sounds can be grouped in the categories of loud/soft and sustained/short, emanating from metal, paper, plastic, or wood sources. Sounds can have pitch or be nonspecific. Considering first those objects which are breakable or scratchable, having the students "play the room" is a good way to experience the musical potential of a classroom.

SAMPLE LESSON: FOUND SOUNDS

A good stop-and-start structure is important here, as is moving from cacophony to an organized sound framework within that structure. Pacing this lesson to group similar sounds quickly is also important. Students must respect others' found sounds as they are demonstrated (by controlling their own). In any sequence of lively experimentation, the goal is to move from the general, to the somewhat specific, to the specific. Jumping a step may result in not utilizing the full range of found sounds in creative ways.

T: Our room is like a symphony waiting to be played. It is full of sound possibilities that may not usually be used for that purpose. We may find that some sounds are useful accompaniments to your original poetry. Will each of you look around the room, and with an object (such as the eraser end of a pencil, an unsharpened pencil, a ruler, or your hand) demonstrate your chosen sound with a short rhythm, one person at a time? Something like

[Teacher claps]

Or, invent your own. I'll give you a minute to look around and a minute to try out your sound softly. [Children scatter and experiment.] I've put some categories on the board. When each of you has demonstrated your sound, the class will find the best category for each. They are [the teacher reads from the board] metal sounds, wooden, paper, plastic, and miscellaneous. Play your rhythm softly one time and one time loudly. [The class calls out a category after each student plays, and the teacher writes on the board.]

Some possible sounds found in a general classroom:

METAL SOUNDS

1. Ruler tapped on the bottom of a metal can from the school kitchen

2. Teacher's bell

3. Pencil or ruler run along the spiral of a notebook

4. Metal leg tapping the floor

5. Metal edge of a ruler tapping a metal cabinet

6. Large metal markers tapped together

MISCELLANEOUS

1. Sound of the pencil sharpener

2. Paper clips shaken in a box

3. Globe thumped with a hand

4. Chair or desk drummed with a hand

5. Hardcover books opened and closed abruptly

6. Chalkboard tapped

7. Venetian blinds played

WOODEN SOUNDS

1. Wooden ruler or pencil tapped on a desk

2. Pencils tapped on pencils

3. Wooden rulers tapped on rulers

4. Unsharpened pencils tapped on a wooden desk, chair, or table

PLASTIC SOUNDS

1. Plastic ruler against ruler

2. Plastic plates tapped together or separately

3. Plastic straws tapped

PAPER SOUNDS

1. Notebook fanned

2. Notebook paper crinkled

3. Newspaper wadded

4. Newspaper folded and whacked against a chair

5. Telephone book on a rug struck with mallet (You can actually get different pitches by opening the book to different sections.)

At another time, consider these sounds in new groupings, such as those sounds that have a mysterious quality, dynamically energetic sounds, milder sounds that continue, sounds that decay quickly, funny sounds, scary sounds, and so forth.

FIRST USES OF FOUND SOUNDS

At the first use of the classroom as a symphony of sounds, students might together create a "rondo rap" using these sounds to frame room, school, or spelling rules. A student-created chant might be as follows:

Chant:
Ev-ery sound in our room says,"fol-low the rule," and
this will make an ex-cep-tion-al school!

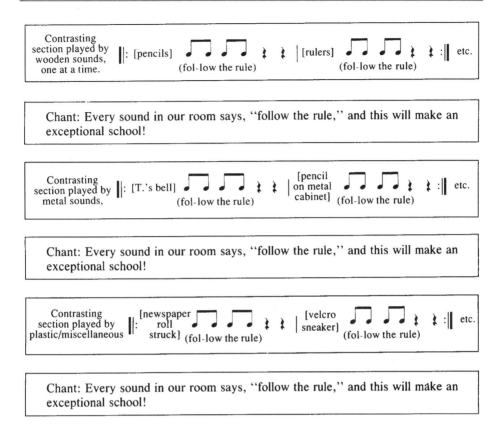

The students will have performed a rondo in ABACA form and will have a new awareness of the infinite variety of objects that make sound, along with the chance to savor those qualities.

Other Easy, Inexpensive Sound Sources

Body Sounds

Some applications not yet used are mouthed whistles (front pucker, side to side), humming, lip pops, buzzing, mouth percussion called "eefen and oafen" used to accompany folk music (particularly from Appalachia), and opening Velcro fasteners on sneakers. The following is an example of "eefen," which provides a wonderful rhythmic accompaniment if you don't hyperventilate.

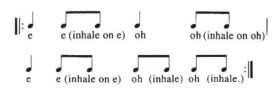

Home Sounds

Aluminum skillet lids make effective sustained gong sounds; soup spoons held as indicated make a wonderful rhythm.

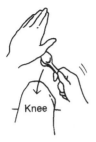

Spoons are struck on right leg and palm of left hand.

Spoons are raked over the stiffly held fingers of the left hand for a fast-note effect.

Pot lids can serve as cymbals, and assorted kitchen implements (e.g., wire whisks) struck together make a host of sounds. Bottles produce organ-like tones when a person blows across the top and can be tuned by varying the water levels within them. Likewise, a dampened finger run over the ridge of a thin wine glass produces a glorious, eerie sound and can also be tuned by water level. Inverted pans struck with wooden, rubber, or metal implements create interesting sounds.

Nature Sounds

Rocks in varying sizes and densities create high and low sounds when struck together. Sticks in varying lengths struck together create pitch. A combination of sticks laid (or nailed) across wood creates a crude xylophone with varied pitches (see following section for mallets).

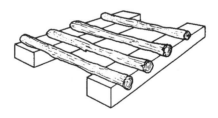

Classroom Sounds

Claves: Dowel sticks cut to 8" or 9" lengths; bamboo fishing poles sawed at joints where the bamboo grows

Woodblocks: Cast-off lumber (ends) from lumberyard or from a child's block set

Drums: Metal cans from the school kitchen hit with hands or mallets; cylindrically shaped oatmeal containers hit with hands or mallets; coffee cans with plastic tops

Mallets: Superball, made by drilling small (1/4") holes three quarters of the way through the ball and inserting a 1/8" dowel stick cut to a 10" length, held in place with white school glue

Reed pipes: Paper soda straws, flattened, trimmed at each corner, and blown to produce different pitches

Straw

Maracas: Small frozen orange juice cans or film containers can be filled with different-size objects to create different sounds: rice, beans, pebbles, and such. Plaster of Paris gauze (found in art stores) dampened and wound around a blown-up balloon creates a container for pebbles. A 3/4" dowel cut to approximately 8" is inserted for the handle and taped into place. The classroom maraca is ready to be decorated using tempera paint.

Balloon

Playing with the Possibilities
Before Applying Them to Poetry

A certain amount of organized experimentation is necessary in order to learn the characteristics of sounds available in a classroom. Loosely structured assignments using these sounds can steer students into a variety of combinations and experiences while giving them a measure of freedom of choice. These sounds are then mentally filed away by the students for later use with poetry.

Here are some possible assignments to promote experimentation and some student solutions. (The students might be working in groups of three or four.)

1. Create a nonrhythmical, sinister piece using sounds of paper clips being shaken in their box, a spiral notebook being scraped, and voices on different pitches singing, "oooooo."

SOLUTION:

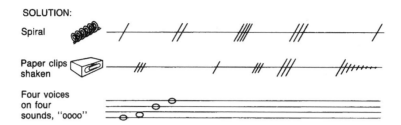

2. Make a humorous rhythm pattern using double-reed pipes, mouth pops, and eefen and oafen.

SOLUTION:

3. Find four metal sounds that are pitched from low to high. Some should be sustained.

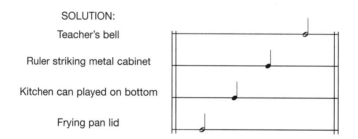

4. Combining wood, metal, and miscellaneous timbres, find three contrasting sounds from low to high and play this pattern.

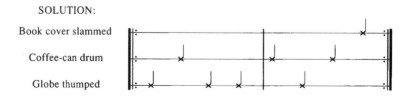

5. Create a soundscape with one instrument continuously playing and others entering in an improvisatory way.

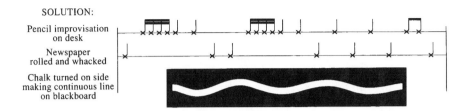

6. Invent a pattern using only contrasting wooden sounds.

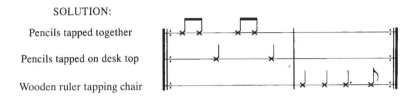

FOUND SOUNDS APPLIED TO STUDENT POETRY

Next should come transitional tasks that will bring the students closer to the goal of using these found sounds to enhance their written work. Word imagery becomes the impetus for finding the right sound, and the students are asked for their ideas. Any task will have more than one solution, and the variations should be honored.

SAMPLE LESSON: CONTINUED

T: Find a way to enhance these lines I've taken from your poetry, using new found sounds. "I grow." (from "What Happens to Me Over Night," p. 105)

S: We could begin with one person tapping with a ruler, and one by one add our sounds to it.

T: You mean like a ruler crescendo?

S: Yes.

T: Let's hear it. You start, and as I move my hand across the room, each person will add his or her ruler tap sound. Begin.

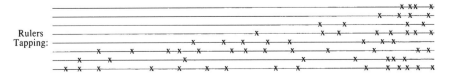

Sometimes, stepping delicately around a suggestion that was not particularly successful, without hurting the feelings of the student who offered it, requires diplomacy and artful dodging. In this example, the class did not like the siren sound and was able to express why. Keeping a neutral stance, the teacher intentionally did not dismiss nor adapt the sound but urged the class to keep the sound in mind while moving on to the next consideration and keeping the student's ego intact.

S: I think we should do it with our voices, too.

T: At the same time as the rulers?

S: Yes.

T: Demonstrate how you want the voices to go.

S: [Sings an upward, continuous siren.]

T: Class, ready to try? Rulers and voices. [They try again]. Raise your hand if you liked the addition of voices. Only a few. Those who didn't vote, can you explain why?

S: I thought it got too thick.

S: I thought it sounded comic and that maybe we didn't want it to be funny.

T: Keep that sound effect and those comments in mind, and try a new one: "I shrink." You are going to want a contrasting sound.

S: What about the paper clip boxes all coming in and then dropping off one by one?

T: We have four boxes. Try it. [They do.]

S: It sounded too much like the ruler-tapping texture.

S: I hear just one sound—like your desk bell or something that keeps ringing—and I see someone moving to the sound, growing very slowly and gradually, then shrinking quickly to the bell sound.

T: Let's do it. Rulers ready? Author, will you read, please?

Author: "I grow." [Rulers begin tapping as author moves up from the floor into a wide shape. They stop when she is fully grown.] "I shrink." [The bell is played as the author moves quickly to a small shape.]

T: Are you satisfied with that, author?

S: Yes.

T: The title of the poem is "What Happens to Me Overnight." Could we try saying that line in a three-part canon—group 1, group 2, group 3?

    Group 1: What happens to me overnight? What happens to me overnight?

        Group 2: What happens to me overnight? What happens to me overnight?

Group 3: What happens to me overnight?
What happens to me overnight?

T: Interesting. What might happen in the next line: "My voice bellows / I sound like / this, RRRRR."

S: I just hear many people doing the RRRRR sound.

T: All right, but the next part lends itself to expansion. You say, "I turn all shapes / all sizes." Class, name a shape."

S: A wide shape, open.

T: Try it. Does anyone hear a sound for that shape?

S: I hear a continuing sound, like that great frying pan lid someone brought to school. It rang for a long time when we hit it with a mallet.

T: Do it, and let's see the class move from a small shape to a wide one. [They try.] What's another shape?

S: Pointed—elbows out, fingers spiky.

T: Angular! Can you go into those shapes suddenly? I hear a sound every day in this room that might be used: your Velcro sneakers? Anyone have a pair on? Let's try four people, rip it open and close it, and as you do, we'll make dab, flick movements to correlate. At last, a use for that sound. Name another shape.

S: Round.

T: Let's see you all go into various round shapes; I see some doing it with arms only. Harriet is using her whole body to make a roundness. Andrew has made a round shape on the floor. What's a round sound?

S: Someone thumping the globe.

S: No, someone thumping the metal can.

S: Try both. [They do.]

T: Can you all practice being round with the globe and metal can sounds? Fine. The poem might use one more shape.

S: What about hooking up more than one person together?

T: Okay. For sound, let's bring the shakers back in with their paper clip boxes and Tic Tac candies. Can you 11 play the moving group into groups of three as they copy your shaking in movement? Make it visually interesting by using your space well—high, low, as we've tried before. [They try it.]

T: There is one more line in the poem to figure out. We need a sound for "I even stretch."

S: That's easy. [Makes the aaahhh sound that a person makes when stretching until it feels good.]

T: Fine. A universal sound. Could we end as we began, with the "What happens to me overnight" in canon? Let me put a map on the board of what we are doing:

Group of movers moving in a wave:

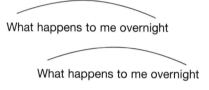

What happens to me overnight

What happens to me overnight

What happens to me overnight
(freeze with body
in a small, tight shape)

S: I grow. (movers grow as rulers tap louder and more rulers enter) I shrink. (bell, movers instantly shrink)

T: My voice sounds like this: [movers adding to RRRRRR and moving gruffly]

I turn all shapes, all sizes.

1. Pan lid: movers, wide

2. Velcro sneakers: movers, angular dabs, pointed movements

3. Globe thump/metal can: movers, round shapes, changing to new rounds with the instrument sounds

4. Shaker paper clips: movers, shaking into groups of three, hooking together in some way to make group cohesive

I grow. (reprise of rulers)

I shrink. (reprise of bell)

I even stretch. (movers stretch languidly with vocal aaaaaaahhs.)

Movers:

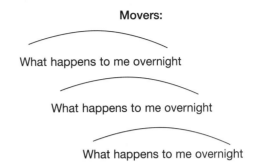

What happens to me overnight

What happens to me overnight

What happens to me overnight

T: So we have created a piece from this poem for voice, movement, globe, paper clip shaker, bell, and pan lid. Well done! Let's look at another poem, "Fantasy." Could someone suggest two contrasting sounds with which we could make an ongoing pattern, an ostinato?

S: You mean two sounds that are not the same at all?

T: Right.

S: How about markers tapped together and pencils tapped together?

T: Let's hear the markers. [They tap.] Now play the pencils. Class, are those sounds different? [The class agrees they contrast in their metal and woodness.] Good. Come up with a pattern for those two sounds. [The class experiments. The teacher looks for two groups that have come up with something usable and showcases those students.] Here's a simple and interesting one—Lydia and Dyson, share yours, please.

S:
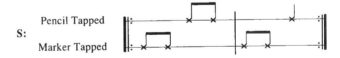

T: It strikes me that this poem lends itself to a strong rhythm. Could one of you please read his first verse while the rest of the class keeps a heartbeat going by patting our legs?

T: Interesting. The first part works very well and the very last, but do you notice how the word *of* gets a big accent, coming on the first beat as it does? *Of* is not an important word and so should not be highlighted by getting an accent. Do you understand that principle? Can anyone use some of the previous ideas, and get the word *of* off the first beat?

S: [reader]

When I am a-sleep I   think of my feet,   they do a   lot   of   work.

T: That works well. Poet, would you like this to be said only once, or since it is brief, repeated?

S: I think twice, but I would like to hear it first.

T: Surely. After we try it out, you still have the final say. Class, can you keep the pencil/marker pattern going under the words, "they run fast as a locomotive"?

Poem:

Pencils:

Markers:
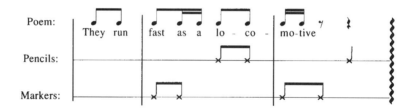
They run | fast as a lo - co - | mo-tive

T: And what sounds would you like to hear following that line?

S: What about the obvious—just feet running helter-skelter?

T: Fine. And following the line,

"are   strong as a   big   foot - ball play - er's legs?"

S: This may sound funny, but I hear four grunts, like the sounds they make sometimes when they are warming up.

T: Four grunts it is. May I hear the class try only four? Let's let the pencil/marker ostinato continue underneath.

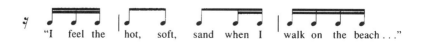
"I   feel the   hot,   soft,   sand   when I   walk on   the beach . . ."

Suggestions for hot, soft sand sounds from our room assortment?

S: What about the sound your finger makes running around the rim of a glass, just one tone?

T: Demonstrate, please. Author, okay? Class satisfied? If that is the hot sound, what will the cold sound be?

S: Let's blow into the bottles with more than one person and make a foghorn sound.

T: All right. We have three bottles. Fill them with different levels of water and let's hear them blown together. [They accidentally get a chord, three sounds stacked up at the interval of a third.]

Bottles:

T: Are you satisfied with those three sounds?

S: I would like to hear it colder. It sounds too sweet. I'll dump some of my water.

[They try again.]

Bottles, second try:

S: That's more like what I think cold water sounds like.

T: Let's work those sounds into the poem. Be ready to blow your bottles together after this next line is read. Pencil/marker ostinato, start please.

Class:

(Introduction)

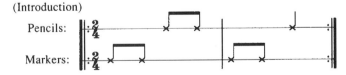

Poet: [states alone in conclusion] "This is my dream."

T: How do you feel about repeating the first verse now?

Poet: I would like to only do it once, but do it again at the very end, after "This is my dream."

T: Is the class in agreement with the poet? Fine. Before we try the whole poem, let me help you by putting an abbreviated map on the board. The key for the map will read like this:

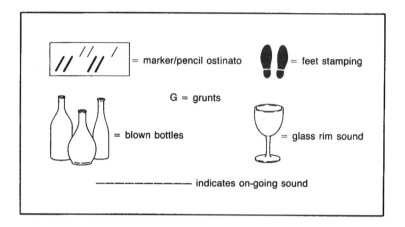

Let's talk through it once from the map to have it well in mind before trying:

GRAPHIC MAP of "When I Am Asleep"

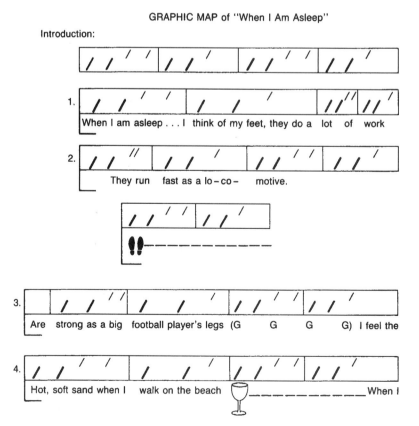

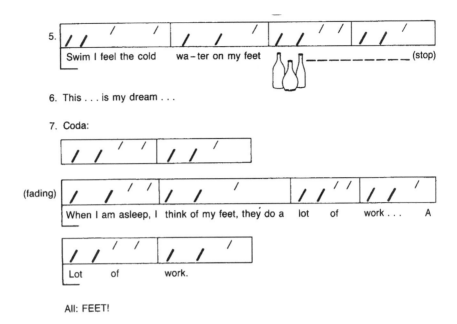

5.
Swim I feel the cold   wa – ter on my feet _____ (stop)

6. This . . . is my dream . . .

7. Coda:

(fading)
When I am asleep, I think of my feet, they do a   lot   of   work . . .   A

Lot   of   work.

All: FEET!

A TASK OF INTERMEDIATE DIFFICULTY

As groups experience facilitated lessons like the preceding one, they become ready to try lessons reaching the next level of difficulty, which is an intermediary step between the supportive lesson and a lesson in which there is little teacher intervention. In this medium-difficulty task, students (approximately 10 years old and older) are given the margins of the assignment, along with the freedom to interact with their peers, working in small groups. There they will experience the social dynamic of that group, argue, agree, build up, tear down, attempt, succeed, and semi-succeed—all of the possible events along the creative way. Sometimes groups will take the task beyond the teacher's design or in a new direction, and this is a good sign that they are stretching and are almost ready to be totally independent and free of teacher intervention. Here's an example of an intermediary sample lesson assignment.

SAMPLE LESSON: CONTINUED

T: Today, instead of working with the whole class, I am going to assign small groups a part of the poem you wrote together, "When I Fall Asleep." I will suggest two or three sounds but how to use them—when and where—will be totally up to your group. You may also use any of the elements we've explored in the past: movement, form, body percussion, texture, canon. Here are the five students I've picked to be group leaders—you can bounce your ideas off of them, and they will help keep the group on the right track. Dyson, John, LaToya, Kim, and Emily, here are the excerpts written out. Please scatter around the room, and the rest of you join the group you prefer—no more than four to a group.

Group 1:   Sounds to include: rocks, vocal; think about movement.

My eyes roll out of my body
like stones, roll
down a mountain, fall into a lake, my bed
      becomes
a river, I
become a mermaid
swim my way
to morning.

Group 2:   Sounds: Use vocal effects, melody, both melodic and modernistic or all over the place (disjunct melody). May also use movement.

My feet become fat
bright green, squishy frogs
and hop all
over the place, my voice becomes
thunder, crashes down
on silent, shadowy
sleeping cities.

Group 3:   Sounds: A rubber ball bouncing. Play with fragments of the poem, using the rhythm of one set of words under another word phrase (e.g., "pepperoni pizza" under "my body").

My body rolls into
a ball and bounces down
Broadway, I become
a pepperoni pizza
at a party, my fingers twist
into pretzels, my ears
blossom into fragrant
flowers, my skin turns
hard and brown as the
bark on trees.

Group 4:   Invent a sad, slow melody for the first thought. Use spiral sounds by scraping a notebook spine; use class-made shakers, and use the dynamic of crescendo in some way.

My eyelashes turn
into tears, my hair

starts to giggle, my eyebrows
become caterpillars and tickle
me till I laugh out loud and wake
myself up.

After 10 minutes of brainstorming, each group could share what they had developed so far. It's expected most groups would not be through. They would constructively critique the ideas in progress and could add a wish to further help the small groups. After those suggestions were absorbed, the groups would reconvene and finish. The poem would then be performed in tandem, with no discussion in between: a classroom performance. Final critiquing would react to the work as a total piece, inquiring if it held together, if there was enough contrast or too much, and so forth. If the group is afforded these preliminary exercises, one day it will be ready to move upward and experience the open assignment. This ideally means turning over a departure poem to small groups with little or no suggestions from the teacher. A fifth-grade class might have come up independently with these artistic solutions to the chosen poem (see p. 109):

The elements that were constant in this piece were the drum/spiral ostinato and the two vocal ostinati. Each time the soloist sang the improvisation, it varied from performance to performance. The teacher's input in this piece consisted of tonal preparation for the improvisation (through singing examples, through small keyboard demonstration, recorder, xylophone, and so forth; see Chapter 5). The scale used in this setting is the minor la pentatonic again, but starting on tone D:

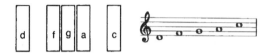

In this older-student, independent setting, the students chose melody, two vocal ostinati, can-drum/spiral-edge ostinato, cymbal pan lid, and teacher's bell as their way to realize the poet's fantasy. Such efforts as these make satisfying pieces to share in programs for other classes and for events to which parents and the public are invited.

SUMMARY: FOUND SOUNDS

This chapter dispels the idea that general classrooms are not equipped with instruments. The found sounds sources may not officially be instruments but can be attractive, interesting, clever, resourceful, and consummately usable sound sources for the creative process, nonetheless. Even music specialists should not overlook sounds available in all classrooms, readily accessible, unique, and often sounding as good as official, nonpitched, percussion instruments!

We've seen how children can collect such sounds over a period of time, working with the teacher in loosely structured assignments designed to acquaint them with the properties of these sounds. The authors observed progression from

- Discovery of sounds

- Categorization

- Simple tasks created by the teacher using these sounds

- Teacher facilitating a group piece

- Small groups performing fairly specific tasks

- Group work where there was tremendous room for student input and experimentation

By varying the amount of text used, length of text, and complexity of expectations, the sequence is adaptable and applicable for both younger and older groups.

PERSONALIZING THE POEM
The How-I-See-Myself/How-Others-See-Me Poem

Up to this point, the assignments have emphasized creative thinking and experimentation with poetic techniques. Students have written about colors, feelings, wishes, daydreams, and fantasies. In a way, writing these types of poems provided the students with a degree of anonymity by promoting the illusion that what was said in the poem was somehow removed from them personally. The emphasis was on the pleasure of words, the beauty of imagery, and the intensity of feeling, without ever requiring the students to place themselves (in the form of *I*) directly into the poems. This distance made it easier to concentrate on creative expression. The poems were written more in a spirit of fun and with less of a sense of accountability. This poetic benefit allowed the imagination to soar and the students to approach their writing feeling unencumbered and uninhibited. At some point, however, it becomes important for students to see their poems as reflections of themselves: they need to understand that what they say, and have said, in their poems reflects who they are and how they feel about themselves and the world around them.

The following lesson is an attempt to personalize the poems, bringing students directly into the images and intention of the poem. At this time, the teacher offers the students an opportunity to write from the "I" point of view to focus on themselves as the subject and expand outward to explore how they see themselves and how (they think) others see them. This ultimate step in the creative writing process requires students to address the meaning and impact of their words.

SAMPLE LESSON: POETRY

This lesson is designed to bring the student directly into the poem, as the subject. In asking the student to recall previous written assignments, the teacher reveals that each poem was really a personal

Teacher: The subject of today's writing assignment is the most important subject in the whole world. Today, we are going to be writing about ourselves! In reality, all of the poems we have written so far have been about ourselves. When you wrote about a color, you were really writing about how you saw that color. When you wrote about a feeling, you were really writing about how you felt about that

statement of self. Drawing on these past experiences, the teacher hopes to explore self-perception in some detail and to inspire written work that will be both poetically rich in language and style and intense and revealing on a personal level.

feeling. And when you wrote about fantasies, they were your fantasies and said something very special about you. And because each of us sees things differently, we used different images, different experiences and memories to enrich our poems and personalize them.

For the purpose of today's lesson, I want you to think of the world as a wheel. Let me draw it on the board. Look at it carefully. John, come on up and place an X where you think you are on that wheel—where you are in the world, not geographically, but personally.

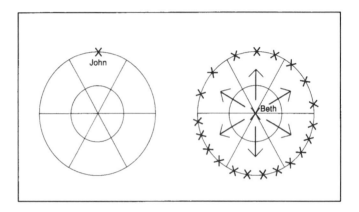

T: Beth, do you see yourself in the same place that John is?

S: No, I don't think so. I see myself right in the center.

T: That's great. Right in the center. Who else sees themselves as being right in the center of the wheel? Lots of hands are up. I think that we are all, probably, right in the center of our own worlds. We look at the world from our point of view, and in the world, John may be exactly where he placed himself on the wheel, but there would be a circle around John that places him in the center of his perception of the world. All of our individual circles overlap, as in the following diagram:

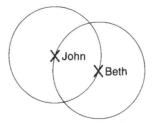

We all think of everything in the world as if it were revolving around us. Do you think that everyone (as indicated by the Xs around the wheel in Diagram 2) sees things exactly as you do? In fact, more to the point, do you think that everyone in your world sees you the way you do?

Here the teacher is using a fast pace, attempting to move the discussion along quickly in the hope that this may alleviate some of the self-consciousness accompanying self-revelation. She purposely does not dwell on responses but rather acknowledges them and moves on. When necessary (later in the lesson), she provides some modeling in the form of an excerpt from a (former) student poem, but mostly this lesson is designed to carry itself along. The hope is that the students will be motivated by their own and one another's insights.

S: No, probably not. I think most people see you in different ways than you see yourself.

T: Give me an example of someone in your life who may see you differently than you see yourself.

S: My mother sees me differently.

T: Someone else?

S: Teachers and friends.

T: Yes. Someone else?

S: Brothers and sisters and relatives.

S: Pets.

T: Absolutely. But let's concentrate on people. Do these people who see us differently than we see ourselves always see us in a good way?

S: No. Sometimes my mother thinks I'm pretty terrific, and sometimes she thinks I'm awful.

T: I think that's probably true of everyone in our lives. Certainly, when we think of other people, there are times when we think of them in a very good, very positive way and then there are times when we think of them in not such a good way. Will someone give me an example of how their mother sees them? Laura?

S: I don't know how she sees me.

T: I don't expect you to know how she sees you. I want you to tell us how you think she sees you.

S: Like a good girl.

T: "Like a good girl." That answers the question but does not answer it poetically. We don't want to forget that we are looking at ourselves, today, through poetry. Our answers need to be images—word pictures—so that all of us will be able to experience them through our senses. Remember all that you know about poetry: images, metaphor, and simile; adjectives, feelings, experiences, and memories; alliteration, onomatopoeia, and, of course, the five senses. Let me give you an example of exactly what I mean.

*My mother sees me as if
I were a house with a hundred
rooms and every day she
has to clean every room
on her hands and knees.*

*My father hears me as if
I were a nail scraping
across a blackboard.*

*I see myself as if I were
a feather floating
on the wind forever.*

These are some lines excerpted from a student poem, and they use imagery, the five senses, and intense feelings to describe how this student thinks his mother and father see him and how he sees himself. Laura, do you think, now, you could create an image for your mother seeing you as a good girl?

S: Maybe she sees me as if I were as good as a newborn kitten.

T: That's much better. Still, I would like for you to look deep inside yourself for those images that will become your poem. When you're looking for images, try to remember the things that you and the person you are writing about like to do together. If you're writing about your mother and you think she sees you in a good way, create your images out of those things that your mother enjoys or the things that you enjoy doing or sharing together. For example, do you and your mom like to shop together? Might she see you as a gigantic sale at her favorite department store? Does she like to cook? Might she see you as a hot chocolate chip cookie straight from the oven? Would someone like to try an image about how they think their mother sees them? Nat?

S: My mother sees me like homemade apple pie with vanilla ice cream.

T: That's the idea. Another image, please.

S: My mother sees me like a red silk dress and long gold earrings.

T: Excellent. How about an image for how your father sees you?

S: My dad sees me like the winning touchdown in the Super Bowl.

S: My dad sees me as a 3-foot fish on the end of his line.

S: My dad sees me as a trash can that's too full.

In this dialogue, it appears as if the student may be aiming for the laugh. The teacher does not attempt to negate the response but acts as a shield to block class reaction and moves the student (through suggestion) toward a more serious contemplation of the assignment. Having elicited a more serious response, the teacher is quick to praise.

T: Those are picturesque images. David came up with one that was not a good feeling. Do you think you can come up with a good feeling image, David?

S: Well, my dad thinks I'm the messiest kid in the world.

T: I think we realized that from your descriptive image. Are there some things that you and your dad like to do together?

S: We ski.

T: Great. Can you come up with a good feeling image using your skiing together as the inspiration?

S: My dad sees me as a ski slope covered with 2 feet of fresh powder.

T: That's the idea, exactly. Good image. Someone give me an image, good feelings or not such good feelings, for the way your teacher sees you.

S: My teacher sees me as a very smart kid.

T: I like the idea, but I'm wondering if it is an image. What do you think?

S: I don't think it is.

T: Would you turn it into one for me?

S: Smart as a library filled with books.

T: Fine. That works much better. Someone else.

S: My teacher sees me as an unsharpened pencil.

T: I like that one. Another.

S: My teacher sees me as if I were a broken record, talking all the time.

T: Those are all strong images. You explored, with humor and in a serious way, the feelings you think other people have about you, and in doing so, you really explored feelings you have about yourself. Let's take that a step further and ask ourselves, directly, how we see ourselves. Ronni, would you please give me an image for how you see yourself?

S: I see myself in lots of different ways.

T: I'm sure you do. We all see ourselves in lots of different ways, depending on what we feel, what's going on around us, what kind of mood we're in. But right this very minute, Ronni, how do you see yourself?

S: Maybe like the sun being blocked out by the clouds.

T: Oh, that's a very powerful image. It says so much and gives us so much to think about. I think an image is even more effective if it leaves some of the interpretation up to the reader. Your image, Ronni, certainly does that. Let's have some more images for how we see ourselves, please.

S: I see myself like an empty refrigerator, hungry!

S: I am a mouse being chased by a cat.

Whenever the opportunity presents itself, the teacher highlights poetic skills being used effectively. She is also choreographing an interplay between students, requiring them to listen and respond interpretively to the imagery of their classmates. Being asked for their opinions affords students a sense of self-importance and involvement. It may also provide the added benefit of students taking their own images more seriously, knowing that their ideas will be put to the group for reaction.

T: Nice metaphor, nice images, creative and thoughtful. By describing yourselves through imagery, you give us, the reader/listener, an opportunity to get involved in the poem. We bring ourselves into the poem through our interpretations of your images. For example, what do you, Robert, think Henry's cat-and-mouse image means?

S: That he feels scared like a mouse does when it's being chased by a cat.

T: Maybe. What else might it mean?

S: That he feels small?

T: Very possibly. You see what I mean about the reader/listener getting involved and becoming part of the poetic experience? We put our reader/listener feelings into your poet images and come up with something that is doubly meaningful for us. Good poetry always provides room for interpretation. Right now, I would like for us to put a list on the board of all of the people in our lives that we might want to include in our poem. Please help me.

> Mother, Father, sisters, brothers, friends, neighbors, teachers, principal, aunts, uncles, cousins, Grandmother, Grandfather, pets, enemies

T: That looks like a pretty complete list to me. What I'd like for you to do now is to select three to five people from that list and write a poem, using all that you know about poetry. Please end the poem by describing how you see yourself. You may, if you like, give us two views (a positive one and a negative one) for each person you write about and for yourself. For example, "Sometimes my mother sees me as if I were a flower blooming in her garden and sometimes she sees me as if I were a bee about to sting her." Please take a moment to think about who you really want to include in your poem and please take the time, as well, to explore your feelings honestly and present them through the poetry of meaningful, visual images.

STUDENT POEMS

HOW OTHERS SEE ME

My dad sees me happy
my mother sees me happy
but my brother sees me
funny and my friends
see me good like a soft,
summer afternoon; but I
see myself like the
pretty blue of the
morning sky.

—SECOND GRADE

ALL ABOUT ME

I think I am as tall
as a tree.
I have eyes
like brown shoe polish.
I am as thin
as my pinky.

My arms
are like steel.
My legs are faster
than a lion's legs.
My hair is fluffy
as a cat's meow.

—SECOND GRADE

ME, MYSELF, AND I

My mom sees me as a
sweet cottage, all tidy
and neat, a place to relax,
sometimes, she sees
me tall as a skyscraper
she has to clean and vacuum
everyday.

My dad sees me as a book
he has to read
all of his days. Sometimes

putting me away in a drawer
is a most relaxing sport for
him.

My grandma sees me as
a flower garden that she
loves to take care of.

My brother sees me as
a toy
all shiny and new, waiting
to play with him.

My grandpa sees me as
a child's toy which he has
no use for.

I see myself like
a leaf falling off a
tree floating far away
far from everyone else.

—Fifth grade

I Like Me

I like me.
I am as pretty
as a star
in the sky!

—Second grade

How I See Myself
and How Others See Me

My brother sees me as
a wacky monkey
who's naughty all the time.

My teacher sees me
as a pencil
doing all its work.

My mother sees
me as a shopping cart

huffing and puffing up and
down the aisles.

My grandpa thinks I am SPECIAL
as an "UPSIDE DOWN
AIRPLANE STAMP."

My gym teacher sees me as
a miniature Lawrence Taylor
d
  i
    v
      i
        n
          g
            diving, diving.

I think of myself
as a wise owl
swiftly scaring away
the hunters
on a cold winter night.

—Sixth grade

How I See Myself

My mom sees me
as a dirty sponge mop.
My father sees
me as a waiter
bringing him ice cream.
My grandmother sees me as a
toy destroyer.
My uncle sees me
as a sportscaster
telling him
the score.
I see myself as a boy
that counts the green
leaves on a tree.

—Fifth grade

SUMMARY: POETRY

This fifth session completes the first section of the poetry introductory stage. We have introduced poetic techniques, experimented with poetic form, and become somewhat more comfortable with the concept of words as tools. Students are daring to use metaphor and simile, alliteration and onomatopoeia, and the five senses with a bit more flair and confidence. Their poems have begun to flow more easily, and they are using language in a somewhat less self-conscious manner than when the sessions began. Teachers need, however, to continue to stress the need for poetic language skills; to rely on repetition to keep the poetry recipe, rainbow of adjectives, and sensory awareness, alive and flourishing in their students' writing.

The creative tree has always borne the most fruitful harvests when nourished by a healthy combination of praise and reward. It is for this reason that one needs to accept student work, particularly in the first draft stage, in a positive and openly receptive way. The need for editing and revision, however, must be emphasized. During the editing stage, teacher input can redirect the student toward application of heightened sensory awareness, clarification of ideas, and inclusion of the essential elements of poetry. Armed with a variety of language techniques, students are ready to explore new music and movement possibilities and, soon, begin applying their skills to daily classroom activities.

SYNTHESIS OF ALL LEARNED MOVEMENT AND MUSIC TECHNIQUES: THE HOW-I-SEE-MYSELF/HOW-OTHERS-SEE-ME POEM

So far, this book has shown diverse developments of movement and music, focusing on specific areas. The sample lessons showed that movement could be used to tell the poem's story in special terms, melody to shape it in sung terms, body percussion and vocal sounds to accompany and enrich, and form to re-create and enhance.

Now we are going to synthesize these areas, using all of the newly recognized creative skills. This chapter recognizes and assumes the exploration that has gone before in order to enable the student to function within the most casual of structures and acknowledges that music and movement skills have been used and reused to keep the possibilities alive and flowing.

SAMPLE LESSON: SYNTHESIS

[*Note:* The following group setting of "Me, Myself, and I" (p. 135) reflects previous experience in music and movement. In this example, the teacher remains totally open to the group's ideas of what should accompany the poem (if anything) and whether the poem lends itself to rhythmical treatment or to being accompanied by vocal or body percussion sounds, if it will work with melody, and what form the poem will take. Thus, the teacher's questions are purposely open, giving the group ample opportunity to initiate ideas based on their earlier experiences from more structured lessons.]

T: You all have copies of the poem we're going to use. Would everyone please silently read this poem?

- Having heard the words in your mind's ear, do any ideas come to you for where we might take this poem?

- You're telling me you see movement in the first verse. Do you see movement throughout the poem?

- Would someone please read it aloud so that we might hear how the word rhythm sounds to you?

- Having heard some ideas regarding the word rhythm, does anyone else envision anything else going on?

John is asked to justify his selection of the tapping sound and rethink his original rhythm choice, as it relates to the rhythmic qualities of the poem. His suggestion is refined by this kind of teacher questioning. The teacher includes the group in the assessment process. This group input provides John with peer backup. By becoming personally involved in the selection process, the teacher retains the right to express an opinion while giving some of the decision-making power to the group. The lesson is then synthesized into a series of group exercises using all of the learned skills.

- John, you hear a pencil tap echoing the word rhythm. Do you hear this tap idea throughout the poem or in special places?

- Class, would you read the first stanza of the word rhythm suggestion, and let John try his pencil-tap idea?

- Class, how do you feel about that arrangement thus far? Then let's hang onto those ideas and continue.

- Christy said earlier that there might be movement. Can you demonstrate what you had in mind, Christy? Would three students volunteer to join her to see what the movement looks like as a group pattern?

- Do you feel that the words chosen to move were effective?

- Group, what words do you feel are key for the movement people to focus on? *Tidy and neat?* What others? Yes, I would agree with your ideas of *skyscraper, wash and vacuum, book, tree, in the yard, toy, leaf.* Movement people, are you hearing the class's preference for words to be moved? Try again.

FACILITATING

Notice that in this questioning, the teacher is not steering toward the focus, as was the earlier case in which there were desired and specific areas to explore (e.g., discovering form, body percussion, and the implications of that to accompaniment, movement qualities). In this facilitator role, the teacher takes the ideas offered by students and becomes the traffic director, suggesting where ideas should be tried and encouraging more input when group jelling has not yet taken place. The teacher is also the interest thermometer, sensing how long to pace the activity: when to divert, when a logjam of ideas is not bearing results, and when the group is really supportive of an idea and willing to make it permanent.

The following group settings are the results of this more open kind of questioning, backed by assumed explorations done in movement and music throughout the year. As you read through these culminations, observe the creative elements used in the pieces, just as you would if you wished to reflect later on the piece you helped facilitate. The following is the fifth-grade example of the results of the word in play.

"Me, Myself, and I" Poem, Group Results

MOVEMENT	POEM AND ACCOMPANIMENT
(Ostinato group of five)	(Ostinato with group of ten.)
Step right on word *me*.	
Touch ankle with left foot on *self*.	Introduction:
Step left on *I*.	
Touch ankle with right foot on the rest	
(silence). Continue through next part.	

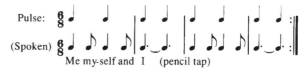

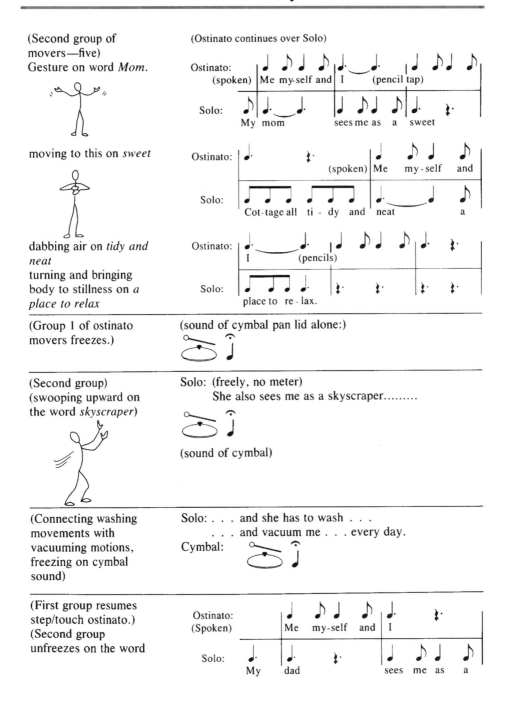

(Second group of movers—five)
Gesture on word *Mom*.

(Ostinato continues over Solo)

Ostinato:
(spoken) Me my-self and I (pencil tap)

Solo: My mom sees me as a sweet

moving to this on *sweet*

Ostinato:
(spoken) Me my-self and

Solo: Cot-tage all ti-dy and neat a

dabbing air on *tidy and neat*
turning and bringing body to stillness on *a place to relax*

Ostinato:
I (pencils)

Solo: place to re-lax.

(Group 1 of ostinato movers freezes.)

(sound of cymbal pan lid alone:)

(Second group)
(swooping upward on the word *skyscraper*)

Solo: (freely, no meter)
She also sees me as a skyscraper.........

(sound of cymbal)

(Connecting washing movements with vacuuming motions, freezing on cymbal sound)

Solo: . . . and she has to wash . . .
. . . and vacuum me . . . every day.
Cymbal:

(First group resumes step/touch ostinato.)
(Second group unfreezes on the word

Ostinato:
(Spoken) Me my-self and I

Solo: My dad sees me as a

book, opening hands
and sweeping air with
rainbow shaped arc,
while turning on *all of
his life*.)

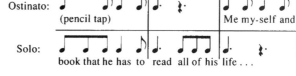

Ostinato:
(pencil tap)   Me my-self and

Solo:
book that he has to read all of his life . . .

Ostinato:
I,   (pencils)

Solo:

(ostinato stops)

(First ostinato stops.)
(Second group freezes
with hands on hips on
sometimes, then mimes
a solid door with hands
outward and stiff on
most, joy of *enjoyable,*
and *sport,* dabbing
three places in space.)

Solo: (freely) Sometimes . . . putting me away in the
closet . . .
is a <u>most</u> . . . en<u>joy</u>able . . . <u>sport</u> . . . for him
. . .

(Group 1 of movers
resumes ostinato.)

(Ostinato resumes with movers, one time, then
continues under poem:)

(Spoken)
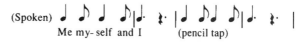
Me my-self and I   (pencil tap)

(Group 1 resumes.)
(Group 2 moves in an
unbroken motion from
grandma shape to tree.)

Ostinato:
(Spoken)   Me   my - self   and

Solo:
My   grand - ma

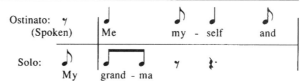

Ostinato:
I   (pencils)

Solo:
sees me   as   a   tree in the yard

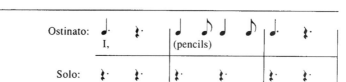

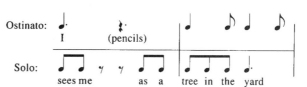

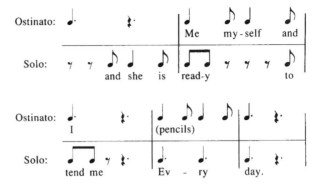

(Group 1: On *play with a toy*, students skip in own circle. They stop and clap the second measure facing the audience. Repeated through next section.)

(New ostinato for voice and clapping)

Solo:
(Spoken)   Play with a   toy   (clap)

(Group 1 moves new ostinato.)

(Group 2, on *brother*, indicates height of child. On the word *toy*, group begins to build an interlocking body toy, moving one at a time to the pulse. Toy moves on the words played with in a rhythmical way.)

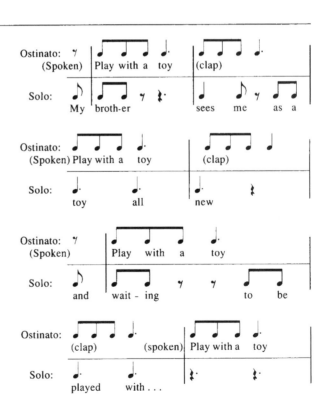

Ostinato:
(Spoken)   Play with a   toy   (clap)

Solo: My broth-er   sees me as a

Ostinato:
(Spoken) Play with a   toy   (clap)

Solo: toy   all   new

Ostinato:
(Spoken)   Play   with   a   toy

Solo: and   wait - ing   to   be

Ostinato: (clap)   (spoken) Play with a   toy

Solo: played   with . . .

(Group 1 stops.)
(Group 2 unlocks toy one person at a time, and walks apart sadly on lines *Grandpa sees me as a child's toy . . . which he has no use for.*)

Ostinato: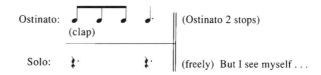
(clap)

(Ostinato 2 stops)

Solo:

(freely) But I see myself . . .

Both groups walk to right making individual circles. *But I see myself,* arms somewhat raised.
(Groups 1 and 2 turn one time and press arms even higher, looking upward at hands on *I see myself.*)

(sound of cymbal)

Solo: (more intensely) I SEE MYSELF . . .

(repeat cymbal)

(Group 1 freezes with hands up.)
(Group 2 begins descending movement scallops with accompanying vocal sounds on *falling off a tree.* They float away from each other on *floating far away from everyone else.*)

Solo: As a leaf . . . falling off a tree . . . floating far away . . . from everyone else.

Group 1 unfreezes to do coda with voice and step-touch-step, holding on last *I* with arms upraised.

Coda:

Group 1:

(Spoken)

Me my-self and I   (pencil tap)

(Shout ME MY-SELF AND I!
forte)   The End

All of the creative elements used within "Me, Myself, and I" reveal a rich assortment:

- Movement

- Speech ostinato accompaniment with movement

- Found sound ostinato accompaniment

- Introduction and coda

- Expansion of form through insertions of ostinati between stanzas

- Use of dynamics

- Use of speech tempo change from rhythmical in 6/8 to free meter

Taking the time to reflect on the strengths and weaknesses (if there were any) of finished pieces develops the power of group critiquing. It gives students (and the teacher) the chance to have wishes and ponder what could have happened differently. This type of evaluation is documented in learning taxonomies as the most significant and demanding to keep creative growth spiraling. In Bloom's dissertation on the taxonomy of learning, he put this kind of critiquing on the sixth, and highest, step of his taxonomy after knowledge, comprehension, application, analysis, and synthesis.

Even younger groups can function in this more open kind of creative framework, provided previous isolation of those elements of speech, movement, and form have been sampled. The next example deals with such a poem from a student in second grade. Here, all of the teacher's good intentions in helping facilitate the group's responses were for naught, and the class remained polarized, half wanting the poem sung and the other half wanting a rhythmical/body percussion setting. The solution was to create two settings.

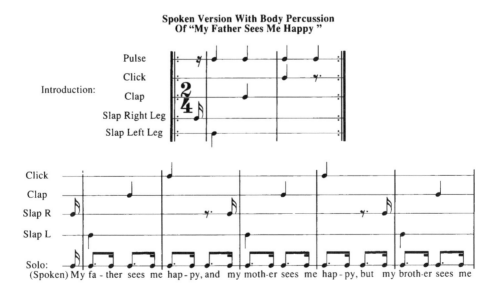

Spoken Version With Body Percussion
Of "My Father Sees Me Happy "

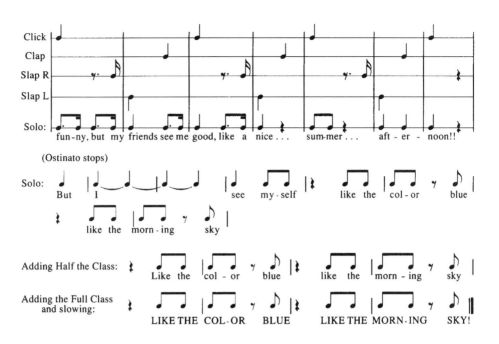

funny, but my friends see me good, like a nice . . . sum-mer . . . aft-er-noon!!

(Ostinato stops)

Solo: But I see my-self like the col-or blue like the morn-ing sky

Adding Half the Class: Like the col-or blue like the morn-ing sky

Adding the Full Class and slowing: LIKE THE COL-OR BLUE LIKE THE MORN-ING SKY!

Melodic Version of "My Father Sees Me Happy"

Do Pentatonic on G

Clapping Group:

Sung Ostinato: All a-bout me Hap-py hap-py hap-py

Solo: My

Clapping:

Sung Ostinato: All a-bout me Hap — py hap-py All a-bout

Solo: fath-er sees me hap-py and my moth-er sees me hap-py but my broth-er sees me

(Group repeats introduction
as coda, pianissimo)

Both versions were convincing to the group. Both had integrity and gave the text its due. Important to note is that neither setting was written down. Once the parts were decided, it was the job of a student conductor to remind the group when to stop and where to continue, as prescribed by the group. The sung ostinato was learned by rote and graphed on the board as a reminder of the pitches:

All
   a-
      bout
         me

The sounds of the pentatonic scale were initially sung by the teacher to get the students' ears into that particular mode (and the scale could have been demonstrated as easily on a recorder or small pitched percussion instrument, as mentioned in earlier chapters).

The following "How I See Myself" poem became a stick puppet show in the hands of the students. The class decided on the important words, and these, when drawn, became the stick puppets. A makeshift curtain was stretched between two students, each holding an end, and the poem with fairly literal sound effects and graphics supplied by the class began.

STICK PUPPET	FOUND SOUND EFFECTS	POEM SPOKEN AS PUPPETS APPEARED
	Improvisation for scraped chairs and tapped tin can following the poem's first line	"My mom sees me as a dirty laundry mat." (Sounds and puppet emerging from behind curtain)
	Improvisation on teacher's bell and delicious mouth sounds	"My father sees me as a waiter that gets him gushy ice cream." (Sounds and puppet)

	Many people making *Mmmmm* contented sounds on many different pitches	"My grandmother sees me as a blanket waiting to be cuddled almost every weekend." (Sounds and puppet)
	Soda cans being stepped on	"My grandpa sees me as a toy crusher."
	Vocal improvisation of baseball announcer calling a homerun with the crowd roaring	"My uncle sees me as a sports magazine that tells him the score."
	Teacher's bell	"I see myself"
(tree slowly rising with other hand slowly showing to count the leaves . . .)	Mark tree made from hanging keys (made by suspending many discarded keys on plastic fishing line. A magical sound occurs when you run your finger along it, and the keys strike each other.) Final ding on bell at end.	"I see myself" "I see myself as a boy . . . who counts the green leaves in a tree."

"How I See Myself" for Solo Group Voice and Movement

There can be great beauty in simple settings, as in this one, based on the "How I See Myself and How Others See Me" poem. The group decided basically on using only speech and movement, the spoken part getting its contrast from solo and group performances and the students who were doing movement taking their ideas from the essence of each line. When someone came up with the idea of doubling the voices and repeating them, another simple but lovely nuance was added. The movement group also had to devise ways to connect movement ideas, one to the next, to avoid looking sporadic.

MOVEMENT	SOLO VOICE	GROUP VOICES
(Four or more people) (Monkey gestures four steps right, four left)	My brother sees me at self defense.	as a crazy monkey who's bad
Multipeople interlocking machine with moveable parts.	My teachers see me all my paperwork.	(automatic voices) as an automatic pencil happily doing
In partners, one pushes and the other is the wheelbarrow.	My mother sees me Huffing and puffing (Retrieving items.)	as a motorized shopping cart Huffing and puffing down the aisles.
Many watching one who is pantomiming licking stamps into an invisible album, feigning interest in the airplane stamp.	My grandpa thinks I'm as special	as the only mint "upside down airplane stamp."
All run with the pass and feign a safe dive to the floor with the arms-up touchdown signal.	My gym teacher sees me diving for a touchdown.	as a miniature Lawrence Taylor diving
Big-eyed owls with sounds flap off in different directions.	I think of myself As a wise owl Swiftly scaring away On a cold, winter night	As a wise owl the hunters (forte) On a cold, winter night. (p)

"I Like Me," Second Grade, ABA Form with Found Sounds

For this next poem, the second-grade class decided they would need star-like sounds that twinkled, so the search began for beautiful, ringing found sounds in the room: fingers around glass rims, glasses struck lightly with rubber erasers, the mark tree made from hanging keys. To lengthen the poem, the group brainstormed all of the constellations they knew to add to the center section and also decided to repeat the first part. An ABA form was created.

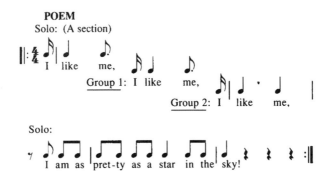

POEM
Solo: (A section)

Group 1: I like me,

Group 2: I like me,

Solo:
I am as pret-ty as a star in the sky!

FOUND SOUNDS

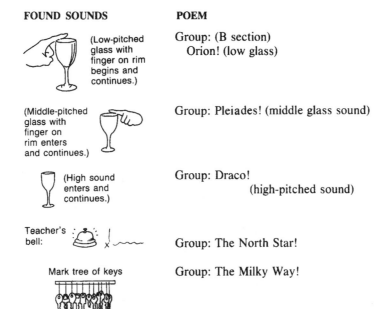

(Low-pitched glass with finger on rim begins and continues.)

(Middle-pitched glass with finger on rim enters and continues.)

(High sound enters and continues.)

Teacher's bell:

Mark tree of keys

POEM

Group: (B section)
  Orion! (low glass)

Group: Pleiades! (middle glass sound)

Group: Draco!
    (high-pitched sound)

Group: The North Star!

Group: The Milky Way!

A section is repeated with final ping on triangle or bell after the word *sky.*

"All About Me" for Bottles, Movement, Improvisation, and Group Refrain (Expansion)

In the next example, "All About Me" uses the minor pentatonic cited in Chapter 3. By this point, the teacher has helped the students enter the mode by conversing in those tones in recitative:

The group decided to have two bottles pitched to the low D so that the breathing could be staggered, making the tone appear to be sustained. This tone also helped the soloist find the home tone or key center (D), which was useful while improvising. Four people were the movers, and the rest of the class sang the ostinato in between the soloist, who was improvising.

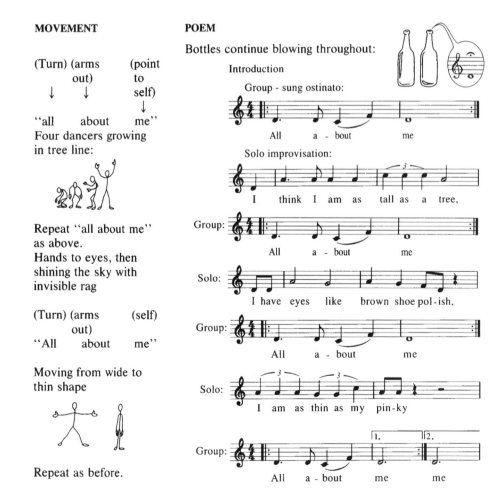

MOVEMENT

(Turn) (arms   (point
         out)   to
   ↓   ↓   self)
                     ↓
"all   about   me"
Four dancers growing
in tree line:

Repeat "all about me"
as above.
Hands to eyes, then
shining the sky with
invisible rag

(Turn) (arms   (self)
         out)
"All   about   me"

Moving from wide to
thin shape

Repeat as before.

POEM

Bottles continue blowing throughout:

Introduction
Group - sung ostinato:

All   a - bout   me

Solo improvisation:

I think I am as tall as a tree,

Group:
All   a - bout   me

Solo:
I have eyes like brown shoe pol-ish,

Group:
All   a - bout   me

Solo:
I am as thin as my pin-ky

Group:
All   a - bout   me   me

Regarding arms,
floating them upward,
then flexing with force
on *steel*

Repeat as before.

MOVEMENT

Movers run in place.

As before

Movers dab hair with
beat.

(turn) (arms   (self)
      out)
"All   about   me"

Repeat above.

Repeat with smaller
motion.

POEM

For purposes of sharing, a melody has been written—fixed—on the page through notation, but the reader should remember that this is an *improvised* melody and therefore not written down at its creation nor would it ever be the same way twice. The only thing that would remain constant would be the chosen mode of la pentatonic. Different soloists would create different melodies within this mode.

SUMMARY

All of the poetic inspirations in Section I of this book began as words on a page or words in the mouth and then through the music and movement experience, became rhythmical and took on additional emphasis through group or solo interpretation and musical and movement enhancement. The poems changed, taking on new forms and new shapes. Like a tree, the poem is a creative miracle in and of itself. Even in winter, it is an elegant linear statement, and then it blossoms, flowers, bears fruit, and changes color—each layering a metamorphosis of the original creative statement.

The students have discovered that the poet's tools, plus movement and music, can be used to explore anything: colors, feelings, fantasies, themselves. And it is through language that students are taught math, history, art, social studies, science, and all other subjects. Words, therefore, are the common tool in all learning environments, thus affording access to the math-oriented student in the language arts classroom as well as the history-oriented student in the math classroom. Subjects are different and unique; however, they are taught and understood through the grace of language. You have now begun to learn how to make words work for you, and how, ultimately, to use them to expand teaching arenas and open all of the interdisciplinary doors to learning.

TROUBLESHOOTING AND TEACHER–STUDENT DYNAMICS

Teaching is an imperfect science, and occasionally plans don't work out in the classroom. Responses from groups and from individual group members are sometimes unexpected, inappropriate, or simply not forthcoming. This is the nature of the teaching environment. Many variables are possible when introducing a new subject or trying a new approach. Students may misinterpret the intent of a lesson and head off in a wrong direction or greet it with silence. One student may dominate the discussion, leaving the other students behind or bored. Any number of divergent factors can and do influence the effectiveness of a lesson. In this chapter, some of the hazards of these variables are addressed. Suggestions, inspired by the authors' experiences, are intended to be helpful in overcoming classroom trouble spots.

It is important to accept the premise that every student response, even those that are problematical or singular, can expand the lesson into new, creative shapes. Thus, the teacher becomes a filter through which ideas are refined and released, not judged or discarded. For example, the student who responded to a lesson on color poems by offering the image, "Blue is the color of wonders" ignited a spark that burned for days. The original classroom reaction was one of puzzled silence. Students seemed unsure of what was meant by wonders or how the word fit the assignment (of finding an image using the five senses for the color blue). They were also unsure of what the teacher's reaction was going to be, and for a moment, the lesson stalled. The teacher rejoined enthusiastically, praising the originality of such an idea and seeking from the classroom as a whole a definition for the word *wonder*. "What are wonders?" The reaction was, "Wonders are wishes, dreams, fantasies, possibilities, and things that lack reality." The teacher began to list student-suggested wonders on the blackboard. Fog was a wonder, as were rainbows, lightning, snowflakes, spider webs, flower petals, bird songs, and many other things. The discussion was animated and intense, and it became inspirational. This is the kind of student-initiated response that one cannot plan for but should be ready to seize. Thus, color poems were unceremoniously abandoned in favor of discovering the nature of wonders. To have ignored this student's serendipitous gift by redirecting the classroom back to a discussion of colors would have been to ignore the miraculous offerings of what wonders are.

In all classroom situations, teachers need to retain an ample degree of flexibility, receptivity, and adventurousness. They also need to approach lessons with a sense of humor, awe, and abandonment. We cannot stress enough the importance of embracing student offerings, whether they seem appropriate or not, being willing to accept the outrageous, and perhaps being a little outrageous as well. This sometimes requires heading north when the original destination was south.

Teachers constantly encourage students to take risks and to allow themselves to be vulnerable. Teachers themselves can do no less. Regardless of an individual's teaching comfort zone, nothing is lost by remaining accessible to possibility. Whether material is taken and used directly from this book, interpreted and applied with a personal touch, or garnered from other sources, a subjective viewpoint is the essential ingredient to any creative lesson. Troubleshooting from this approach promises the greatest chance of reclaiming and renewing a lesson that seems to be going astray.

GROUP SITUATIONS AND SUGGESTED SOLUTIONS

The remainder of the chapter covers various possible classroom situations that cause difficulties or disrupt the lesson. Situations that are addressed here include silence, negative classroom interactions, lack of student leadership, unfocused (or inappropriately focused) energy, and difficulties resulting from transitions from one activity or class to another. Each section describes a situation and possible solutions.

Silence

Silence in the classroom is almost always a recognizable puzzled silence. Questions elicit little or no response, and through attempted application, it becomes clear that students are unsure of what is being asked of them. However, the teacher must avoid the temptation to interpret this kind of silence as student inattentiveness or blatant unwillingness to participate. Indeed, the teacher must be willing to immediately evaluate the effectiveness of his or her presentation. If unclear communication appears to be the problem, the teacher can indicate this to the class: "Perhaps I didn't present this clearly. Let me explain it again." At this time, it may be helpful to offer the lesson in a number of different ways, watching carefully for student signs of understanding and enthusiasm.

The following is an example of this kind of teacher self-evaluation. Having presented a lesson designed to stimulate a writing experience about the sea, the teacher encounters blank looks and silence. He or she presents the lesson again, coming at it from a number of different vantage points, asking the questions, and giving examples: "The sea is as green as a frog's back. The sea is white with foam. The sea is rough. Which of these, if any, is an image?" "How can we turn those that are not images into images? Should they be similes or metaphors?" "The sea is as rough as what? Sandpaper? A cat's tongue? A hurricane? Thunder?" The silence usually gives way to a discussion of imagery (a subject with which students are familiar). At this point, it might be helpful for the teacher to record (on the chalkboard or on paper) the students' images as they are suggested. The teacher can then point out to the students that they have, in fact, been verbally writing the poem they were confused about and discussing the poem (through imagery) they thought they couldn't create. Very often, their delight in the beauty and clarity of their own images stimulates further discussion.

Thus, in dealing with the kind of silence resulting from unclear teacher presentation, it is essential to innovate in unexpected and varied directions. Here, a strong but vulnerable teacher voice is important: "I think the sea is as gentle as my granddaughter's eyes." Through personalization, the teacher offers images from her own experiences, and the lesson is clarified. Students now have viable examples and a promising point of departure.

Inadequate Teacher Modeling

Another possible cause of students' puzzled silence could be inadequate teacher modeling. Some of the solutions for silence due to unclear teacher presentation may be equally applicable here. Examples of modeling occur in most areas of this text. Using a movement lesson as the canvas, the teacher should try to illustrate verbal instructions with clear and easily interpreted movement examples, while leaving room for student exploration. Likewise, in any melodic work, the teacher must be prepared to demonstrate examples in the sets of tones (keys) in which the students will be working. Seeding any initial lesson with teacher-given examples can ensure that students will see the teacher as a willing participant, ready to join in the risk-taking (an important aspect mentioned before), and that the students will recognize that opportunities enter the inception stages of a task, moving toward revelation and nonthreatening progression. Through this process, a sense of security is initially established. Succinctly, the progression is:

1. Observe: "Watch me."

2. Copy, echo, or imitate: "You do it."

3. Create: "Try your own ideas."

4. Copy a peer's idea for reinforcement: "Try doing what Jamie is doing."

5. Create longer forms: "Why don't you combine your idea with Jamie's?"

6. Analyze: "Describe what you did."

7. Upgrade language: "Tell me again, but use movement terms."

8. Synthesize: "Okay, now, put it all together."

It is generally the case that student discovery is a more powerful teaching technique than information feeding. Note in the sample lesson in Chapter 1, the teacher illustrated the mystery color through a movement demonstration, inviting students to use their observation powers to bridge the gap between a color and a movement. At the same time, students were discovering the language of movement by listening to the teacher. In the question framed by the teacher, there was margin for interpretation, leaving the students free to choose from many right answers. When the students were asked to do the teacher movement, they could respond within a safety zone because they were merely following the teacher's lead. The invitation to try another motion of a student design added weight to the amount of investment and thought demanded from students, and encouraged them to bring the motion into space. Discussing the results of their movements from a subjective point of view provided students with criterion for determining the quality of a movement. Labeling these movement qualities (using the Laban terminology) offered students a richer vocabulary with which to evaluate or analyze their efforts.

Chapter 2 illustrates a music lesson in which the modeling of tones is accomplished through musical conversation before being used in student improvisations. In Chapter 4, a masterwork is used as a model for a parallel poetry writing lesson.

Negative Classroom Interactions

The types of problems that arise in a classroom as a result of poor group dynamics are legion and almost always lead to problematic interactions. In Section I of the book, we have chosen to present good group dynamic situations to portray optimum lesson flow. Teachers are aware that the ideal lesson is very seldom the case. Several elements can cause negative classroom interactions, including fear of ridicule from peers and negative or aggressive peer responses to student suggestions (e.g., derisive laughter).

Fear of Ridicule

One of the most inhibiting and potentially destructive elements in the classroom is student fear of ridicule or a negative reaction from peers (e.g., derisive comments, laughter). This type of student negative brew serves up a silent response and muted enthusiasm for creative lessons, which require verbal interaction and input.

First, all teachers must analyze the group persona to determine if a poor group dynamic is the result of peer fear. Having made that diagnosis and realizing at the beginning of a lesson that the verbal responses will not be rich, the teacher can use the following suggestions to nurture students and tap the temporarily blocked creative energy:

- In a language lesson, have older students write their responses to the initial presentation. Have each student then exchange his or her response with a fellow student, and have them read each other's works aloud. This may alleviate some of the pressure of sharing one's own work with the entire class. It may also give students an opportunity to get more deeply involved in one another's work, and by so doing, develop a more empathetic stance.

- Younger students, lacking sophisticated writing skills, have a different problem. The teacher might suggest that students respond by drawing a picture of the image that comes to mind. This means of expression is appealing to students and thus increases the chance for an uninhibited response.

- Assess and deal with the negative feelings that may arise by openly exploring student feelings.

Make it a classroom rule that students in general will share their work. Maintaining focus allows students to respond honestly. If the response is a negative one, turn the discussion into an analysis of how these negative responses might make one feel. The following is a possible script of how this scenario might proceed:

Teacher: Mary, how did it make you feel when John laughed at your comment?

Mary: It made me feel very bad.

T: Did it make you feel anything else?

Mary: Angry.

T: John, how do you think you would feel if someone laughed at your comment?

John: Not too good, I guess.

T: Can we all discuss the feelings that we have about speaking aloud in class? Does it make you feel good to get up and share your thoughts with the group? Does it make you feel proud? Does it make you feel frightened? Please write down on a piece of paper three feelings you get when asked to share aloud your ideas with the rest of the class. [Students write down their feelings. The teacher invites each student to read aloud what he or she has written.] Okay, I see that three common feelings are angry, frightened, and nervous.

The teacher then might turn the lesson toward a positive language experience by asking the following questions:

- Angry as what?

- Frightened as what?

- Nervous as what?

The students may then be encouraged to take their feelings and turn them into images (the beginning of a poem):

- Angry as a charging bull

- Frightened as a mouse being chased by a cat

- Nervous as a tooth about to be pulled

In an actual writing experience responding to negative classroom feedback, the poem "The Nag" was written (see Chapter 2, p. 36). The teacher could then extend the lesson into an ongoing poem or discussion about negative feelings, and poetry can then become a cathartic experience for the class as a whole. The lesson can become a point of reference should the behavior reappear.

Another solution is to establish class atmosphere by direct teacher intervention. The following script gives an example of this:

T: [reacting to derisive laughter] Julie, in this class, we want to feel free to try new things and to express ourselves without being afraid to make a mistake. When you laugh at someone's response, you no longer allow this to happen. Exploration is one of the most important things we do in our classroom. I'm going to ask that all of you, from this point on, greet the efforts of your classmates with positive comments only.

There is perhaps no more stifling type of behavior than aggressive and/or negative response, and it must be addressed through teacher–student input or through quick and decisive positive teacher intervention.

Lack of Student Leadership

It is not uncommon to have a group with no clear student leadership. Most groups do best verbally when there is a lead to follow. For example, one student will respond to the teacher's modeling, giving not only an example to the rest of the class but also perhaps needed courage. A lack of student leadership can lead to confusion and a weak lesson. When no leadership is evident, the following suggestions may help spark participation.

For lessons involving language, one option is to assign roles to particular students before the lesson is presented. The following teacher script illustrates how this might be done:

T: Joseph, I'm going to be talking today about colors. Before I begin, let me remind you of our discussions in the past about using your five senses when writing poetry. When I finish talking to you about colors, I want you to be ready to write down (or tell me) three responses to the colors using the sense of touch. Mary, I want you to have three responses to the colors using the sense of hearing. I will then ask you to share them with the class.

Using advance assignments before the task ensures that the class will have verbal leads to follow. For lessons involving movement, set up tasks in small groups and assign leaders, thus giving students the opportunity to flex their leadership qualities in a controlled, comfortable, and nonthreatening environment. The following teacher script shows an example of this tactic:

T: We've been exploring verbs and what these words can prompt us to do in movement. I have demonstrated some of these verbs for you. Take any from the board that I have not moved, and (in groups of four) be prepared to present these words in movement to the class. I will assign a leader for each group, and you can bounce your ideas off of that leader.

This manageable, preassigned group activity results in mosaics that, when combined, become the focus for a larger class piece.

For lessons involving music, when no leadership propels the class in a forward direction, the teacher may choose to assume the role of leader. The teacher may give numerous examples, use repetition, and provide positive stroking for student effort. When the teacher feels reticent or lacks musical skills, using a music specialist may be appropriate and desirable.

Unfocused Energy

Too much, too fast: the group dynamic in a classroom with unfocused energy can result in an overly zealous atmosphere in which a significant number of students wish to lead the class and have their suggestions adopted. The teacher may find him- or herself battling verbal traffic, high volatility, and inattention.

Verbal Traffic

A classroom with a lot of verbal traffic can get chaotic and confused. Good ideas may get pulled under and lost in the tide of enthusiasm. It can also lead to squabbling and negative feelings that actually result from a positive outflow of ideas. Classes of this type require a strong teacher presence and a clear outline of how the class will function. The teacher becomes, in effect, a skilled and sensitive facilitator of verbal traffic. He or she must point out that ideas need soil in which to be nurtured and that the soil is the attention of fellow classmates. It is important to establish the realization that listening is not a passive role and that the listener is contributing by digesting, analyzing, and reshaping what is being said. Specifically, creative control of this type of group may be accomplished by one or more of the following methods:

- Break the larger group into units of two, allowing them to share their ideas aloud, enjoying the immediacy of a response while not interfering with class flow. Once the initial need to share has been satisfied, the entire group can be reformed and ideas can be exchanged in a more relaxed format.

- Make sure that pacing is considered when clearing space for individual ideas (e.g., allot time frames for opening discussion, for quiet thought, for class group input, for teacher reflection and redirection, and for selection of ideas through a variety of methods).

- Tell students, "Vote for the idea (or the melody or movement) that you think will propel the piece the most successfully."

- Use trial and error by selecting at random ideas on which to act as a group, and then ask the group to decide which were the most effective.

If the pacing needs to be faster, the teacher can simply arbitrarily select (having allowed for widespread student input) those ideas, melodies, or movements that he or she thinks will best satisfy the goals of the lesson.

High Volatility

Although having an enthusiastic, responsive group can be delightful, it is important to remember that creativity comes in a variety of forms and sounds. The too-quiet classroom can be stifling but so can the too-loud classroom. What is needed is a variety of "sound carpets" on which to create: the quiet hum of students sharing in small groups, the absolute silence of individual contemplation, the hypnotic timbre of a single voice expressing a view or in dialogue with a teacher, the explosive joy of laughter, enthusiasm, and sheer reaction, and, sometimes (but not always or for too long) the cacophony of too much, too fast.

Transition Difficulties

Transition difficulties come in many forms, from an overcrowded curriculum, to student tension, to difficult emotional transitions from previous activities. Teachers can use several solutions to cope with these issues.

An Overcrowded, Distracting Curriculum

The obvious problem in a classroom with an overcrowded curriculum is that the teacher may have great difficulty maintaining a flow of ideas that are pertinent to the topic at hand. The class becomes splayed and fractured and seems to be going off in all directions at once. This is not uncommon and is due in large part to the nature of today's curriculum, which takes students from place to place at a rather har-

ried pace. Using this book can help teachers address the issue by offering interrelated and cross-curriculum approaches to teaching, which provides an environment that fosters a more cohesive and bonded class.

Student Tension

Tension, both physical and mental, is not uncommon even on the elementary level.
Students must have receptive minds and relaxed bodies if a lesson is to blossom to
its full potential. Reducing tension may be accomplished by providing students with
an opportunity to physically unwind (e.g., a stretch, a deep breath that is let out
without a sound), or it may be helpful to suggest focusing on an image (e.g., "As you
silently exhale, think of a starry sky with a million dots of light. Focus on one star.
Block everything else out. Mentally touch the star. Listen to the sound of its silence.
Use your five senses to explore the darkness and the light.") This may be a lead-in
to a lesson, or it may simply be a deep mental breath, an opportunity to clear the
mind and prepare a clean, fresh mental sheet on which to create. Gentle exercises,
which stretch the body and bring the breath to play, and colorful teacher imagery
are beneficial in helping children of all ages to relax and focus.

Difficult Emotional Transitions

If a group appears to be caught up with a previous activity (e.g., playing a volatile
baseball game, hatching chickens, watching an emotional dispute between two class
members, viewing a captivating film), the teacher may have to change direction and
move with the class in the wake of their enthusiasm, despair, excitement, exaltation,
or preoccupation. The teacher is a receiver as well as a giver and has to be able to
assimilate the mood and disposition of the class and allow this input to shape the
moment. This invokes the joy, the challenge, and the artistry of teaching.

Creating Anticipation

The class that is unfocused because it meets between an outdoor gym class and
school dismissal time, for example, is not going to be terribly open or motivated to
participate in a language/music/movement lesson. One solution is to tell the
students about the lesson in advance, so that they enter the room in an anticipatory
and excited mood. For example, as the class is leaving for lunch, the teacher might
suggest to them that during their language arts class, scheduled for later that afternoon, "We will be using as our focus for writing the most important subject in the
world." Invariably, the students say, "What is that?" The answer that the teacher
could give is, "You'll find out as soon as you arrive from gym today." This seeding
almost always provides the advantage of at least a few of the students coming in
with the question on their lips, "What is the most important subject in the world?"

Anticipating the possibility that the class will have difficulty focusing on the lesson, it might be helpful to instruct them prior to the lunch break to bring something
back with them to the classroom—a nature sound they heard while out on the playground, a movement they witnessed in nature (e.g., trees waving in the wind, cloud
movement, birds), or any other number of things that could prove to be the focus of
the day's lesson.

INDIVIDUAL DYNAMICS AND POSSIBLE SOLUTIONS

Occasionally, the issue is with an individual student, rather than with the class as a whole. Some possible situations include students deliberately misunderstanding the assignment, giving rambling responses, offering innocent non sequiturs, getting lost or left behind, being uncooperative or disruptive, dominating classroom discussion, or simply feeling creatively blocked. Each of the following sections addresses a possible situation with an individual student and offers some solutions and ways of improving the individual dynamic.

Student Deliberately Misunderstands Assignment, Teacher, or Cue

A student may deliberately misunderstand the assignment, the teacher's instructions, or an agreed-upon cue. Often when this happens, the student is going for the laugh. The teacher must remember that he or she can cope with even this type of response in a positive way, thereby reducing its disruptive effect. For example, in the course of preliminary discussion about poems dealing with the topic "The People of My World," Brad was called on to volunteer what he had brainstormed about this subject. He had chosen to talk about his neighbors. As he began, it became clear that he was extemporizing beyond his original notes. It also became clear that he was heading in a direction designed to provide a bit of unscheduled humor. He included a wealth of salient details about his neighbors' reactions to his dog's visit to their lawns. He spared no detail. The class began to follow his lead. At this moment, the session could be either won or lost, depending on the teacher's reaction. To acknowledge that what Brad said was inappropriate would negatively reinforce his intention. To divert the trend or try to find pertinent worth in what was said would instead take the wind out of his sails and add substance to the classroom discussion. Thus, the teacher took a deep breath and reflectively said, "We have learned a lot about you today, Brad. We've learned that you are a person who keenly observes the behavior of your pet and of your neighbors and that you are very much aware of their likes and dislikes. It takes a sensitive person to be that observant. In poetry, we need to develop just those types of skills."

In these situations, the teacher, in essence, acts as a shield to deflect the remark that may destroy the direction, mood, and intent of the discussion. He or she must respond quickly and gracefully, so as not to deflate the misguided student who is contributing (in his or her fashion) to the discussion nor add fuel to the fire.

Student Offers a Rambling Response

It is not uncommon for a student to respond to a topic in an unintended or unfocused manner. This may happen when the teacher presents the topic for discussion and the student, in responding to that topic, hits the periphery of the idea, getting caught up in his or her narrative. When an entire classroom of students have this experience, it is sometimes most productive to go with the flow (see pp. 100–102). When only one or two students are responding to the lesson in unintended ways, the teacher may elect instead to subtly insist on a return to topic. The following sample illustrates an example of a student offering a rambling response and the teacher leading him back to the topic at hand.

T:　Could anyone, using imagery, express the nature of sadness? Jim?

S:　Once my brother got the measles, and we were supposed to go on vacation, and he got all the attention, and we didn't get to go, and everyone sent him presents, and my mother said I couldn't watch TV because it was noisy, and I couldn't have any friends come over and play and—

T:　[gently interjecting] How did all these events make you feel? Did they make you feel sad?

S:　[thinking] I guess I was more mad than sad.

T:　Does anybody in the class see sadness in Jim's story? Is it sad not to go on vacation when you're excited about it and ready to go? Is disappointment the same as sadness?

Here the teacher has attempted to find elements within Jim's fairly unfocused account that will keep the class concentrating on task. It is germane to point out that this type of rambling story usually inspires students to volunteer their stories about vacations, siblings, illness, and a variety of subjects that are not related to the lesson. Without seeming disinterested in their offerings, the teacher must set time limits and attempt to refocus the group:

T:　We've heard Jim's story, and there are still hands in the air, but today our goal is to explore feelings, in particular sadness, and to write poetry about this feeling. I'm encouraged by the fact that you are calling on personal experiences to stimulate a flow of emotion; however, at this point, we need to focus not only on the stimulus but on the emotion itself. So take a quiet moment to reflect on those stories that best illustrate the feeling or emotion of sadness, and then please tell us why you've chosen that story.

Student Offers the Innocent Non Sequitur

Often a student response made with the best of intentions derails the group's focus. The class may react to the unorthodox response with disruptive laughter, derisive comments, or puzzled silence. The teacher must immediately interject a sense of balance to offset the tilting class equilibrium. He or she may choose to address the non sequitur head on and in so doing move the lesson back on track, or the teacher may choose to appeal to the student's evaluative powers for self-help or the analytical powers of the group for peer advice. The teacher could also use this non sequitur as a contrasting springboard to widen the scope of the lesson. Here is an example:

T:　As I say the verbs you have helped me list on the board, I would like you to put those action words somewhere in your body, and try to show me the verb in movement: ooze.

　　　All of the children except one are slowly moving their arms and torsos in a weighted motion, in all directions. Tom, the exception, is slashing the air wildly.

T: And relax. Tom, I wonder if you're silently saying the word *ooze* in your own mind as you were moving. Did you notice how much quicker your movements were than the rest of the class? What sorts of things ooze? Do birds ooze as they fly? Does a fire engine ooze out of the firehouse? [The teacher is appealing to the child's ability to self-help.] Tom is silent, indicating that he may be unsure of the word's meaning.] I think perhaps we need to define the meaning of the word *ooze*. Can someone give Tom an example of something that oozes? [Here the teacher is appealing to the group for peer advice.]

S: Catsup oozes.

S: Honey.

S: Toothpaste.

T: Tom—turn your arm into that toothpaste and show me an oozing motion. [Tom wiggles his arm slowly forward.] That was a convincing definition of that verb.

Using Tom's original movement to widen the scope of the lesson, the teacher might wish to point out that Tom's motion was antithetical to the original verb and in doing develop other contrasting motions using opposites. This might ostensibly lead to a deepening of the lesson. In a poetry writing session, this type of unrelated response is not uncommon and, in fact, should be anticipated.

T: Since school is just beginning, and we are in the process of getting to know one another, it might be helpful and fun to concentrate today on poems that help us discover things about ourselves. We often see ourselves, I think, in ways quite different from others around us, particularly those who are closest to us. I'd like to begin the lesson by listing on the board people in our lives who may see us differently from how we see ourselves. Tamika, can you suggest someone in your life who may see you differently from how you see yourself?

Tamika: My aunt was over at the house yesterday with her new baby boy.

S: [calling out] My mother has a new baby!

S: [joining in] My cat had kittens! And Ginny's Mom is going to have a baby.

The teacher becomes painfully aware that somehow he or she has lost the lesson threads and that the plan for the poem is rapidly unraveling.

T: Tamika, I'm sure your aunt is very excited about her new baby—and wasn't it wonderful that she brought the baby over to meet his cousin? When your cousin grows up, he may be someone in your life who sees you differently than you see yourself. He's too young now, but your aunt has known you since you were born. How do you think she sees you? Sometimes in a good way, sometimes in a bad way?

Again, choosing one element of Tamika's diversion, the teacher leads the class back through the front door.

Student Gets Lost or Left Behind

Each child moves at his or her own pace, and there are as many tempi as there are students in a class. But at any given time or in any given lesson, a single student may (for any number of reasons) get left out or left behind. It may be for lack of interest on the student's part or lack of understanding, self-confidence skills, or abilities. It may just be a bad day for that student. Whatever the reason, it behooves the teacher to try to help this student become engaged with the activity and help him or her to benefit from the day's lesson. This may include simply encouraging the child by feeding responses from which he or she can work:

T: [addressing a "lost" child] Barry, I haven't heard you offer an image for any of the colors we've been discussing today. Do you have a favorite color? Red? Blue?

Barry: Red's nice.

T: Do you have anything at home that's red? A toy? A favorite shirt? Something in nature that's red that you particularly like?

Barry: [picking up interest and energy] I like fire engines.

The teacher has singled Barry out in a positive way and allowed him to feel that his views contribute something to the group discussion. The teacher has provided him with a means of responding that is nonthreatening and that gives him center stage and promises good results for him and the class. If the student resists being drawn out into the group, offering a special task that may be presented at a later time could propel him or her into a more comfortable situation without relieving the student of all responsibility to the group.

T: Beth, you've indicated that you have no wishes, dreams, or fantasies to contribute today to our discussion. Perhaps you might sit quietly over by the window where there's a lovely view of the beech tree, and imagine yourself living under that tree, like an elf, or a wood nymph. Take a piece of paper and pencil with you and jot down ideas as they come. The class will look forward to you sharing your ideas with them later.

Sometimes nothing seems to work, and the student simply refuses to be a part in any form of the day's activity. In teaching, sometimes the reality is not pleasant and no solution presents itself. Experience, however, teaches that "hope is the thing with feathers"[1] and that tomorrow is another day.

Student Is Uncooperative or Uses Energy in a Misdirected Way

Every teacher has had to deal with a student who is uncooperative or who misdirects his or her energy. The problem presents itself on all grade levels and in all group dynamics. As a common classroom phenomenon, it is never easy to address. The reasons for this type of behavior cannot be categorized in this text because the number of possibilities is unwieldy. Recognizing that generalities may not be applicable, here are some suggestions for re-engaging a student who has this issue.

• Channel negative energy into positive outlets (e.g., observe certain repetitive motions and invent a way to use these motions as a movement piece—pencil tapping nervously on desk, knee bouncing, finger fidgeting—or as a rhythm behind student texts). Motions might also be used as image stimuli for motions found in nature (e.g., What taps? What has a quick, repetitive motion?).

---

[1]From "Hope Is the Thing with Feathers" by Emily Dickinson.

- Place a uncooperative student with a cooperative one for a long enough period of time for peer influence to have a possible effect but short enough not to frustrate the better-focused student. The hope here is that by having the cooperative student react to the uncooperative student's work, a degree of motivation is provided through their interaction.

- Find ways to use misguided energy as inspiration for class activities (e.g., the student who seems unable to sit still, continually balancing his chair on two legs, rocking, moving things about on the desk's surface may be used as an image for the restlessness of nature—the movement of leaves on trees, the swaying of branches in a storm, or the ocean's tide depositing treasures on the beach and then removing them). The teacher may, in fact, ask this student to be the demonstrator, while the rest of the class observes and tries to draw parallels that may later become the images used in writing poetry. There is the risk, of course, that by highlighting this behavior, the teacher may be encouraging its continuance. Yet, there is the hopeful possibility that the student will flourish through this attention and that positive attention may be the very element he or she is seeking.

Student Dominates Classroom Discussion

The student who dominates classroom discussion presents a unique and difficult problem because more often than not this student has much to offer. He or she is usually self-confident, excited by the lesson, and eager to make his or her opinions known to the class as a whole. The thin line the teacher has to walk is how to contain this child's enthusiasm—without dampening it—and restore a sense of equality to the various members of the group. Two possible troubling repercussions might be:

1. Fostering jealousy on the part of the other students because of deserved teacher recognition and praise

2. Group self-denigration because of feelings of not being able to rise to the perceived level of excellence

It is essential to recognize that these problems may surface and to try and head them off before they do. The teacher and students alike need to be able to delight in the contributions made by the overzealous student. Note the temperature of the group, the other students' reactions to the overzealous student's contributions and to your reactions as a teacher. Know when to strike a better balance and when the largest number of students will be best served by playing down the individual's role. This is the key to utilizing the strengths of this exceptional student without adversely affecting the group dynamic. These suggestions are by necessity subjective because there is no panacea or simple solution for dealing with group interactions. We do, however, offer the following somewhat more concrete suggestions:

- Instill a sense of discrimination in the overzealous student by suggesting that more is not necessarily better and that he or she needs mentally to edit class contributions before presenting them.

  S: [raising hand for fifth time in 5 minutes in response to the teacher's call for adjectives that describe the sun] Round, yellow, smooth, hot, pretty, bright—

T: [gently interrupting] Thank you for all of those appropriate and visual adjectives that help us to picture the sun. What I would like you to do now is select two of the many adjectives you've offered and silently form full images in your mind. Choose only those two adjectives that will best describe the sun. Please take your time. Can someone else please suggest new and colorful adjectives?

In offering this overzealous student the opportunity to extend two adjectives into full images (i.e., "the sun is yellow as a dandelion," "the sun is bright as a gold coin"), he or she has been presented with an advanced assignment that acknowledges his or her abilities and the fact that he or she is moving at a faster pace than the rest of the group. By separating his or her activity from the rest of the group's, the teacher has tactfully excluded him or her from further vocalization. This gives the rest of the group the opportunity to catch up.

• Emphasize to the exceptional student the essential role that listening plays in a classroom. Assign this student the task of listening as an analytical observer, so that he or she may offer reaction, criticism, and praise later in the discussion, thus becoming a valuable peer resource.

T: Which of the suggested adjectives do you think are the most vivid? Which do you think best describes the sun?

• Reassure the exceptional student that the fear of having his or her silences misinterpreted as ignorance are unfounded. The teacher knows that he or she knows.

T: You have provided us with a feast of adjectives this morning, and I'm sure you still have others you would like to share. However, I would like to hear your full images now and then have other students share full images for their adjectives.

Student Is Blocked

It is frustrating to both teacher and student when a response is not forthcoming. Sometimes the cause is simply that a child cannot respond in the learning mode that is being used at that moment. For example, every teacher has had a student who is vocal and vibrant during a class discussion and immobilized by the command to write. This is perhaps the most commonly encountered blockage; however, some students suffer from the reverse dilemma, contributing nothing to the class discussion but producing an outstanding piece of written work. Still others who can do neither find the abstract language of movement and music welcome realms in which to be creative. In particular, these students who have a strong penchant for one learning style or mode may benefit greatly from working the word through many mediums. Success in one area may provide the student with the courage and curiosity to explore those heretofore inaccessible learning arenas.

We have attempted to address those problems that seem to arise most frequently. Dozens of other troubling snags may thwart the flow and effectiveness of a lesson, but conversely, there are just as many wondrous, spontaneous moments when the words, the movement, and the music "like stars, turn the classroom bright."

IMPLEMENTATION AND EXTENSIONS

At first the word
was just a word, long
and flat like a shadow cast
across the page and then
your eyes rounded
on a thought,
the word
stirred, shifted, filled
with a deep breath
of imagination;
became
sky
storm
sunset
dreams as big as laughter
spilled off the page and ran
like a river around the room
and the word became
words; turning, tumbling
towards completion
of a thought and carried us
along a flood
of sight
and sound
and smell
and taste
and texture pressed
like love against the mind; then
like the rivers restless
rhythm the words moved
musically in space, in time, became

the rush of voices and the flow
of song and that one
flat word fattened into more
than memory alone could hold; reached
through us to embrace
the soul.
So do not clench the words
like sunshine in your fist
and miss the magic
of their light; LET GO,
LET THEM FLOW until
like stars they turn
the darkness bright.

—SUSAN A. KATZ

In the first section of this book, we examine evocative techniques in the areas of language, movement, and music. Each isolated technique presented in the first section is, by itself, relatively easy to assimilate and apply. Synthesizing these techniques is challenging because one must be sensitive to

- The group temperament and dynamic—its unique possibilities and background

- The individual imprint within the group and the importance that the individual plays in defining the group

- The initial inspiration for the student poetry and the applicable elements in the enhancement of the experience: which poems will sing, which will move, and which will adapt to rhythmical treatment

- Which experiences are the most appropriate to the school environment, given the time constraints of school day and year

- Serendipitous opportunities, such as writing about the fragility and interdependence of life on this planet in response to a headline environmental disaster

- The ongoing possibilities and the individual lessons that may serve as an entry to the larger concentric curriculum

This, then, represents the ultimate challenge of teaching: blending all of these variables into a cohesive, natural flow. This brand of teaching invites and intrigues both student and teacher. It deepens, widens, and spirals into an expansive wordplay learning experience. This is the orchestration of teaching, which never gets less challenging, nor should it.

Having accepted the unpredictability of creative teaching, the teacher now needs to believe that the process is reciprocal and that much of what will ultimately contribute to exciting classroom experiences must come from the students as well as the teacher. So it follows that the teacher must be willing to relinquish a measure of classroom control. It is a leap of faith that allows the student to generate creative energy that may propel the class in promising directions. As ideas rebound among students and the teacher, a kind of creative chaos results in which, to paraphrase Theodore Roethke, students and teachers learn by going where they have to go. This mutually expansive experience provides each student with a sense of self and contributes to his or her feeling of significance. There is joy to be found in this type of scholastic adventure.

An example of this type of teaching might occur in a science class. In addition to exploring geodes in the traditional teaching style of asking for properties, origin, and geographical location, the teacher can layer the experience, suggesting that students expand the ideas of applying colors, feelings, sensory perceptions, sound, movement, or other techniques. This may result in a totally new juxtaposition of concepts. The discussion may veer to the "secrets of stones," "smooth as an ice cave," "rough as the bottom of the ocean," "shiny as the inside of the moon." The geode design itself, with its undulating lines, may lead to a many-voiced aleatoric interpretation, or the qualities of the stones may inspire alliteration, as expressed in a third grader's poem: "Solid, shiny, sensuous, sinking, silent stones." This alliteration can then be interpreted in movement: heavy, flicking, flowing, floating, falling.

Chapter 8 shows how a science lesson might be crafted into a language arts, movement, music gestalt of layered learning. When focusing in a purposeful way on the multiple facets of a singular experience, opportunities can be provided that deepen, widen, intensify, and enhance the learning experience, thus making it more memorable. This is in keeping with the philosophy of Dr. Eliott Eisner, who entreats us to "slow down perception" in order to "cultivate the senses."

In another actual classroom experience, third-grade students were asked to suggest images for colors. One student insisted she was unable to think of an image. The class went through the spectrum of colors with no response from the student. Images were listed on the board such as "blue is the color of blueberries," "blue is the color of the summer sky," and "blue is the color of a robin's egg." Finally, the reluctant student's hand went up, and with some trepidation, she offered the image "blue is the color of wonders." That offering led the class down a side street of wonders more evocative and exciting than the original course. A far more effective series of lessons followed than had been originally planned. The teacher sometimes has to be willing to say, "I planted tomatoes, and I got a watermelon but it's a *great* watermelon!" The kind of teaching presented in this book suggests that ideas can come from anywhere at any time and can implement and enlarge on that which has to be taught.

The first section of this book provides detailed scripts that a teacher may use to evoke creative language responses and then incorporate music and movement activities. This groundwork requires the infusion of more in-depth information into the classroom:

- Poetry recipes: The five senses, imagery, metaphor, alliteration, and onomatopoeia

- Differences between a poem and a story

- Editing: Structures of poems, including form, line breaks, and how a poem looks on paper

- Music concepts such as melody, dynamics, tempi, canon, and form

- Speech and rhythm play

- Body percussion, vocal sounds, and found sounds

- Exploration of movement qualities

Section II shows readers how to use these elements within the context of the everyday curriculum. Contexts include field trips and science explorations, and themes include environmental issues, seasonal changes, and current events. Suggestions are offered, based on experience and experimentation; however, each teacher should rely on his or her own creative instincts to make the event *singular*. The hope is that the word in play will orchestrate the multiple voices of learning into a resounding chorus.

FIELD TRIP EXPERIENCE

A school field trip is an extended learning experience. It reaches beyond the limits of the classroom to explore familiar and unfamiliar worlds and suggests, by its inherent qualities, adventure and discovery. For these reasons, we have chosen the extended field trip experience to serve as a laboratory presentation, an introductory chapter to Section II, and an in-depth outline for application of the skills discussed in Section I.

Any school field trip can offer opportunities for richly integrated amalgams. When the teacher conducts and shares research with the group prior to the trip, student anticipation and expectation are heightened, making it possible to reap greater rewards. Reflections and projects occurring after a trip bring closure and deepen the effects of the event. The attention paid by the teacher to inherent possibilities (i.e., movement, speech, song, found-instrument sounds, art, poetry) can elevate a field trip into a singular happening.

The trip described in this chapter was taken to Storm King Art Center in Mountainville, New York, with 10-year-old students from Upper Nyack Elementary School. Storm King, a world-class sculpture garden, is located approximately 2 hours north of New York City. It melds megalithic sculptures with the rolling topography of more than 400 acres. The sculptures have great visual appeal, ranging in size from monumental to moderate, by such famous sculptors as Alexander Liberman, Alexander Calder, Louise Nevelson, Henry Moore, David Smith, Isamu Noguchi, Kenneth Snelson, Mark Di Suvero, and Tal Streeter (to name nine of the hundreds of sculptors represented).

The art teacher, poet-in-the-school, and music teacher collaborated, starting with a reconnaissance photography trip. Black-and-white prints were taken and used as visual motivation in the classroom prior to the trip. Because this was an intracurriculum experience, the goals were many and varied:

- To break through any of the children's preconceived notions of what constitutes museums and to share abstract and nonobjective art in an outdoor environment

- To open students' eyes to the monumentality of the creations

- To be aware of the ambition inherent in creativity: how a person can make his or her initial creative impulse lead to something real

- To be aware of the exceptional professional skills in engineering, materials, design, and landscaping brought together in this particular environment

- To lead the students into a realization of the relationship between visual sculpture and its translation into sound, movement, and language

- To apply creative language skills (e.g., metaphor, simile, alliteration, onomatopoeia) to that which has form and substance

- To select appropriate adjectives that enhance the image and describe feeling and subject as applicable to the individual sculptures

- To use the sculptures' creative energy as a stimulus for initiating new student creations

- For each student to experience the impact of the work on a sensory level, to internalize it, and to make it uniquely his or her own

- For students to feel the worth of their own contributions

- To heighten visual acuity through sketching the sculptures, later to be used for interpretive work in the art classroom

What follows are the specific events that brought us to these goals.

Nine principal sculptors were chosen to be key for recognition of style. These sculptors were intentionally chosen because their works were in abundance in the park and particularly dramatic. Through a quick study of the photographs, the students were soon able to analyze style and apply this new skill in identifying other sculptures by the same artist (e.g., Alexander Liberman predominantly uses large, cylindrical shapes; Kenneth Snelson often uses cross-thatching of narrow, metal poles).

These nine sculptors' names were offered as possible rhythm building blocks. The students individually spoke the sculptors' names in possible rhythm combinations, and together the class figured out the corresponding rhythmic notation:

LESSON IMPLEMENTATION

Combinations of these patterns were explored.

These combinations translated into body percussion patterns, over which individual students improvised (e.g., clapping, hand drum, desk top, metal chair, leg).

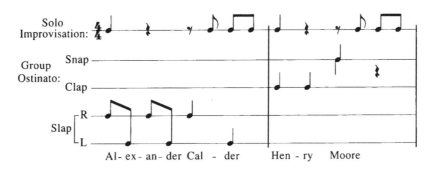

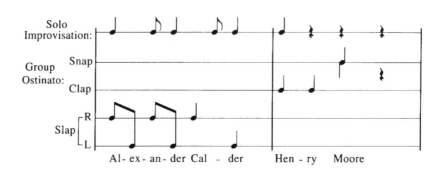

Next, they were transferred to small percussion and also used beneath student improvisations.

The group was then asked to explore a musical order for all of the nine sculptors mentioned—an order that would have variety while allowing students to say their names without distorting them. They came up with this:

A | ‖: Alexander Liberman, Louise ——— Nevelson,
    Alexander Calder, Hen - ry - Moore :‖

B ‖: Kenneth   Snelson   Isamu Noguchi
     Tal Streeter David Smith   Mark ——— Di Suvero :‖

There was a lot of playing around with inflection (Isamu Noguchi's name seemed to invite it!) and dynamics, with the majority determining the outcome: first time forte (loud), repeat piano (soft), ABA form. The students discovered that this form worked well canonically, and so it became a speech canon.

Ⓐ Ⓑ Ⓐ

This then became the basis for a melodic setting. The task in this instance was to use a mode recently studied, *dorian* (which occurs when you play from D to D on a piano).

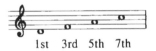

Furthermore, the group-written melody was to work as a canon by constructing the melody so that every strong beat landed on the first, third, and fifth note of the dorian scale, ensuring a harmony when sung in canon. The seventh tone was a possibility as well.

1st   3rd   5th   7th

The resulting canon came from a collection of many students' ideas, by trying the ideas out, singing them, playing them on recorders, and honing the results.

Tal Stree-ter Da - vid Smith Mark Di Su - ver - o

Layering Through Language

Familiar now with the sculptors' styles and comfortable with their names from having spoken the speech piece and sung the canon, we began to look deeper into the works by using metaphor, simile, and alliteration. Through the application of these poetic skills, we reshaped the strange and exotic sculptures into words.

In layering the field trip experience through language, we selected a particular sculpture and asked the students to brainstorm aloud (with the teacher listing the words). Students were invited to suggest words that seemed to best capture the spirit, the flow, the movement, and the energy of the piece under scrutiny. For example, students responded to this particular sculpture with the following words:

• Thin	• Hard	• Thunderous	• Shiny
• Spidery	• Floating	• Suspended	• Stretching
• Flowing	• Angular	• Light	• Smooth
• Elastic	• Heavy	• Broken	• Wistful
• Wiry	• Big	• Bright	• Large

Kenneth Snelson, *Free Ride Home,* with students.
Storm King Art Center, Mountainville, New York

Once the words were listed, students were asked to think of them in two ways: first, as descriptive of the sculpture and, second, as possible images that either described the sculpture or enhanced it:

- Hard as what?

- Floating like what?

- Spidery as what?

Encouraged to remember all of their language skills, students shared images aloud: "heavy as a bridge," "loud as a crackle of thunder," "sharp as a prickle" "shiny as a new, black car," "shiny as a crystal mirror," "flowing like hair in the wind." Sharing the ideas and images helped to expand creative possibilities. The sculpture became more than form and substance. Lines moved and interacted, one with the other, through imaginative interpretation.

Each student was then asked to select a single sculpture from an assortment of photocopied photographs. It was suggested that each student choose the sculpture with which he or she felt most comfortable and that seemed to offer the widest variety of creative possibilities. Students were then asked to list adjectives that described the scope of that particular sculpture. Having listed the words, they were asked to create images and then extend the images into language sculptures that took on new shape and form.

STUDENT POEMS

POETRY

Big
Tall
Hard
As big as a bridge, as
tall as a mountain,
a skyscraper as hard as
a diamond.

—FOURTH GRADE

Alexander Liberman, *Iliad.*
Storm King Art Center, Mountainville, New York

WORDS

Round	as the sun
Deep	as the ocean
Strange	as outer space
Flowing	as the wind
Wiggly	as a worm

—FOURTH GRADE

Alexander Liberman, *Iliad*.
Storm King Art Center, Mountainville, New York

POETRY

1. Hard as wood
2. Heavy as buildings
3. Big as a castle
4. Climbing like a monkey
5. Trapped like in a cave
6. Tall as a skyscraper
7. Licking like waves at the ocean

1. A black knight defending its castle with a sword
2. A dog guarding a yard
3. An eagle flying in the sky
4. Dancing at a party
5. A tiger running to its destination
6. A buried treasure from underneath a million years ago

—FOURTH GRADE

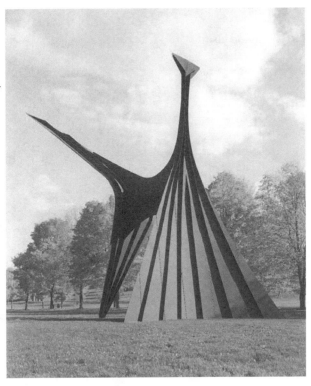

Alexander Calder, *The Arch*.
Storm King Art Center, Mountainville, New York

WOODPILE

Think of trees, straight,
woodpiles, hollow and
      heavy
perhaps you see stars
in a night sky
perhaps you walk
a balance beam tight-rope
      walker
careful not to bend or
      break
the branches under your
      weight
Think of trees,
tall and straight

—FOURTH GRADE

Alexander Liberman, *Adonai.*
Storm King Art Center, Mountainville, New York

PAINTER

The small painter paints
      on his
extraordinary triangular
      canvas.
He is dipping his tiny
      brush in the
depth of the sea of
      sparkling turquoise.
He envisions the finished
      masterpiece
in his mind.
His brush pulls across the
      rough canvas
making colorful lines and
      shapes.
He dips it gingerly into
      the rippling
crystal water.
With a flourishing stroke
      he closes
his imagination's door for
      a day.

—FOURTH GRADE

Alexander Liberman, *Adam.*
Storm King Art Center, Mountainville, New York

Egg

One-half egg
I am inside it
Its walls are smooth
like plastic on gravel
the shell is shiny
like glaze on pottery
it is bumpy
it's cozy but I hear
a voice
my mother
I depart from my egg.

—Fourth grade

Isamu Noguchi, *Momo Taro.*
Storm King Art Center, Mountainville, New York

Throughout this experience, language elements have appeared in a natural and effective manner. In the following poem, notice the use of many of the techniques and skills addressed in the first part of this book.

Coconut

A big, broken coconut	[alliteration]
Sad and lonely	[emotion]
Heavy and warm	
Round and standing still	[alliteration]
Like a fat, lazy rock	[simile]
with a beautiful shining color,	[adjectives]
Lying on the hot earth	[imagery]
with a few tree branches	[imagery]
on top of its head.	[imagery]
It's waiting	[imagery]
For a gigantic dog	[imagery]
to lick its head.	[imagery]
It can't move	[imagery]
From left to right	[imagery]
It's trying to move its head	
Scratch	
But no hands.	
The hot sun is in love	[imagery]

with the broken coconut   [metaphorical]
Trying to move west   [imagery]
so the coconut's juicy water
Won't dry.

    —FOURTH GRADE

STUDENT POEMS: CONTINUED

MAN

Man holds a statue
with a finger,
yet he never touches it.
It is leaning; falling;
yet it is straight
held in the ground
with cold winds
blowing around it;
whipping;
one more blow, it
will topple over
like a teetering nestling
on the edge of its nest.
Two separate pieces
connected.

    —FOURTH GRADE

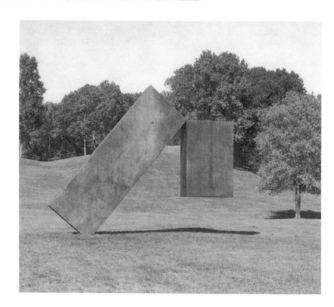

Menashe Kadishman, *Suspended.*
Storm King Art Center, Mountainville, New York

LOLLYPOPP

A swirled
lollypop
a pin in a
crystal ball
that is ready
to destroy
the world.

—FOURTH GRADE

GLOBE

A globe
Shining and spinning
in its own
queer stillness
Sitting in
eerie light and feeling
Inside it,
a life is growing
changing, learning.

—FOURTH GRADE

Jerome Kirk, *Orbit.*
Storm King Art Center, Mountainville, New York

COLUMN

It seems to reach out to
    the cloudless
bare sky and start to
    daydream.
It seems to fold and flicker
    up and down
as if there is danger and
    he must be hidden.
It seems to bounce at the
    sky to
say "let me come up too."
It seems to smell the
    wetness of a rain cloud.
It sees the clouds floating
    and flying around,
It seems to hear the musical
    chirping of birds,
And feels the fuzzy rabbits
Snuggling it.

—FOURTH GRADE

Tal Streeter, *Endless Column.*
Storm King Art Center, Mountainville, New York

ROADRUNNER

Here comes the roadrunner,
   short and lean,
Daniel Boone takes off his
   hat
to the big, full moon.

—FOURTH GRADE

Isaac Witkin, *Kumo.*
Storm King Art Center, Mountainville, New York

In "Roadrunner," it is exciting to note that the student poet stretched the assignment beyond its limits of sculpture, language, and field trip and included something learned in another classroom. In a small but significant way, this illustrates the kind of curriculum interaction this book is suggesting. This is a particularly fine example of imagery and the poet's ability to move from image to real-world knowledge and still have the poem maintain its integrity and emotional impact.

STUDENT POEMS: CONTINUED

STATUE

Old oak trees after a storm,
Crumpled with fear.
A little child's pick-up-
   sticks
Crashing to the ground.
A first grader's stick figures.
Cowboys and Indians.
Bang bang.

—FOURTH GRADE

Kenneth Snelson, *Free Ride Home.*
Storm King Art Center, Mountainville, New York

SPACE EGGS

These round
eggs sent
from space
awaiting the
time to awake and
hatch.

—FOURTH GRADE

Grace Knowlton, *Spheres*.
Storm King Art Center, Mountainville, New York

The classes were inspired melodically by the sculpture as well as verbally. "Endless Column," Tal Streeter's work, led one fourth-grade class into a sequence, in which a melody patterns itself higher or lower. If you follow the contour of the melody, you can see the sculpture ascending, then descending. The task this time was to write a group piece in Aeolian mode, which begins on E and is as follows:

Resulting Melodic Interpretation of Graphics

Endless Column

The other class created a halting, disjunct, angular piece for the same sculpture. It also led them into a new written concept of mixed meter (more than one meter).

Vocal Sound Experimentation

Before interpreting the sculpture photographs in sound and movement, those vocalizations that can be made with the mouth were explored. With the teacher modeling a variety of consonant and vowel sounds for the class to imitate (or echo), the students were helped to feel comfortable with extremely high and low sounds and extremes in dynamics:

T: Puh puh BUH!   **S:** Puh puh BUH!

T: T-T-Ssssssssssssss   **S:** (echo)

T: MmmmmmmmmmmmmmmJAH!   **S:** (echo)

T: ZzzzzzzzzzzzzzzzKUHmmmmmmmmmm   **S:** (echo)

The teacher modeled plosive sounds (P, B, T), affricates (J, CH), sibilants (S, Z), continuants (M, J, N), and vowels and demonstrated a variety of tempi, high and low sounds, and dynamics. One good warm-up game was to have the group sit in a circle and, starting with the teacher, each make a hand or arm motion and accompany that motion with a sound, passing it on to the next person when finished.

At this point, it was natural to advance from sound and movement to sound inspired by graphics, the ultimate graphic being the photograph of the sculpture. Presenting simplified graphics for interpretation was a good intermediary step before going to the actual sculptures, which were more sophisticated and thus required more advanced skills. Students made up these graphics on large craft paper in small groups or individually. The graphics were then performed with one person conducting, time-line fashion, with his or her finger slowly moving along the bottom of the graphic to suggest when a sound was to occur or with individuals interpreting their own graphics. The graphics could be read from left to right, right to left (or both simultaneously with two groups), or upside down. Dots alone were the simplest to interpret, followed by dots and lines, and most difficult, dots, lines, and planes.

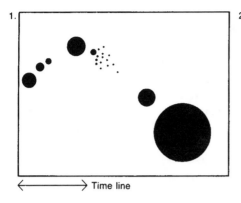

← → Time line

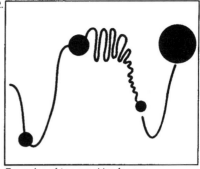

Examples of two graphics for one
group's interpretation

3. Dots and lines (for three groups
of vocalists)

4. The most difficult aspect of this graphic is
deciding how to create a sound for the plane
of color on the lower part of the graphic.

Group 1

Group 2

Group 3

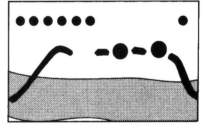

Movement and Sound Games

Before interpreting the simplified graphics in movement and using them as floor patterns, another game that stimulated the students' imagination was "follow the dancer." Starting with a seated circle around one person in the middle who was the leader, the group was challenged to make a collective sound that best represented the movements of that leader. The leader was encouraged to make large and thereby "loud" gestures, using all of his or her body; likewise, small gestures and angular ones were made for soft and separated sounds.

When the group had the idea, two leaders were placed in the center, and each got to choose his or her favorite movement: short/sudden/small (dab, flick); sudden and angular (slash/punch); weighted and slow (wring/press); or light and continuous (float/glide). The circle was divided, and each half followed their leader. The two leaders thus created the sound piece not only as they improvised it but also as the results that they heard were dictated: Sometimes the sounds would call for being together, sometimes separate. With older groups (ages 10 and older), the teacher can assign as many as three or four leaders. The more people in the center, the thicker the texture and thereby the more difficult the creation. With this kind of warming up, the presentation of a sculpture for interpretation in movement is a logical extension for the student, and the results should be rich and satisfying.

A student and teacher conduct a speech piece that is composed of sculptors' names.

Exploring vocal
possibilities to ensure interesting
and varied results when putting
sounds and movement to the sculptures.

A teacher and a
student demonstrating some
circular movement possibilities
when working with a partner.

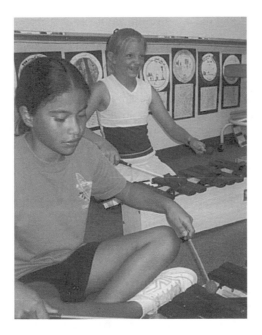

Students respond
musically to circular shapes.

Teacher accompanies students
as they move "Nevelson/
Lieberman/Nevelson" (ABA).

Girls demonstrating movement solutions with
gestures inspired by the Nevelson sculpture for the
class. Letting students observe each other and make
positive suggestions often strengthens the movement task.

Teacher: What kind of motion would this sculpture make? Can you do it with your knee? hip? nose? shoulder? How would you walk this sculpture if it were suddenly a floor pattern? Can you accompany your walk with a sound that tells me the character of this sculpture? Can you increase your tempo? Your dynamics? Now can you do the pattern with your arms, adding the sound, while you are moving the floor pattern? Everyone choose a way or a combination of ways to move this sculpture and stop when you hear the sound of the cymbal.

SAMPLE LESSON

Interpreting Sculptures in Sound

T: Look through these photographs with me, and stop me when you see one that is the opposite of the Tal Streeter style. I see you picked the Liberman with flowing circles, connected instead of disjointed—truly a good example of the opposite. Can you now make a hand motion that represents the shape of this Liberman you chose? Let this motion go into your elbow, head, arms. Take the circles into your space and see how many places you can make them. Keep going. Can you add a sound that reflects your smooth, continuous, flowing, floating motions? Good! Breathe when no one else is breathing so your sound is continuous, which is called *staggered breathing.* Listen to the group as you make your sound. Nice. There is a darker circle in this picture. May I hear that also in your soundscape? Again, can you keep your air pattern going in circular motions but add a circular floor pattern as well? It can be the size of a manhole cover or the whole room. It's your circle. Notice others as you do your own and relate to a circle passing by. Next, could we combine these two graphics, the Streeter and the Liberman, to create a larger movement form, ABA?

Do you want to stay only with vocal sound, or add an additional color from a small percussion instrument or found sound?

S: I hear the cymbal in the B section.

T: A big crash?

S: No, soft and continuous.

T: Fine. Who would like to be the musicians?

Using these techniques, students created a variety of movement forms that were beautiful, focused, abstract, and believable. The integrity of the subject matter and the power the sculptures conveyed were responsible for generating this artistic bonding.

During the trip, students carried clipboards with eight mystery sculptures pictured. They were asked to identify these works by title and sculptor as they were discovered. They were also given paper on which to sketch one favorite sculpture. Earlier we discovered a little accidental arena at the base of Calder's "Arc," and we used this for a concluding mini-program. Excerpts from the students' poetry were shared, as well as the songs, speech canons, and movement forms created in class. Then, led by one of the classroom teachers, we wound through the sculpture in an exuberant line, much like people did in the 12th century, when whole villages did "Estampies" through the town. For us, it was across the field and back to the waiting buses.

SUMMARY

Back in the classroom, subsequent closure involved more poetry writing and reacting to the trip and the sculptures; in the art room, it led to creating junk sculptures with a new eye and understanding of balance and integrity of dimensional design. The field trip experience, with all of its implications and enrichment possibilities, could as easily have been applied to a trip to the zoo, the botanical garden, a historical village, a natural history museum, a traditional art museum, or any number of other places. It is equally apparent that the age range of students is not a factor—the techniques slide easily through grade levels.

The emphasis in this book is on erasing the lines between curricula. Consequently, we believe that a field trip that is well planned and well orchestrated might easily filter through every aspect of the curriculum. The possibilities for using this kind of experience are as limitless as the individuals who are willing to experiment with them.

SCIENCE LESSON

Science, an arena of discovery, lends itself naturally to the extension process. We are working with ideas that often start in the abstract and are channeled through experimentation into facts and finite notions; knowledge unfolds slowly. With each unfolding, there is new awareness. This type of creative scrutiny, through imaginative exploration, becomes a new science teaching tool. When children examine a snowflake and say it "bit like a freezing breeze," "sailed like a ballerina," and "lurked like a butler in a mansion," they have embraced a metaphorical way of defining its properties. The snowflake is still a snowflake, but it is now much more. In the words of Aristotle, "The greatest thing by far is to have command of metaphor. This alone cannot be imparted to another; it is the mark of genius, for to make good metaphors implies an eye for resemblances."

STUDENT POETRY AND MUSIC/MOVEMENT EXTENSIONS: SNOW

Grades 1 through 6 wrote poems in response to science lessons on snow. Students were instructed to examine snow during storms, watching it fall, examining its movement in space, letting it settle on the hand, drawing pictures, and using all acquired poetry skills and the five senses.

STUDENT POEMS

SNOW

Snow is white
Sun makes
it sparkle
At night snow is
plain as white.

—FIRST GRADE

COLD WINTER DAYS

The snow is cold
as ice below
frost
bites like
freezing breezes
on my hands.

—SECOND GRADE

SNOW

Snowflakes slid
silently.
Snow sailed across the sky
like a ballerina,
slept like a baby,
hopped from cloud to cloud
like a kangaroo,
and lurked like a butler
in a mansion.

A white polar bear,
snow sailed spryly—springing
from side to side
to side swiftly
snow settled
suctioned by
gravity.

—SIXTH GRADE

Extension Possibilities

Find a white sound (e.g., a finger running around a glass rim, many voices singing "ah" on different pitches). Find a sound that sparkles (e.g., a homemade mark tree made from dangling keys, a bonafide bell tree). Explore ways of slowing down the poem through silences or repetition to create spaces in which to use the sounds. In "Snow," which has a driving rhythm, what body percussion ostinato could accompany the words? After the body percussion is solidified with the words, try the poem in canon, with the second group entering at the ice. Create a slow, soft, sound ostinato with musical or found sounds. For example,

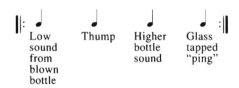

Add other sounds over that ostinato for "sailing across the sky," "jumped . . . like a kangaroo," and "suctioned by gravity."

STUDENT POETRY AND MUSIC/
MOVEMENT EXTENSIONS: EGG HATCHING

The poetry and music lessons that follow were in response to a science lesson in which students observed, in the classroom, the egg-hatching process in an incubator over a period of weeks. Through poetry, music, and movement, students were asked to translate the experience, once again by using their five senses, by applying their poetry and music skills, and by investing themselves emotionally into the evolving process.

THE EGG

Crack.
The chick pops out!
Small, black, yellow.
Sticky like glue,
Wet like having been
Caught in the rain.

—FOURTH GRADE

THE SQUISHY DAY

I felt squishy.
My egg was too small.
With my sharp beak
I pecked,
pecked,
pecked . . .
I rested and pecked,
rested and pecked 'til
I was free! 'til
I was me!

—FOURTH GRADE

SAMPLE LESSON

Teacher: Can you become the shape of the little chicken inside the egg, round, tightly tucked? Feel the watery fluid around you, how it feels to be gently rolled over every now and then so you will grow healthy and well formed. See the darkness. Know when it is time to hatch, to come into the world. Feel the shell against your egg tooth and how much energy it takes to break out of your egg prison. Peck the shell with all your might, then rest and peck again until you have a small hole formed. Rest. Keep working at getting out of the house that has held you for many weeks. Your bill is out — one wing — the top of your body — one leg — you're free! But very wet and very weak. You must rest, but soon you dare to try to stand. You are wobbly, and you take a few unsure steps. You fall, you rest, and you try again. The light from your incubator feels warm on your back. You look for another chicken. There is only another egg, but a hole in the shell holds promise! You may have a sister or brother chicken soon. You try drinking the water and eating the mash. You feel stronger. You are able to peep and hop — you are becoming a very fine baby chick!

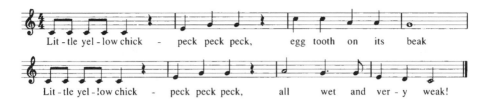

Lit - tle yel - low chick - peck peck peck, egg tooth on its beak

Lit - tle yel - low chick - peck peck peck, all wet and ver - y weak!

This piece was written by a first-grade class at Upper Nyack Elementary School, with word and melody suggestions by students. It uses the form ABAC and the do pentatonic on C.

STUDENT POEMS

CHICKENS HATCHING

I am a ball
of wet wool
skinny
and wet
When I dry I'm
fluffy
I sound like this—
Peep! Peep! Peep!

—FOURTH GRADE

A CHICKEN IS BORN

First you see an egg, white
as vanilla ice cream.
cracking, cracking
a chick wet, not
fluffy yet,
chirping sounds soft
as music.

—FOURTH GRADE

The text in the following piece of music was written in response to the teacher's question, "And what happened next?" The order of the words was determined by the first graders.

He pecked, he peeked, he kicked, he hatched

Lit - tle chick chick lit - tle chick chick.

THE NATURAL WORLD

These poetic examples were written in response to a series of science lessons that explored the natural world. Students were asked to creatively interpret elements that sparked their imaginations. The focus was on using personification, metaphor, and simile and experiencing the natural world through the five senses.

STUDENT POEMS

SUNLIGHT

Sunlight is sweet candy.
soft as satin, rays
scatter
singing sleepily
Sunlight hides shadows,
scariness, and sorrow.
It is successful
steady
still and strange.
sunlight is splendid.

—FIFTH GRADE

STARS

The stars are scattered in a swarm,
snowflakes fall in storm,
sculptures made of stone,
steeled in solar homes,
stars swim across a nighttime sky,
wild static,
rattling bones,
sweet, white sugar,
pollen from a rose.

—FIFTH GRADE

SANDS

Moon makes
reflections on
water.

Water hits
shores.
Grass sways softly
Sand crabs scurry
wild on sand.

—FIFTH GRADE

STORMS

Sand storms swoop
lightning flashes
in the fierce black sky.
Rain roars
Thunder thumps
Rainbows appear

—FIFTH GRADE

RIVERS

Rivers creep
like stalking cats
Rivers tumble
like falling rocks
Rivers move
like turtles walking
Rivers skip
and soar
and roar
like lions
that are hunting

—FOURTH GRADE

EXPLORATIONS OF ROCKS AS MUSICAL INSTRUMENTS

Geology has universal appeal. First, all of humanity is fixed onto the rock of the earth, which provides our fundament. But even more, rocks feel good to the touch and may provide cool comfort in a pocket, as with a worry stone. They are beautiful in texture, shape, and color. Rocks sound interesting when struck together, and flat ones skip nicely across the surface of a pond; almost everyone has a favorite rock somewhere in the house. Acknowledging the universal fascination with them, it's a logical progression to enjoy their possibilities through language (i.e., poetry), movement, speech, rhythms, form, improvisation, melodic invention, and instrumental playing.

Rocks as Instruments

When students clap two stones together to determine high or low sound (i.e., pitch), they are in the brotherhood of those who played stones in ancient China when Confucius lived. The instrument was called the *pien ching,* stone chimes, and was played with a stick. Confucius was said to have marveled to hear "dumb stones sing" and mused that he probably would never hear anything sweeter in his life.

A speech pattern could be invented, framing four rock sounds, high to low, to savor the quality and timbre of the rocks:

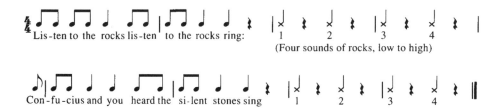

Lis-ten to the rocks lis-ten to the rocks ring: 1   2   3   4
(Four sounds of rocks, low to high)

Con-fu-cius and you heard the si-lent stones sing   1   2   3   4

Add a B section, in which each of the four rocks improvises for eight beats. Return to A section. When students invent a grid piece for the three or four "colors" of sound created by different rocks, they are in the brotherhood of some African, Caribbean, and Polynesian cultures whose music can be conveyed through grids.

	1	2	3	4	5	6	7	8
High sounding rock	X			X			X	X
Medium sounding rock		X	X			X		
Low sounding rock	X			X	X			

Students count to eight and play on the X'ed number.

When students invent rock-passing games with rhythmic speech, they are in the ancient brotherhood of all people who have practiced such activities since the beginning of time. (Students seated in a circle, each with a palm-size rock in their right hand)

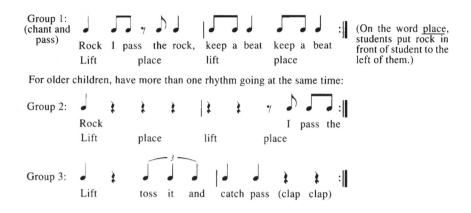

Group 1:
(chant and pass)

Rock I pass the rock, keep a beat keep a beat
Lift   place   lift   place

(On the word <u>place</u>, students put rock in front of student to the left of them.)

For older children, have more than one rhythm going at the same time:

Group 2:

Rock   I pass the
Lift   place   lift   place

Group 3:

Lift   toss it and catch pass (clap clap)

Rocks in Speech Play

Mineral names feel good in the mouth and can be arranged in orders that have an interesting rhythmic feel. Students can be asked to invent these rock-name chains and can lengthen the form by inserting a rock improvisation in between sections, for a rondo form.

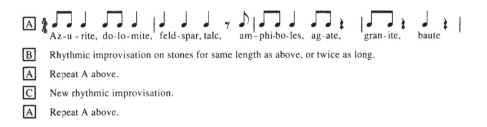

[A] Az-u-rite, do-lo-mite, feld-spar, talc, am-phi-bo-les, ag-ate, gran-ite, baute
[B] Rhythmic improvisation on stones for same length as above, or twice as long.
[A] Repeat A above.
[C] New rhythmic improvisation.
[A] Repeat A above.

As a way to remember the exotic mineral names, this kind of speech drill could also be transferred to body percussion, with the teacher taking student suggestions, and could then become a piece based on the mineral names with a rock ostinato accompaniment.

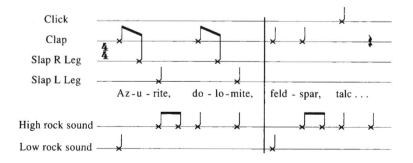

Click
Clap
Slap R Leg
Slap L Leg

Az-u-rite,   do-lo-mite,   feld-spar,   talc...

High rock sound
Low rock sound

A student uses the five senses to
experience the properties of a geode.

Learning the geode by touch.

A Rock Rondo Using Student Poetry

The three main categories of rocks and their properties could be transferred to interesting nonpitched percussion, adding one melodic line. This, in turn, could become Section A of a rondo in which student poems become the contrasting Sections
B, C, D, and so forth. Section A:

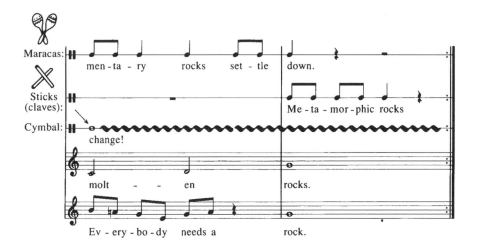

Section B:

STONES

Stones are as sweet
as flowers
in a summer garden,

perfect as
a curved, carved
sculpture.

SHARP as
broken glass.

Sparkling as the
blinding sun

Round as
shooting comets
s - h - o - o - t - i - n - g
across the skies.

Happy as fireworks
on the fourth of July.

—THIRD GRADE

A section repeats:

Rocks as Visual Aids

There are movement forms and stories within the diverse patterns found in geode slices. One such beautiful rock could be:

- The departure of a contemporary tale, revolving around the mysterious circles within one geode

- The basis for a group sound, which might then serve as a backdrop for a student poem

- The basis for a group rhythm, which might serve as a backdrop for relevant vocabulary (e.g., eolithic, paleolithic, neolithic)

- Grouped with other geodes to make a movement form—one geode danced and the second vocalized, with the piece concluding as a danced geode

Rocks and stones hold secrets waiting to be released, not only through scientific exploration but also through those diverse roads found in language arts and music.

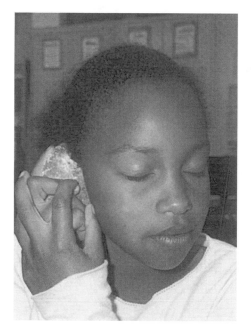

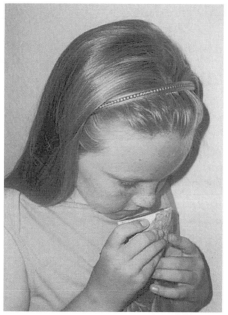

A student listening to a geode.   A student smelling a geode.

Students exploring the tactile imagery of geodes.

STUDENT POEMS

STONES

As beautiful as
pretty silver rings,
bumpy as mountains
smooth as ice.

Stones are rough as wood,
yummy and sweet as
chocolate chip cookies.

Quiet as
a still tree
standing TALL.

Stones are bright
and beautiful as
diamond earrings,
bright as
shining stars
in the night sky.

—THIRD GRADE

STONES

Stones are like crystals
twinkling in the sun
on a warm day in the fall.

They are a bird nest
filled with cute, fluffy,
baby birds

Stones are rough
armadillo skin.

—SECOND GRADE

SUMMARY

In the process of extending science through language, music, and movement, the natural world becomes real, while taking on surreal qualities. The geode has been explored and explained scientifically in the science lesson, but by extending the focus of the geode beyond the limits of scientific discovery, the students are able to gain access to a vast selection of creative possibilities. There are now sounds in the stones, movement to be interpreted through the crystal formations, and sensory images that extend the geode into the realms of the imagination to be seen as "an ocean stirring silently in the night," "a light breeze of wind at the beach," or "rough armadillo skin." The geode becomes "splashing, splattering stones," a "wolf moaning on a mountain peak," and "loud slapping, popping, clanking, screeching tires on the road." By exploring the natural world through heightened and extended imagination, original investigated elements are enlarged, and more meaningful learning takes place.

Endangered Species Lesson

All life is dependent on all life, and as such, issues of creature survival are a recurrent theme in almost all subject areas. For example, in American history we study the exploration of the frontier and its negative impact on native wildlife, which in turn drastically affected native human populations. In science, we study the cyclical effects of humankind's interference in the natural world (e.g., insecticides, air pollution, acid rain, habitat destruction, global warming), all of which threaten the interdependent chain of life. In language arts, poems, stories, and plays depict the conflict and competition between humans and animals. From the walls of prehistoric cave paintings to the walls of modern museums, we view this struggle. It echoes through the music and myths of the world.

Our realization that diminishing world wildlife populations diminish humans as well leads us to understand that the link between humans and our fellow creatures is symbiotic. These perceptions, poignant and compelling, instruct teachers to use endangered species as a focus for extended study. Because these issues arise as an integral part of the curriculum, they compel students to confront and acknowledge irrevocable survival truths:

1. The problems and long-range ramifications of ignoring the issues could prove universally fatal.

2. Humans are dependent on the survival of all creatures for our own survival.

3. Humans are the caretakers of our world and must accept our role and responsibility in effecting positive global change.

4. We are not helpless or alone in this effort. There are organizations that strive through legal, informational, and direct affirmative action to reverse negative global trends and to which people can contribute and lend support.

There is a need to understand the life force that exists in all creatures if students are to become sensitive to their right to exist. By introducing into the classroom the voices of creatures that call beneath the sea and cry in the air, and reverberate from mountaintop to valley, teachers individualize and personalize them.

Some musicians unite the human and creature worlds by weaving the strands of our divergent lives together. One such musician is Paul Winter, who celebrates himself and "creatures from whose song we can learn and take heart" in his record "Common Ground." Poet Gerald Clarke, who celebrates the wolf in his book *Mon-*

toya, reveals his understanding of "the nature of the predator, but not the predatory nature of man." In the field, scientists have collected and documented the haunting whale songs that echo through the oceans of the world. And we learn that a creature who speaks, even in a language we don't understand, communicates the relevancy and essence of its life to us. We begin to comprehend that we share certain finite life qualities, and thus it becomes easier to empathize and identify with our fellow creatures through poems, music, and innovative study.

ENDANGERED SPECIES LESSON

When students become involved in studying endangered species, whether as a result of a science or social studies lessons, they often have dramatic emotional poetic responses. In this writing assignment, the teachers are asking students to empathize with the reality of life for another species. Students are also asked to try and envision the world through the animal's eyes. Some examples include writing from the point of view of "I am the last whale" or "I am the last wolf," exploring all of the ramifications of that creature's precarious hold on life. Attempting to use any and all poetic tools at their command, students are often intuitively able to reduce the immensity of the situation to its most basic, imperative level, exposing a single animal's fears and perceptions.

STUDENT POEMS

THE BIG HUNT

I went deer hunting
in the old wood
air smelling
of sap on the trees.

I heard a noise
picked up my gun
shot the deer in its side.
Blood like a red rose
dripped in the sun.

He dropped.
His fur was tattered.
The woods would be empty
without that deer.

—FIFTH GRADE

GLEAMING EAGLES

White eagles gleaming
like the moon
shining high
glowing, glowing,
glowing, in the night
and flying, on wings like
little winds,
eagles sitting in
their nests hatching
little ones, clap, clap, clap
and the nice breeze flowing
with the eagles as they fly

—FIFTH GRADE

KOALA BEAR

I am the last koala
light brown with eyes
like the sky.
I am in a forest
with trees,
lonely as a cloud
in an endless sky.

—FOURTH GRADE

I AM THE LAST WHALE

I see a black sea.
A whale dies
Tears.
Sadness.

—THIRD GRADE

DOLPHIN

If you ever saw
a dolphin with eyes
like silvery diamonds
and his slick, powder blue
gleaming body,
and heard his splash with joy
against the waves
you would want to
save him.

—FOURTH GRADE

WIND

The wind is talking
to the birds.
The whale is talking
to the sea
and I'm very sad.

—SECOND GRADE

THE WHALE POEM

When I was young
I used to be afraid
of the wind and
the whale was so
big it was 100 feet
long and it sings good
when I was a baby
I used to be afraid
of the whale singing
and then when I grew
up it sang so sadly
I almost cried
then I tried to
stop and I did
and the whale was
killed then the
ocean was empty
all was left were
little goldfish
and the sky
was full of
clouds.

—THIRD GRADE

Original "Ocean Child" Music and Poetry

These next examples of poetry were collated into a book that, when sold at the school bazaar, became the means to adopt real whales through the Whale Adoption Project in Massachusetts. Other animal welfare societies and zoos also have such programs in place, making it possible for students to use their art to aid the world's creatures. The melodies were inspired by Paul Winter's "Ocean Dream" from the recording "Common Ground," in which the whale is referred to as an ocean child, and melodies sung by real humpback whales are woven into the arrangement. The notes used are the first five notes of a mode called lydian, which creates a mysterious mood because of the raised fourth tone: F, G, A, B natural, C.

STUDENT POEMS

ANIMAL

I am the wonder of ocean
I am ancient song.
I am form.
I am the sky,
I am the sand.
I am the ocean child.
Call me home.

—FOURTH GRADE

CALL

Call me
back to the sea,
ancient song of the ocean
I love, sea creatures,
snuggle beside me
at night.

—FOURTH GRADE

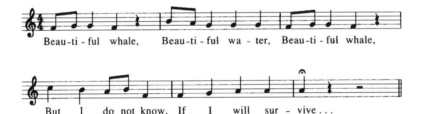

Beau-ti-ful whale, Beau-ti-ful wa-ter, Beau-ti-ful whale,

But I do not know, If I will sur-vive...

SUMMARY

As a result of the work dealing with endangered species, students became interested in finding out more about groups that are actively protecting wildlife. The following is a list of some of the organizations that the students chose to support through school fundraisers.

1. International Fund for Animal Welfare, P.O. Box 193, Yarmouth Port, MA 02675; www.ifaw.org

2. Bat Conservational International, P.O. Box 162603, Austin, TX 78746 www.batcon.org

3. American Eagle Foundation, P.O. Box 333, Pigeon Forge, TN 37868 www.eagles.org

4. Endangered Species Information, U.S. Fish and Wildlife Service, 4401 North Fairfax Drive, Room 420, Arlington, VA 22203 endangered.fws.gov

5. SchoolWorld Endangered Species Project
   www.schoolworld.asn.au

6. Greenpeace, P.O. Box 3720, Washington, DC 20007
   www.greenpeace.org/~climate

7. Sierra Club, 85th Street, 2nd Floor, San Francisco, CA 94105
   www.sierraclub.org

8. Cousteau Society, 710 Settlers Landing Road, Hampton, VA 23669
   www.cousteau.org

9. U.S. World Wildlife Fund–Endangered Species, P.O. Box 97180,
   Washington, DC 20090
   www.worldwildlife.org/species

10. The Whale Adoption Project, International Wildlife Coalition, 634 North Fal-
    mouth Highway, P.O. Box 388, North Falmouth, Massachusetts 02556-0388

The extension process enabled students to tap the intensity of their concerns and
feelings for the creatures that share their world and gave them a language (of words
and movement) with which to speak their passion.

NATURE AND SEASONAL LESSON

Working with nature settings and the changing seasons provides students with a laboratory of possibilities for isolating and fine-tuning their perceptions. Through intense sensory awareness, they begin to discover how one sense can stimulate another and how intellectually potent responsive observation can be. So much of the world is lost through inactive senses. When asked to describe their walk to school (the same walk taken every day), students often give a very perfunctory account of trees, buildings, the playground, and so forth. Retracing those same steps with instructions to isolate their senses—that is, using first the hearing sense (closing their eyes), using the sense of smell (to the exclusion of the other senses), using the tactile sense (skin, fingers)—they are treated to a new and sometimes startling assortment of stimuli.

This sensory approach to nature results in students' recognizing that their world is made up of many parts. The tree, which previously had been seen in its entirety, is now perceived through its component sections—trunk, bark, branches, twigs, leaves, flowers, and seeds—and each one of these facets, in turn, has its own taxonomy and set of properties. Different elements appeal to different senses and create new sensory reactions and images:

- The bark is rough and scratchy beneath the hand and to the finger and often reminds students of rocks and stones, of sandpaper, or of beach sand.

- The leaves are soft and pliable and can be crumpled, sniffed, or manipulated. They create a kaleidoscope of imagery, including that of "crinkly paper," "mother's perfume," "cotton balls," "animal fur," and "mint," among others.

- The wind moves across the surface of the leaves, creating light patterns on the ground and as the leaves brush against one another, soundscapes that whisper, sing, moan, and intrigue.

Students are further instructed to think of their senses as antennae capable of receiving all of nature's signals. While they are experiencing the abundance of nature's energy through their senses, they are becoming sensitized to rhythms, patterns, sounds, silences, and the changing seasons. In essence, each student is asked to remember this: that which you are not focused on will pass you by. The bird may be singing, but unless we are listening, we will not hear it.

In addressing this lesson, it is important to remember that poetry and music movement extensions using nature and the seasons as stimuli can result from the study of

- Snow, eggs, chrysali, insects, or other natural phenomena in science

- Bird calls and the nuance of animal movements in music

- Literary masterworks in language arts, such as William Wordsworth's "I Wandered Lonely as a Cloud" and "My Heart Leaps Up When I Behold"

- Natural geometric shapes, such as beehives and ice crystals, in the math classroom

Not every classroom is situated in an environment that lends itself to a nature walk or the firsthand observation of a burgeoning spring or crystalline winter. Environmental sound experiences are available on compact discs, audiotapes, and records that give realistic replication of outdoor soundscapes: "Among the Giant Trees of the Wild Pacific Coast," "Spring Morning on the Prairies," "Ocean Landscapes," "Canoe to Loon Lake," and "Dawn by a Gentle Stream." (See Appendix C for more information.) These sound experiences invite listeners to use their hearing sense as a gateway to all of their other senses. The poems resulting from this kind of listening experience are as valid as those written in the natural setting. The imagery is as stunning and the perceptions as keen, so that teachers and students in urban settings should not feel there is a reduction in the intensity of the experience by using these tools. The fifth-graders' poetic response to "Among the Giant Trees of the Wild Pacific Coast" gives eloquent credence to the impact of the listening experience.

STUDENT POEMS

A Journey Through the Forest

The waves are hitting rocks,
birds chirp like
squeaky instruments,
thunder starts softly,
wind blows and the sky
turns dark
like the soft fur
of a black cat.

Birds stop
singing and we

smell the dampness of
the ground,
rain, thunder, lightning,
trees waving
in the wind, our hair is
wet.

The sun comes out,
muddy ground is like
sand at the beach, and
the air smells like
roses in the garden,

crickets sound like
someone who has the
hiccups, leaves are
dropping drizzles

of rain on our heads,
bugs chirp like
violins in an orchestra.

—FIFTH GRADE

TEACHER IMPETUS IN STUDENT OUTDOOR WRITING

A nature or seasonal extension lesson might begin with a walk outdoors on a spring morning or after a snowstorm. Each child would have a pencil, paper, and a clipboard. After stepping outside, students might be asked to stand perfectly still, not moving or talking, but simply absorbing the atmosphere around them. The teacher can suggest that students jot down their perceptions as soon as one of their senses becomes acutely aware of a sensation. Very often their first reaction would be to the tactile sense: the cold air on their skin or the warm sun on their faces and bare arms.

This introductory phase, when students are gently eased into becoming solitary receptors, might last from 5 to 10 minutes. Following this, students begin to seek specifics through teacher suggestions such as the following:

Teacher: Observe the sky colors, cloud formations, movement of clouds across the sky, the position of the sun, the intensity of color contrasts. Observe the ground, its color, the sound when you walk on it, the feel of it underfoot and to your hand. Smell the air deeply with your eyes closed. Listen to the sounds of nature around you and of your movement through the natural environment. Feel the bark of a tree, and rub a leaf against your cheek. Taste winter or spring on your tongue.

All the while, the impressions are being preserved by students on paper. At the conclusion of the walk, which may last for a half hour or more, students may, if the area is suitable, find a quiet outdoor place to write or move back into the classroom to extend their impressions into images and images into poetry.

One student poem, "Autumn," begins with a series of impressions: "Autumn is the time / of year when / leaves turn brilliant / colors. . . . Autumn smells like / Chinese food. . . . It sounds like a / small child crying. . . ." Before the student wrote the poem, her teacher suggested that she look for metaphors and similes that might extend and enhance her original impressions. Of what did the brilliant autumn colors remind her? What does Chinese food smell like? And how could she extend the image of autumn being a "small child crying" into something that the reader of her poem could experience through his or her senses? Included in the poems that follow, "Autumn" is the culmination of this process.

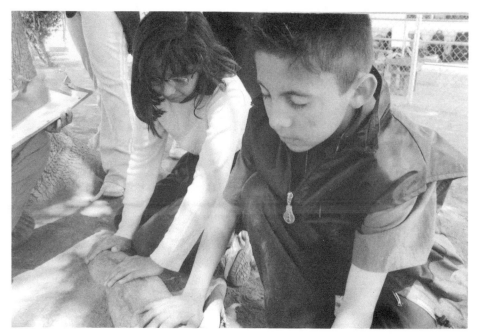

The up-close experience of nature on a spring day.

Learning to know with hands.

Touching a tree trunk.

Discovering a beech tree's beard.

Experiencing a tree intensely.

Letting the tree flow through us.

Putting the tree on paper.

Exchanging ideas and images.

Touching the tree's skin.

STUDENT POEMS

AUTUMN

Autumn is the time
of year when
leaves turn brilliant
colors, golden as
corn muffins, the sad
look of a whimpering
puppy's eyes,
a crackling fire.

It is a time of mourning and
memories, like a
dreary, cold day.

Autumn smells like
Chinese food, creamy
and saucy, a freshly
cooked turkey,
thick custard
pumpkin pie.

It sounds like a
small child crying
quietly in a corner,
wind whipping
leaves out of
trees, sounds of a
faraway echo in a

grassy valley.
Autumn.

—FIFTH GRADE

MY SUMMER POEM

Summer,
a piece of shiny gold in a
pot of rainbows
after sun-showers.

Summer tastes like
ice cream melting,
a tall glass of
lemonade by the side
of a lake.

Summer sounds like the
soft purr of a cat,
the chitter-chatter of
crickets on
dark nights.

Summer feels like cool soft wind on
    warm nights,
feathers drifting.

Summer smells of
roses on cool mornings,
like perfume and
crystal clear wind.

—SIXTH GRADE

SPRING

Spring is as bright
as buttercups, the
smell of oranges,
birds chirping
loud as you can sing.

Spring tastes
of lemonade ﹀
as delicious as a
professional pianist
playing a tune.

Spring smells
of roses, filling
the air with honeysuckle.

—THIRD GRADE

Using a Single Sense: The Sounds of the Season

Sometimes, to achieve a sharper focus, it is helpful to concentrate on a single sense.
The following poem is an example from an assignment that required students to listen to the season and write a poem entitled "The Sounds of the Season."

THE SOUNDS OF THE SEASON

Yelling people
sledding down a bumpy
hill, through crunching snow.

The crackling of fire
on cold nights,
honking of geese,
slushings
through snow.

—THIRD GRADE

USING THE NATURE AND
SEASONAL EXPERIENCE AS A SCHOOL PROGRAM FORMAT

Frequently in the course of the school year, a particularly exciting or innovative idea for a lesson will present itself. At Upper Nyack Elementary, the following all-school focus resulted in a poetry, music, and movement experience. This Apple Festival reached far beyond the walls of the general classroom and ended up entering the curriculum through art, music, math, language arts, and science. It also reached into the community, involving a variety of people and resources.

The following is a sample teacher/administrative brainstorming session that preceded the actual autumn unit.

"What about an all-school apple festival for next fall?"

"We could borrow the 150-year-old apple press from the Historical Society."

"My car will hold it."

"Who would write to the Apple Institute of America for free materials and perhaps a film if they have one?"

"We could use apples this month in math and in classroom cooking."

"The Poet-in-the-School will be here in September; we could ask her to focus some of her lessons with the third graders on apples."

"Let's have an all-school assembly at the end of the full-day event with freshly squeezed apple cider!"

"We could ask the PTA for volunteers and to foot the bill for the apples."

"I'll man the press."

"I was going out to the Davies' orchards this year anyway."

"Know any apple chants?"

"And what about extending it to the following week in the evening for parents by hiring an English country dance caller?"

"Why not put together another throw-together chorus like we did for Bach-to-Bach night and do early American music?"

The actual event bonded children, parents, and teachers into creative unity. The following program illustrates the fusion of improvisation, movement (using English country dances and English wassailing songs), original poetry, music, orchestration, and joyful all-school singing.

The Apple Festival Music/Movement/Poetry Program

The opening was written by Dr. Angelo Patri and read by the principal: "The apple is the loveliest of earth's fruits. There is no flavor like that of a ripe apple. It is the children's fruit, cherished in the school bags waiting for recess or given over to a special teacher. Apples have always been children's favorites and for good reason:

Apples put sparkle in their eyes, polish on their teeth, joy in their stomachs, and health all over! As for grown-ups, apples make the great culinary triumph of these United States—apple pie. That in itself is enough to call for this hymn of praise."

Apple callers (improvisation): Five children throughout auditorium

Apple wassail song, Carhampton, England (Sung by the quintet, then by the entire school as the curtain opens to first grade on stage. Third and fourth graders sing the counter melody):

Rome,   Rome,   Gran-ny   Smith   Ap - ples, ap - ples   lov - li - est of earth's fruit

"Winding up the Apple Tree" (as on the Twelfth Night in England), Traditional English Song, first grades

"Old Roger Is Gone and Buried and Dead," English Traditional Chant, second grades

"Haste to the Wedding," English Country Dance, third grades

Original apple poems by selected third graders (read between the third and fourth original song. The apple poems were written with poet Susan A. Katz as part of the Poet-in-the-Schools program.)

STUDENT POEMS

APPLES

As sticky as honey
Falling out of a beehive,
As red as a
Red, red cherry,
As smooth as the
Color of pink,
A secret you
Won't tell anybody,
A treasure buried
Under the sand,
A golden bracelet
Twirling around the
Queen's wrist,

A heart beating
With love,
A lovely unicorn
Flying through the air,
I LOVE APPLES.

—THIRD GRADE

INSIDE APPLES

As white as
A headband in your
Hair.
A seed trapped
Inside a cocoon,

As smooth as a
Piece of chalk,
Skin as silky as fur,
As light as the
Falling snow.

A unicorn flying
In the clouds,
As white as a

Cloud on a sunny
Day.

As fluttery as
Hair in the wind.
As soft as
A piano playing
In the night.

—THIRD GRADE

"Look for the Star in the Center of the Apple" (Fourth-grade original text and
    music, harmonized with a i, VII harmony and orchestrated for Orff instruments)

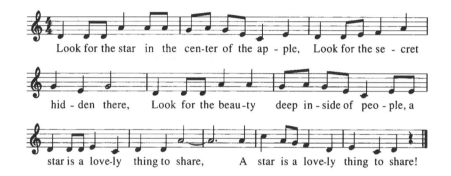

Look for the star in the cen-ter of the ap - ple, Look for the se - cret

hid - den there,   Look for the beau -ty   deep in - side of peo - ple, a

star is a love-ly thing to share,   A star is a love-ly thing to share!

Reprise of "Old Apple Tree, We'll Wassail Thee," followed by a fresh cider-making
    demonstration.

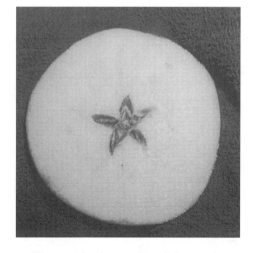

The star in the center of the apple.

THE STAR IN THE CENTER OF THE APPLE

The words, melody, and orchestration for "The Star in the Center of the Apple" was written collectively by a fourth-grade class.

In the same way that students were inspired to write poetry and music by discovering the secrets within the hearts of apples, the resident poet was inspired by the secrets revealed within the student poetry. Each poem contained some of the same magic that filled the classroom, as the hearts of apples were exposed. Just as art inspires art, the honesty and vulnerability that students revealed through their poetry inspired a heart-felt response.

THE HEARTS OF APPLES

Beneath the shiny, smiling
skin of apples the hard flesh
holds secrets, wishes,
dreams: in silent chambers
the future waits
to be born.

Within the seed, black
and bottomless as a doll's
eye, a life holds
on to itself, holds on
to instinct's memory
of sun and soil.

In the souls
of children, there lives
the energy of love
and laughter, the high
stepping life that marches
to the beat of trumpets
and drums.

In the eyes
of children, there is
a light that speaks
of things that we,
who store our dreams
in boxes, only half
remember, a light
that shines beneath
the surface, that penetrates
the clouds, that tempts
the robin into song.

In the hearts
of apples, there is
magic and mystery, there
is the tree's core;
in the hearts
of children, forgiveness
and truth and, much,
much more.

—Susan A. Katz

SUMMARY

Highlighting student work results in positive feedback to the students. Publication also generates intimate communication with classmates, fellow students, and parents and provides student authors with a sense of pride and accomplishment. School newspapers, newsletters, bulletin boards, and programs are vehicles for this type of student-work celebration. In the Upper Nyack School, each creative effort resulting from a "Spring Is " writing assignment was first published in its entirety in the individual classroom. To make these works more visible, excerpts from each poem were later selected to appear in a group poem, which was presented by the group in tandem during a fourth-grade "Moving Up" Program.

Spring Is

Spring is
The little white flowers that surround
You as you lay
On a hill looking at the sky
Strolling in a big field when the sun begins to rise
Playing in a tree
The sun playing hot
spot lights on you
Spring feels like the soft, wrinkly
skin on a baby. It smells of wind,

flowers, roses,
Laying on a beach, pushing my hands
Through the crystal clear sand
Spring is the taste of ice
Cream and the sound of crickets singing loudly
Feels like the wind blowing in the trees
Tastes like watermelon
Tastes like the starting of a new life
Looks like a red-breasted robin with a worm and her young
Is the creak of a swing going back and forth, back and forth
Rolling down a steep, flowered hill
Green grass stretching up to the sky
Bugs biting people!
Spring tastes like green
Apples just being picked
Spring is taking a stroll on the
Beach with the moon lighting your path
Feels like one rose petal that fell slowly to the ground
Spring is like a gold coin sitting
In the sky, like a flow of birds come back
From the south
Is a baby in the field
Tastes like wild cherries
Spring is the wind telling you to "come here"
Feels like a very comfortable grass pillow. It is leaves falling and
Finding a new home
Smells like my father
Just mowed the lawn and sounds like the
Grand Canyon
Smells like a cherry pie just taken out of the oven
Sounds like paper bags crumpling
Up as the wind blows
Against the trees
Sounds like a lily pad in a breeze
Tastes like lime soda
Looks like an ant lifting up the
World like it was a round picnic basket
Sounds as graceful as a California condor soaring through the air
Spring is with me like a dog following you through your lovable and
Cherished life
Spring has a wonderful feeling!

—GROUP POEM

CURRENT EVENTS LESSON

In the broadest sense, the extended experiences that result from exploring current events can run in any direction—moving forward to explore the future or moving backward in time to redefine the past. Newspaper articles, local events, world issues—all are fodder for the creative interplay of ideas that may result in poems, movement pieces, or musical presentations.

Writing assignments that lead into further explorations are thought expanders for students. Acting like the spokes in a wheel, the process begins with a central focus ("We the People," "The American Flag," "Freedom") and often extends far beyond the original point of inspiration. On many occasions, themes have overlapped and "We the People" became the window through which "Freedom" was explored. Many Americans' patriotic acts after September 11 illuminated their pride in and gratitude for being a citizen of the United States of America. A teacher introduction might have been:

Teacher: Having been brought up in an environment where freedom is a comfortable given, we tend to take it for granted. Can you imagine a life where freedom does not exist? Where the simplest of goals cannot be achieved? Where your life and your actions are directed by others? Now, explore personally and poetically, within the framework of your own life, what freedom is, and what it means to you.

The continuation of the extended lesson might be introduced in the following way:

T: Taking the group poem "We the People Means" as one example, what simple melody might we put to the essence of "Freedom feels like raindrops?" Thinking in a minor mode, can anyone mentally envision a melody using these tones? (T. demonstrates the sound of la pentatonic, D, F, G, A, C. One student volunteers a melody.) A good start. Can the group echo that idea? Do you think the rest of the poem should be sung as a recitative or spoken?

STUDENT POEMS

WE THE PEOPLE MEANS

Freedom feels like
the tiny pitterpattering of
soft wet raindrops
falling on a new
white and sweet-smelling
rose.
Freedom tastes like an
appetizing
breakfast on
a cool clear summer
Fourth of July.
Freedom smells like
the newly sewn
and crisply ironed
red white, and blue
flag.
Freedom sounds like
the rusty colored
liberty bell ringing
for you for the first
time.
Freedom feels like
holding the
white feathery
quill when you
sign the
Constitution.

—FOURTH-GRADE GROUP

EXTENDED VERSION CREATED BY CLASS SUGGESTIONS

Fixed melody, agreed on by the class to be sung by the group:

Group in Canon:

Solo [spoken during the humming]: The tiny pitterpattering of
soft, wet, raindrops
falling on a new
white and sweet-smelling
rose

Solo [spoken during the humming]: Like an
appetizing
breakfast on

a cool, clear summer
Fourth of July.

Free - dom smells like a new flag   (hum)

Solo [spoken during the humming]: Like
the newly sewn
and crisply ironed
red, white, and blue
flag.

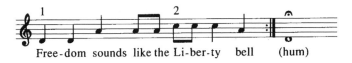

Free - dom sounds like the Li-ber-ty bell   (hum)

Solo [spoken during the humming]: Like
the rusty colored
Liberty bell ringing
for you for the first
time.

Free - dom feels like a feath-er- y quill   (hum)

Solo [spoken during the humming]: Like
holding the
white feathery
quill when you
sign the
Constitution.
Group [singing on low D and holding]: Freedom. [singing on A and holding]
    Freedom.

—FOURTH-GRADE GROUP

FREEDOM

Freedom tastes like
Pizza
fresh from the oven
hot, flaky
with herbs and spices.

Freedom smells like
a turkey feast with
rich, brown gravy.

Freedom looks like
two huskies playing
joyfully in the
cold winter snow.

Freedom feels like
the affection of a
fluffy, snow white kitten.

—FOURTH GRADE

We The People

America is sweet
as the smell of roses.
I like the freedom to speak
in America, to do
what you want in America.
The Constitution makes us
free in America.

—Third grade

The Tattered Flag

Waving in the sky
like a wounded
red, white, and blue bird,
standing proud
for my country,
I was held by George Washington
in the Revolution, and I still
lead my country,
my people.
I stand for the United States:
I am tattered but still
the American flag
after September Eleven.

—Fifth grade

WE THE PEOPLE

We the people means ———————
    we have freedom so we can go to
    the store when we want to go.

We the people means
    love so
    we can love anyone
    we want to love.

We the people means
    food so
    we can go to the
    store and eat hot dogs
    and drink soda.

We the people means ———————
    clothes we can go out and go
    shopping so that we can look
    pretty for school tomorrow.

We the people means
    Thanksgiving so we can
    celebrate and eat
    turkey and stuffing.

We the people means
    we only have to feed who we
    want to feed.

That's called freedom.
We have it here
in America.

There is a strong repetitive framework here that lends itself to group movement, contrasted with solo improvisation. All-class movement choir, repeating refrain in ensemble each time it appears.

"We" the   "people"   "means"
(pointing   (turning,   (palms up—
to self)   all-encom-   freezing motion
                passing   while solo moves
                gesture)   stanzas in
                                between.)

Solo: (speaking/moving the poem in between
the group refrain with improvised movement)

FREEDOM IN AMERICA

Freedom feels like
a copper coin deep inside of
you, filling you with
heat 'til you burst into
flames.
Freedom is a
red, white, and blue
flower, growing
in the hot, dry desert where
the sun glows and
rain falls to make
plants grow.

Freedom is sweet like
a cinnamon apple pie,
Sounds of people
cheering, crying,
caring.
Freedom looks like a
rainbow with
everlasting colors.
Freedom feels like
the sick getting well and
the dead rising
for a new life in America

—FOURTH GRADE

SUMMARY

The poetic focus within the context of these vast themes was the personalization of subcategories, such as citizenship, unity in the face of a national tragedy, and patriotic pride. Flexing their knowledge of poetic techniques, each student adapted his or her own experiences into the scope of the central theme. Creatively examining freedom, personal pride, and liberties provides new insights into citizenship and elucidates the role of each American within his or her own community and the world as well.

Environment Lesson

In this chapter, we share a culminating experience that rose above the sum of its parts to become a moving, memorable, all-encompassing school event. Selecting a single, relevant theme that could be extended over a period of weeks within the structure of routine school and classroom activities, we were able to play with all of the skills and techniques addressed in the first section of this book. Furthermore, the intention was to move beyond the classroom into the special resources available in the music room (i.e., Orff instruments and nonpitched percussion). It was the intention of the music specialist to enhance the poetry writing experience through possibilities inherent in the Orff-Schulwerk approach.

In an elementary school (kindergarten through fourth grade), students in second, third, and fourth grades were selected to participate in this experience. The third-grade students, already primed in poetic skills through the five workshop sessions scripted in the first section, were targeted to receive the environment workshops. Meetings were held with classroom teachers who would be involved in the total process, and a focus was agreed on. The lessons were designed to run for 8 weeks: six poetry classes spread over 3 weeks, six editing and refining sessions spread over 3 weeks, and a 2-week follow-up period to ready the music extension phase. The ultimate goal was to present an assembly that framed the student poetry in melody, movement, instruments, and vocalization, as well to create structures that showcased individual works in a dramatic and meaningful format.

The theme ultimately selected was influenced by a number of factors:

- The school itself was in the midst of building expansion, which resulted in a chaotic environment inside and out.

- Community efforts (sponsored by the local garden club) were under way for creating natural habitats and beautification of school grounds.

- Environmental issues dominated the news (i.e., oil spills, acid rain, ozone depletion, endangered species, conflict over fishing practices, global warming, and so forth).

- In previous months, class emphasis had been placed on awareness of individual worth.

- The school was involved in efforts to help students become aware of their own powers to effect positive change in their world.

With these elements in mind, a far-reaching theme of "This Is My World: I Choose" was chosen. The plan was to begin with a simple kind of stimulus. The familiar subjects, colors, and feelings were selected because they had been used earlier to teach poetry techniques. It was hoped that students would address these comfortable subjects on a more personal level. Classroom discussions focused on establishing the intimate relationships between the subjects, the student, and his or her world.

OUTLINE FOR SIX POETRY WORKSHOP SESSIONS

The six poetry workshop sessions each had a separate theme. The following outline became the worksheet from which the sessions began:

1. "The Colors of My World" will explore the colors of the natural world and encompass the use of basic poetry techniques.

2. "The Feelings of My World" will investigate emotions that are evoked through an awareness of the world: seasons, holidays, environment, and so forth.

3. "The People of My World" will delve into the differences and similarities between people and will define the people of the student's world and their roles in his or her life through imagery, as well as the common denominators among peoples and cultures. Discussion will emphasize the benefits of differences, similarities, and contributions of people as individuals and as groups.

4. "The Creatures of My World" will examine endangered species, the living world, and the students' role in it. We will attempt to coordinate with planned school programs (e.g., Garden Club planting, habitat; Carnival of Animals; "Horton the Elephant" fourth-grade Recorder Club Musical).

5. "The Places of My World" will explore environments: mountains, deserts, oceans, and so forth. Discussion will be geared toward environmental issues, threats to the environment world-wide and locally, and individual responsibilities and abilities to make a difference.

6. "This Is My World: I Choose" will focus on each student's individual place in the world, what he or she loves about it, what the student needs to do to make a better world for the people and creatures in it, and his or her responsibility toward the environment.

Although these lessons were carried out by a language specialist, the techniques used could just as easily have been implemented by the classroom teacher. All of the techniques had been introduced earlier, and the real emphasis in these lessons was on classroom discussion, student participation, and a meaningful personalization of pertinent themes. Students were asked to explore, in depth, their feelings about each subject. Poetry became the vehicle through which ideas and feelings were explored and ultimately took shape.

In between the poetry sessions (which were on Mondays and Wednesdays), classroom teachers worked with students to refine and edit their poems. Further

A student explores
his world on a topographic map.

work was done during the language arts time. This involvement with the poems became part of the normal language arts class, using poetry to teach whatever was on
the teaching agenda, such as punctuation or spelling. These revised copies were then
passed on to the music teacher, who culled the works with an eye toward those
poems that would best lend themselves to extension. The student groups made the
decision that ultimately shaped the presentations of the teacher-selected poems
(e.g., melodic setting, rhythmic setting, soundscape-behind-word setting, extended
form). In the four 35-minute music periods (over the 2 weeks), roughly two poems
were expanded in each of the three third-grade groups. The three fourth-grade
groups chose an excerpted format, using a collaborative music refrain (text by them,
music by the teacher) to highlight individual lines from approximately 50 student
works.

The ideas spilled beyond the classroom and became

- Bulletin boards in the hallways focusing on environments: air, sea, land, and subsequent pollution

- Individual student suggestions for ways to improve home and neighborhood
environments

- Plans to raise monies to contribute toward saving elephants and adopting whales
or wolves as classroom and school projects

- Student-published poetry arranged into topical booklets, suitable for selling

- Donations requested for admission to the fourth-grade elephant-theme musical,
which were then given to environmental agencies

An idea from one of the third-grade Upper Nyack Elementary School teachers, Marion Anderson, led to a particularly educational facet of the bulletin board
happening: school-wide art displays reflecting various environments such as ocean,
desert, mountain, and sky.

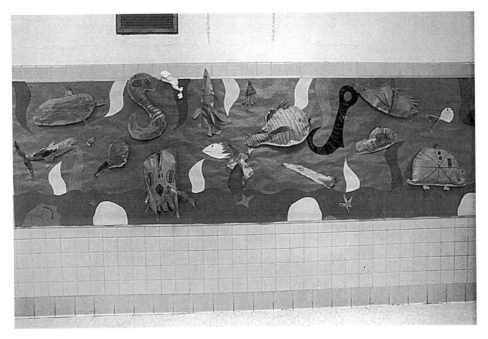

Bulletin board depicting the underwater environment.

Environmental bulletin board.

The idea was to have students begin with a clean environment. (Students did the work for these bulletin boards in art class, involving yet another discipline.) They then littered that environment by tacking up the type of litter collected from their own schoolyard. This illustrated visually, for the entire school body, the devastating effects of various forms of litter:

- Bottle tops

- Candy wrappers

- Plastic soda connecting rings

- Styrofoam packaging

- Plastic bags

The learning exercise involved devising methods to affect the neighborhood and school. These community actions would then entitle students to clean up, remove litter, and then restore the original bulletin board environment.

Through all of these plans and activities, it became apparent that the excitement throughout the school required teachers to follow their students' lead, and new student ideas were discussed and enacted on a daily basis. This kind of spontaneous creative combustion is perhaps the most exhilarating of all teaching experiences.

STUDENT POEMS

THE COLORS OF MY WORLD

Blue is loud as rain
beating on city sidewalks,
sparkling as a pond
in a cool evening breeze,
cold as the whistling wind
in chilling winter,
sweet as sugar
from the sugar bowl.

Blue is a tear
on a baby's face.

—THIRD GRADE

THE FEELINGS OF MY WORLD

Loneliness is as blank as
a single piece of paper

in a stack of 1,000.
Happiness is soft as a
colt newly born.
Unhappiness is
a duckling that has waddled
away from its nest
and never found its way back.
Sadness is a blue tear
On a child's face.
Fright is something
in the fog
you can't make out.

—THIRD GRADE

THE PEOPLE OF MY WORLD

Carpenters are busy
as beavers in the woods.

Teachers are smart
as owls at night.
Children are curious
as monkeys in the zoo.
Parents are caring as
mother cats with their kittens.
Babies are happy
as the song of birds.
Poets are sweet as strawberries in a
    bowl.

—THIRD GRADE

THE CREATURES OF MY WORLD

Dolphins are
beautiful like
rainbows lighting
up the sky.
Birds are musical
as flutes,
raccoons are soft
as clouds floating
in summer skies
seals are smooth
as a baby's skin.
Animals make me
feel special
and without them,
I wouldn't.

—THIRD GRADE

THIS IS MY WORLD: I CHOOSE

I choose to love poetry
bright as a flickering candle
in a dark cave.
I choose to hear animals,
smell their fragrance of
green grass,
fresh as fruit.
I choose to see birds,
gentle as playful kittens
romping with a piece of yarn,
a dancer gliding
across a stage,
trees standing
big and strong
as soldiers.

—THIRD GRADE

THIS IS MY WORLD

I choose to love the
forest that
hides the hidden streams.

I choose to love
mountains
that touch the
morning sky.

I choose to love
the feelings
of the world,
clean and free.

—THIRD GRADE

STUDENT ORCHESTRATION OF "MY PEOPLE" BY LANGSTON HUGHES

The student excitement and delight in their written work carried over into the creative task of intensifying the poems through music and movement. In reality, this music process began not with a student work but with a Langston Hughes poem ("My People"), which a second-grade class learned in language arts class. Having memorized it as a choral reading, the class, still full of the moment, shared their accomplishment with the music teacher. The class decided (and the music teacher approved of the idea) to work with this poem and turn it into "poetry-plus" as an introduction to the planned "This Is My World: I Choose" assembly.

MY PEOPLE

The night is beautiful,
So the faces of my people.

The stars are beautiful,
So the eyes of my people.

Beautiful also is the sun,
Beautiful also are the souls of my people.

—LANGSTON HUGHES[1]

When the music teacher first heard this poem, she was struck by the key words and asked the students to recite it again and listen for those words and others that they felt were key to the meaning and feeling of the poem. They found *night, stars, sun,* and *souls.* The next task was to find musical sounds that paralleled their word selections. The Orff instruments were available to the students.[2]

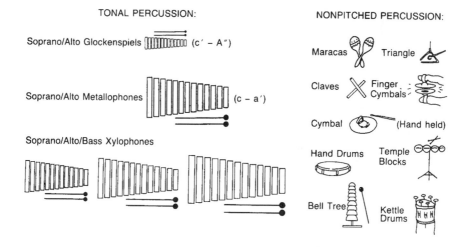

For *night,* one child invented a four-note theme on the bass xylophone that the group agreed sounded dark:

[1]From THE COLLECTED POEMS OF LANGSTON HUGHES by Langston Hughes, copyright © 1994 by The Estate of Langston Hughes. Used by permission of Alfred A. Knopf, a division of Random House, Inc.
[2]These instruments were developed by composer Carl Orff, who was inspired by world models, such as the gamelan found in Indonesia and the drums and nonpitched percussion found in parts of Africa. The instruments make it possible for young children to play in ensemble at an early age. They provide accompaniment to the children's singing and movement and enable them to improvise and compose in a wide variety of melodic patterns and elemental harmonies. Carl Orff intended his approach to be taught in a way that integrates movement, singing, speech rhythmic play, the playing of elemental instruments, and improvisation. Teaching musical concepts using this approach also offers the possibilities of enhancing poetry, drama, and general learning.

For *stars,* they chose an improvised motif on the glockenspiels (tuned to: E G A B D). The *sun* became the sound of the sustained cymbal, and the *souls* became the sound of the bell tree. The children felt a short melodic pattern would be nice at the end of each line, and a number of these were invented and shared. Ultimately the class chose this one:

Scored, the completed work looked like the following and became the introductory piece in the assembly:

For one of the selected poems in "The Creatures of My World" category, a musical refrain was decided on after the class built four layers over the pattern supplied by the teacher.

This resulted in a piece that was driven by the insistence of the patterns created by the students (drum included) and the reiterative melody of the refrain sung by the students. Scored, the resulting student creation looked like this:

The Creatures of My World

The second selection for the "Creatures of Our World" category involved dolphins and lent itself to a simple format of the student reading over the metallophone's musical punctuation.

DOLPHINS

Dolphins* are as gentle as
A new baby* and
As soft as
The water they live in*
They are as gentle as
Quiet whispers,*
But tomorrow*
They will be
As nothing.*
Dolphins* are as sweet
As sugar,*
but the water
That they live in*
Is sour.

—THIRD GRADE

The third "Creatures of Our World" selection was treated as a movement poem with the jubilant arched dolphin leap as the impetus for finding choice sustained sounds. The children then took words from the poem as guideposts for their movements. They designed a movement interpretation that played with large pieces of billowy chiffon and scarves to duplicate the shimmery underwater effect. Students

used locomotion, air space, and floor patterns, and they incorporated the qualities
of float, flick, glide, dab, press in their choreography. The score follows:

DOLPHINS

Solo: DOLPHINS!
(metallophones) (arched
leap)

JUMP like dancers and FLY like birds over the water . . . they seem
to have wings!

DOLPHINS!

. . . sing and dance, and
laugh . . .

DOLPHINS!   . . . keep them in your world
. . . let them sing for you. Let
them dance, and glide over the
water for you. Don't kill them . . .

DOLPHINS!   . . . love the world.

DOLPHINS!   . . . love the sea.

DOLPHINS!   . . . love you . . . please love
them. Their eyes twinkle
[glockenspiel improvisation]
like stars that fall from the sky
that you found in your back
yard . . . that you found,
shining in the dew [add
metallophone glissando].

DOLPHINS!   . . . enjoy the world, but with
you, they can't enjoy it for
long. They are dying
. . . from you . . .

Vocal and Movement Extension

The "Feelings of My World" were conveyed through a poem by a third-grade student to which movement and vocal sound were added by the class. The narrator controlled the length of the movement by hitting the hand-held cymbal to indicate everyone was to freeze.

Narrator: *Uncomfortable is being squeezed into a tight place.*

Students converged with disjointed, automatic movements into a center spot, accompanying the crunch with appropriate improvisation and sounds.

Narrator: *Bored is having nothing to do on an exciting day.*

Group melted apart and floated into disparate shapes all over the stage with bored sounds.

Narrator: *Mad makes you want to tear your pillow apart and then throw it out the window.*

Group made punching and slashing motions in all directions with accompanying loud sounds.

Narrator: *Sadness is losing something you really loved.*

Group all walked toward stage front with arms outstretched, then crossed them, then put their heads down with a sad sound and held the final motion. A soft cymbal sound ended the piece.

Students used the Orff instruments as sound effects for "The Places of My World" by a third-grade student. A single triangle sound was the signal agreed on to hold the movement for the next stanza.

Narrator: *The ocean is a wavy, wonderful, wacky, watery rain forest.*

Metallophones did glissandos. One student who did a solo wave used his whole air space from the lowest to the highest, while the group did waves that stayed low and undulating.

Narrator: *Mountains are as high as skyscrapers as they seem to touch the sky.*

Xylophone and temple blocks played ascending improvisation at the same time. At the triangle, the group froze with arms in skyscraper positions.

Narrator: *Clouds* [metallophone glissando] *are as white and wondrous as a desert.*

Group, using high air space, floated in slow-motion.

Narrator: *The desert is as deserted as an empty cookie jar.*

The group feigns a hunger for cookies, saying the word *cookie* at all speeds and vocal ranges, reaching outward with their hands.

Narrator: *The ice caps* [sound of the bell tree] *are as cold and slippery as a 200 below zero day.*

Musicians played glissandos on metallophones and bell tree, as movement group slid and slipped on the stage.

Narrator: *These are the places of my world.*

The group holds the final position for approximately 3 seconds.

The third-grade students who were considering the poem "The People of My World" for expansion agreed that the author's words sounded very rhythmical, which led them to the need for a short, layered rhythm pattern in between lines. An African piece from Ghana using a hand drum, maracas, claves, a small drum, and a large drum had been learned earlier by the class, and it was this piece that ultimately found a new usage in "The People of My World."

RHYTHM PATTERN:

A triangle was used to embellish four of the lines, and to add contrast. The poem was read over the heartbeat of the African piece, as follows.

Introduction

The instruments came in, one layer at a time until all were playing the rhythm pattern and then stopped together to let the narrator begin:

Narrator: *Policemen are like blue soldiers.*

RHYTHM PATTERN:

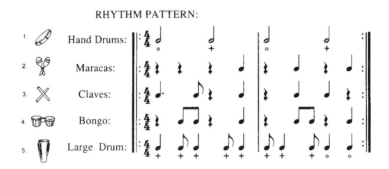

Narrator: *Teachers are like junior scientists!*

            The rhythm pattern played.

Narrator: *Nurses are Band-Aids, barbers are scissors.*

            The rhythm pattern played.

Narrator: *Presidents are bosses, mailmen are letters.*

            The rhythm pattern played.

Narrator: *Neighbors are the next thing, children are toys.* ◁

            Fishermen are people who catch nature. ◁

            Doctors are germ killers, bankers are money. ◁

            Soldiers are gates that are locked. ◁ ◁ ◁

Narrator: *Babysitters are baby cradles.*

            The rhythm pattern played.

Narrator: *Friends are on the same rope.*

            The rhythm pattern and one more beat were played all together to end the piece.

Melodic Improvisation

In setting two edited fourth-grade poems from the "This Is My World" theme, the first task became one of singing recitative in a mode recently studied with the fourth-grade students: dorian (D, E, F, G, A, B, C, D).

A i, IV harmony was borrowed from another dorian song, and a group-invented melody was found for the first line of each stanza of the poem.

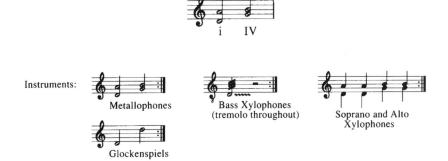

The preceding notation approximates the improvisation done by the fourth graders.

Poem with Related Sounds

Another edited fourth-grade poem shared in the assembly had great contrast in the stanzas. The students decided there should be a set of good sounds, whatever that constituted, and a set of rougher, more strident, bad sounds to parallel the poem. The good sounds were as follows:

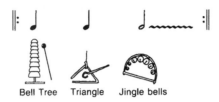

Bell Tree   Triangle   Jingle bells

This pattern was played slowly under the brighter parts of the poem. The students with sounds representing the bad parts of the poem assembled and, playing in tandem, found four different drum sounds, followed by maracas, a single bell, and a guiro. The pattern became

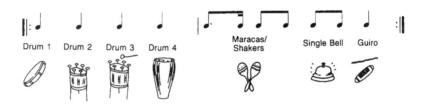

Drum 1   Drum 2   Drum 3   Drum 4   Maracas/   Single Bell   Guiro
                                          Shakers

The sequence of the poem, the good sounds, and the bad sounds follows.

This is My World

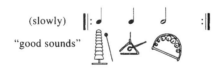

(slowly)

"good sounds"

Narrator [reading over good sounds]:   *This is my world*

I love the nature,
and I love the rain. [The good sounds stop.]

Narrator [shouting]:   *Not the junk and the acid rain!* [The bad sounds follow.]

(quickly)

"bad sounds"   1   2   3   4   Shaker   Single   Guiro
                                                    Bell

Narrator [reading over good sounds]:   *I love to watch the birds fly*

In the clear sky. [The good sounds stop.]

Narrator [shouting]:   *Not the junk all around and the dust in my eye!* [The bad sounds follow.]

Narrator [reading over good sounds]:   *I love to watch the stream go past*

And the wind blowing the grass. [The good sounds stop.]

Narrator [shouting]:   *Not the muddy stream or the dirt flying around!* [The bad sounds follow.]

Excerpted Poetry Using a Rondo Form

In an effort to allow as many students as possible to share their wonderful insights and wishes for their world, a large rondo was created for the finale of the assembly. Approximately 50 fourth-grade students chose a stanza or two from their completed poems to read, one after the other, stopping every eight people to sing the A theme of the rondo with the whole school. This A theme song, though written by the teacher, had words written by the students. It could easily have been written by the students, only the limited time frame in putting the program together negated this possibility. So the form of the final segment became:

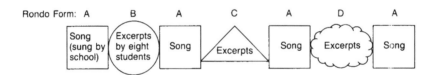

The A theme song follows, with selected "This Is My World" poems and excerpts. The words are by the fourth-grade students and the music is by Judith Thomas.

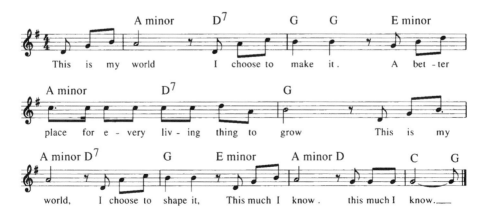

A student
accompanies the
group on an Orff instrument.

Teachers join in, celebrating
student work in a culminating assembly.

STUDENT POEMS

THIS IS MY WORLD: I CHOOSE

My world is green grass,
valleys, mountains
tall and high.

My world is peace,
love, kindness,
no more wars.

My world is caring
for animals and people
It is a world of free land,
free people.

It is a world without
pollution, violence
fear.

This is my world!

—FOURTH GRADE

THIS IS MY WORLD

A world with a spring breeze
An area full of trees with leaves
A nonpolluted air.
My world would be a handshake
For every man you meet.

—FOURTH GRADE

This is My World

I choose to see
the sun setting over the ocean,
not coffee cups, beer bottles,
litter.

This is my world
I choose to hear seagulls
soaring over the ocean,
not seeing the news
someone got shot.

This is my world
I choose to see
snow fall
from my windows,
not homeless people
on the streets of cities.

—Fourth grade

This is My World

Lakes sparkle in sunshine, geese
fly above,
grass sways gracefully,
springs of water spurt
up in the air,
fish jump around
the ball of life.
Eyes of Indian children amazed
at magic they hear,
whales stay near the surface
close to man,
bells on a horse-drawn sleigh
ring out in the snow,
baby seals sleep in peace.
This is my world.

—Fourth grade

SUMMARY

Within the framework of "This Is My World: I Choose," the process was designed to be ongoing. When the language and music specialists completed their input, environmental themes were projected into all of the various school disciplines. Possible math projects were considered, science lessons designed, and history lessons planned that would compare past, present, and future environments. Earth Day activities were on the agenda, and a follow-up outdoor spring poetry/music day was planned for the end of the school year.

The point of concluding the section with this particular extended environment-related experience is to illustrate the positive aspects of educational layering. For us, this school-wide event reinforced the degree to which cross-curriculum teaching can affect, and enhance, the total learning gestalt. The goal throughout this book has been to strive to achieve this level of teaching using creative techniques in a way that is curriculum-kind (i.e., it permits the teacher to work within his or her own format without additional material interjection). An exciting, energized classroom combines teacher skills, student participation, a bit of faith, and a bit of magic. By yielding to this evocative process, the student is released creatively and more able to find delight in the word in play.

Teachers as Participants (TAPS)

Before the Word

— To the teacher-students of George Mason University

"Of all those arts in which the wise excel,
Nature's chief masterpiece is writing well."
—John Sheffield, "Essay on Poetry"

Before the word is formed
senses bend like branches
beneath snow, weighted
by a need to know
the spirit of the thing
that we would tame, dynamic
in the mind, settling
on the tongue, answering
to red, orange, blue,
love anger, hate, every
state and hue emotion
colors to.

We walked a while in warm
companionship, shared a heady
brew of words seductive
as warm cinnamon
and cider on a winter's night
soothing the chill
of silence, frost
of thoughts lost unformed
by language.

Each face, a foreign country
mapped by poems
led us to some inner
truth, gifted us with common
causes, fears, desires
and despair; words fell
light pooled, ran

into corners, unmasked shadows
dispelled even the memory
of gloom.

We gave words to the air
and they came back as poems
each one perfect as a single
drop of rain feeding
the hungry stream, joining
into rivers
of one another's dreams.

Beyond the word
the poem.
The world!

—SUSAN A. KATZ

We conducted poetry/music/movement workshops for teachers as participants (TAPS) at education, language arts, and Orff-Schulwerk music conferences; for school staff enrichment and districtwide development programs; for arts-based groups and events such as the Westchester Philharmonic, the International Arts and Ideas Festival, and the Yale Playing for Keeps Conference; and as part of teacher-training courses at colleges and universities. We adapted these workshops to meet the requests and needs of each organization or group (e.g., field trips, curriculum slants, special events). Audiences have varied in size from 15 college faculty members to more than 200 people at large national conferences. An introductory workshop program takes a minimum of 2–3 hours, and longer workshops span 2–3 days and sometimes last up to a full week.

REACTIONS TO THE WORKSHOPS BY TEACHERS AS PARTICIPANTS

The benefits of these TAPS sessions are reflected in the words of former participants:

- "This [workshop] had very effective and useful techniques and suggestions connecting language and music for both classroom teachers and music specialists." —Music Department Chairman, Trevor Day School, Manhattan, New York

- "Every moment was packed with creative, imaginative, easily used in the classroom information. I didn't miss a beat the whole time!" —A fifth-grade teacher at the Vista Academy of Visual and Performing Arts, San Clemente, California

- "The workshop was a very powerful and moving experience. Not only were music and language brought together, but so were the people! There was so much sharing and opening-up to one another. It was magical." —A second-grade teacher at the Vista Academy of Visual and Performing Arts, San Clemente, California

- "It is this kind of curriculum blending [that] is rarely found in classrooms and music rooms, but is so valuable, which Judith and Susan bring to teachers with such skill. We were so lucky to have this unique and talented pair!" —An Orff-Schulwerk specialist, American Orff-Schulwerk Association National Conference, Seattle, Washington

- "I know of no other source as rich as Judith, Susan, and their book, for demonstrating the process of how one melds original language and music so masterfully — a delight!" — An Orff-Schulwerk specialist, Canada Orff-Schulwerk National Conference

- "This workshop inspired me to look deeper and longer at the richness of simple things: the star in the apple, the fire of red, the peacefulness of blue." — A teacher at the Vista Academy of Visual and Performing Arts, San Clemente, California

- "I was inspired, not only as a teacher, but as an individual able to improve my own communication skills." — A third-grade teacher at Vista Academy of Visual and Performing Arts, San Clemente, California

- "This workshop demonstrated to teachers how to incorporate original poetry into their classes using it as a springboard for musical works. The workshop was superb and provided terrific models!" — A professor of Music Education, Los Angeles Chapter of the American Orff-Schulwerk Association

Having observed TAPS in action at these sessions and having read the subsequent comments on evaluation forms, we believe that the prevailing sentiments of participants were overwhelmingly positive. They reflected a sense of personal accomplishment and a newfound confidence in bringing what they had experienced and learned back to their students in the classroom.

ROLE REVERSAL AS RATIONALE FOR TAPS WORKSHOPS

This third section addresses the importance of role reversal, in which teachers became students of poetry and extension in order to experience and to better understand the many challenges inherent in any creative process. The authors present this section as a way of enabling the reader to observe from an adult perspective, the delineation of the following:

- The application of the intricacies of the poetry and extension process at work

- The realization of the degree of personal clarity that can be achieved by TAPS going where students are asked to go

- The amplification of the scope of adult creativity, sensitivity, and sensory awareness

- The practice of poetic and extension vocabulary elements

- The expansion of comfort zones and attainment of greater familiarity with the process, allowing for enhanced ease of adaptation with students

- The discovery of and experimentation with personal visions in the creation of poems in TAPS workshops

- The integration and layering of music and movement elements

- The observation of the metamorphosis of an initial creative product from inception to editing, from extension to culminating event

- The recognition within the curriculum for potential creative development of any meaningful experience

The workshops presented in this section represent interaction with a small portion of the TAPS with whom the authors have worked over the years. We presented most of the workshops in actual classroom settings with TAPS acting as observers and collaborators. This section provides teachers with salient enrichment and guidelines for honing individual skills and at the same time, alerts them to an array of germane classroom possibilities:

- Whether attending a poetry writing workshop at a conference

- In a local faculty setting

- Deciding to become an initiator of a workshop

- Simply engaging in poetry-pertinent dialogues with fellow teachers in casual settings

- Responding to any poignant occasion or compelling event in poetic form

PREVIEW OF CHAPTERS

Chapter 13: Exploring Water Worlds: Without, Within, With Wonder

Chapter 13 shows how we responded to the needs of the Vista Academy of Visual and Performing Arts' faculty. They wanted to familiarize themselves with a water setting, which was to become the focus of subsequent schoolwide field trips for their students. This TAPS workshop trip was unique in that it involved almost the whole school faculty, provided reconnaissance information in a stimulating ocean setting, and spanned an entire weekend, encouraging the strengthening of bonds between teachers. It was for all of these reasons that this workshop became the first chapter in Section III.

Chapter 14: Seeding the Garden of Language:
From the Word to the Narrative to the Poem and Beyond

The faculty of Walker Elementary School in Poway, California, chose a theme of gardens and growing. This particular school was fortunate to have multiple gardens throughout a maze of courtyards, connecting school buildings, which were actively utilized by all grade levels. The experiences generated by planting, nurturing, and harvesting these sites became the focal point of many interrelated lessons that centered on the refinement of language from the individual word to the narrative to the poem and beyond. This workshop was chosen primarily because the theme was universal and it was an interesting approach through the narrative.

Chapter 15: Mozart in Motion:
Integrating "Eine Kleine Nachtmusik" into the Curriculum

The Westchester Philharmonic in Westchester, New York, has a unique artistic outreach program that invites students to participate in music appreciation workshops prior to attending philharmonic concerts. The TAPS involved in this program are offered workshops designed to help them make the most of this experience with their students. We were invited to conduct such a workshop with 65 participants who were eager to find ways to bring children to music and music to children. We began our workshop by introducing a visual map of "Eine Kleine Nachtmusik," which was then translated into movement. The experience was enlarged and enriched through interpretation and expression of the music in the form of feelings, words, imagery, and ultimately poetry.

Chapter 16: The Circle of My World: Personalizing Commitment to the Poem and Beyond

This workshop described in Chapter 16 was developed as an outgrowth of a graduate course in education taught by Dr. Rosemary Omniewski at Edinboro University in Erie, Pennsylvania. Her education students were required to read and apply the skills and techniques discussed in the first two sections of the first edition of this text. As a follow-up and reinforcement to this course, Dr. Omniewski invited us to facilitate a 1-day intensive workshop using the topic "The Circle of My World." Relevant to the exploration of this theme was the inherent need to turn inward to seek inspiration through self-awareness. It was this reversal of perspective (coming to the experience from the viewpoint of "self" rather than "observer") that made inclusion of this workshop meaningful.

Chapter 17: REACT: Reaching Emotion through Arts-Based Creative Teaching

We presented a workshop designed to help TAPS respond to the events of September 11, 2001, and a growing awareness of violence in schools through poetry and arts-based extension. The workshop was sponsored by the Yale Prevention Research Center and presented at Mead Elementary School in Ansonia, Connecticut. The workshop was intended to help TAPS use their insights to show fifth-grade students how to vent their emotions in acceptable and productive ways, through poetry, movement, music. Toward this aim, an initial TAPS workshop was presented with follow-up student workshops planned that would result in ongoing, international, interethnic dialogues.

EDGING IN

The creative classroom is one in which the boundaries of education are marked only by the evolving reach of the imagination. Here, ideas are translated into innovative forms through poetry, music, and movement. It is for this reason that TAPS workshops begin, as do student workshops, with a basic introduction to the fundamentals of language, music, and movement (see Section I).

Section I of this text presents basic skills and demonstrates, through repetition and experimentation, an adventurous and expanding view of the creative classroom. The goal is to promote an educational environment that fosters self-discovery through integration of the arts. It reveals how to exercise imagination by giving it voice, one word at a time, until words become poems, and poems become music/ movement extensions.

Introductory TAPS Lesson

The introductory lesson at TAPS workshops that lays the groundwork for this recondite educational experience can have its foundation in any academic subject—history, social studies, science—so long as the teacher remembers that language unifies and connects the elements of learning. The theme for the introductory TAPS lesson, storms, was chosen because it has universal significance, it lends itself in very specific ways to emotional and artistic responses, and it is a topic that teachers may be called upon to address in the classroom. We could have chosen a different subject, such as nutrition, urban and rural landscapes, history of transportation, pond life and activity, or an innumerable array of subjects. Lessons, whatever the focus or grade level, are adaptable as language arts experiences, as inspiration in the art or music room, and ultimately as guides to intercurricular development. This introductory experience has been presented in TAPS workshops as an entry to the concept of using the arts to enrich curriculum and blend lines between subjects.

As an example, TAPS may be asked to write down their impressions of storms by recalling a particular one that they had witnessed or heard about. An array of recollections might be noted: gray clouds, rain falling, wind blowing, and trees bending. These initial thoughts, through the application of language skills, might be channeled into personalized, powerful sensory images:

THE STORM

The sky scowled	[visual image, personification, alliteration]
wind like whips tamed	[alliteration, simile, onomatopoeia]
the trees; rain	[dramatic line break]
sorrowing	[personification]
strained the ground	[visual image]

—SUSAN A. KATZ

The appearance of a poem can add meaning to the words and enrich the metaphor. Here the poem appears wind-blown on the page in an attempt to visually create a sense of chaotic movement.

Using a storm theme as a science TAPS lesson, we began with a discussion of clouds and cloud formations, listing names and definitions collected by the facilitators:

Cirrocumulus: Thin, wispy, fluffy mounds or ripples; signal possible rain

Cirrus: Thin, creamy white, ribbon-like strands; indicate good weather

Cirrostratus: Very thin papery layers; may mean a change in the weather is imminent

Altocumulus: Scattered, rounded, white or gray clouds; signal that rain is likely

Altostratus: Smooth planes of grayish clouds; possible light rain or snow

Stratocumulus: Soft, heavy layers of globular gray or white clouds co-joined; indicate the possibility of light rain

Cumulus: Thick, heavy, fluffy, white clouds that rise up from a flat bottom; indicate good weather

Stratus: Low, even layers stretching outward; indicate vacillating weather

Nimbostratus: Dense layers of dark gray to blackish clouds hanging low to the ground; indicate rain or snow

Lenticular: Globe-shaped clouds that are the result of waves of air moving downwind from the tops of mountains

Cumulonimbus: High, rising, gloomy-colored clouds spreading out to form a massive top; indicate heavy rain, thunderstorms, and possibly even hail or tornadoes

Poetic Possibilities of Clouds

These uncommonly used scientific names provide fertile language possibilities. They offer interesting rhythmic opportunities when used alone, highlighting their multi-syllabic qualities, or in combinations for creating rhythmic strands. They can feel good in the mouth and on the tongue, are fun to speak aloud, and are illustrative of language energized through alliteration. (Each subject will reveal through in-depth exploration its own vocabulary of words and phrases that can become the inspiration for a poetry/music/movement lesson. See Appendix C, p. 375)

A rich and varied vocabulary provides a myriad of opportunities for poetic exercises. By applying learned poetic techniques, such as alliteration, personification, internal rhyme, and imagery, words can be crafted into lines, and lines extended into poems.

In these examples, we have used a storm theme as a departure point for playing with words, but for teachers interested in taking this type of assignment back

Alliteration, also called head rhyme, echoes the beginning sound of several words.	Cumulus clouds cavort like circus clowns across the cavernous cerulean canvas of the sky
Personification attributes human qualities to nonhuman things. This poem also uses internal rhyme (i.e., *doom* and *gloom*).	Cumulonimbus clouds tower threateningly, menacing with eyes like flame voice of doom, hammering with balled fists of rain, hiding behind descending gloom
Metaphor illustrates a relationship or similarity between two things without using *like* or *as*. (In this case, *stone* is like life.)	Battered by wayward winds my soul is stripped to bone, but deep beneath the reach of rain my roots hold fast to stone

into their classrooms, any pertinent subject could serve as well. Having played with the words, the lesson can now be enriched through layering.

Music/Movement Extension Possibilities

The rationale for using music and movement stems from the benefits inherent in revisiting a poem in countless ways. It offers an opportunity to cultivate the senses in powerfully explicit ways, put artistic energy into play, and examine a chosen topic from multiple views. This slows down the process and leads to savoring and thus deeper understanding.

From a music/movement extension perspective, the sounds of scientific terms themselves might form a rhythm chain that could serve as an introduction or an accompaniment to a poem. The chain could be spoken, or stand alone as a chant, using a variety of dynamics, tempos, textures, and forms to create interest.

Types of storms could be the basis for movement pieces, reinforcing the definitions. A *tornado* is a devastatingly strong, swirling wind accompanied by a funnel-shaped rotating cloud that moves in narrowly defined paths over land. After a TAPS read the definition aloud, the group spoke the word "tornado" in ensemble, with one muted cymbal crash struck after the word. The cymbal, hit repeatedly with increasing energy, began a long and gradual crescendo. While the cymbal was played, one TAPS represented the tornado by twisting and whirling his way through standing TAPS who responded to the tornado's presence by making a blowing sound randomly. The cymbal made one final loud, muted crash, and the whole group ended the mini-movement by yelling "tornado!" and making a strong body gesture with the final word.

A *typhoon* is a strong, tropical hurricane, most commonly found in the western Pacific Ocean. The movement and accompaniment was similar to that for the tornado, with the added sounds of a rainstick and reinforced water sounds. These water sounds were made by patting the lap, clapping, crumpling newspapers, and making plosive "droplet" sounds with the mouth, and they were added gradually. More than one person performed the part of the wind.

A *tidal wave* is an unusually huge rise or surge of water along a coast line, caused by an earthquake or very strong winds. A tone on one Orff instrument (bass xylophone) repeated in octaves created an ominous mood, as the cymbal surged from very soft to loud to loudest. Six TAPS used this sound-surge to move the shape of the wave, standing side by side in place. They bowed at first and grew in height and velocity as the cymbal grew in sound. At the loudest point, TAPS called out, "tidal wave," which was the signal for the TAPS representing the water to run full height from one side of the room to the other as though crashing onto the shore.

A *thunderstorm* is a storm characterized by lightning and thunder that unleashes heavy rain, often leading to flooding. TAPS performed the movement responding in texture and dynamics to the storm soundscape created by small percussion instruments and vocal sounds. Mouth clicks (as droplets) were accompanied by occasional pats on lap and then soft claps, which gained in tempo and loudness. Rattling paper was added, and at the loudest point, intermittent drum rolls were added for thunder, representing the storm's full intensity. A ratchet, representing lightning, punctuated the activity at intervals. When the storm was at its apex, the TAPS were the most physically active and then slowly reversed the process to indicate the storm's end.

The group decided to excerpt the definitions and turn them into repeated phrases, to be spoken together in order to create layered pieces.

Example with 8-beat ostinati

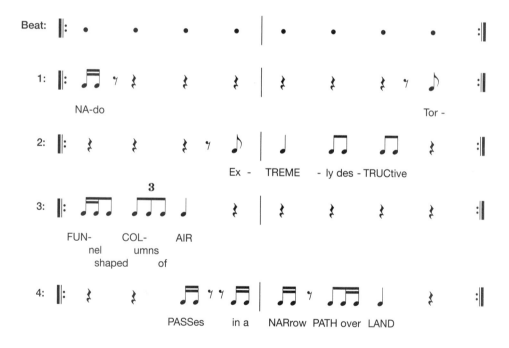

Another group activity focused on the poem "The Storm" for music/movement enhancement. For the first line "The sky scowled," TAPS suggested dark sounds to play repeatedly on drums beneath the poem to solidify the mood, adding a group sound of a variety of soft, sustained pitches sung at the same time. They also moved in a way that depicted darkness through body shape and exploration of lower space, deciding the poetic line would be most effectively read in ensemble rather than by one person.

For the second line "winds like whips tamed," the ongoing dark sounds were punctuated by crackling inserts of percussion instruments, and the wind took the form of drum heads brushed by fingers. The movement group extended the sound enhancement, creating more time between lines. During the lines "the trees, rain/ sorrowing," a group of TAPS created a rainstorm through hand and mouth clicks, in combination with the rattling of crumpled newspaper. They then played a ringing sound with the triangle before the word "sorrowing" as a way of emphasizing its significance, speaking and extending the word through movement. They repeated the word "sorrowing" overlapping canonically, pitched downward. The line "stained the ground" was extended into a multi-pitched cluster, sung slowly by all and then repeated. The chosen dark sound continued on for a brief codetta, which then faded.

This type of many-layered group activity uses multiple learning modes: speech, rhythm, movement, group interaction, repetition, and visual, aural, kinesthetic, and written reinforcement, resulting in a memorable, significantly enriched learning experience. When the TAPS take this lesson experience back into the classroom, the topic of storms can be used in a social studies classroom for a discussion of the economic and social impacts of storms, which may in turn lead to yet another poem, or it can be incorporated in the math classroom where wind velocity, storm size, and speed could be calculated. The art classroom might then host the next extension in which colors could give shape, form, and individual personas to real or imagined storms. The circular motion of this teaching/learning experience creates enriched school environments that deepen and thrive on the integration of subject matter and continuity of ideas.

Following these facilitator-led activities and before the final phase of the TAPS workshop, some TAPS volunteered their completed, edited, and refined poems for group expansion. At this juncture, the TAPS became their own core facilitators for six smaller groups. Each group consisted of approximately seven people and were formed to develop the core leader's poem through group consensus into music/ movement extensions. The presentation of these six theater pieces was the culminating event of the workshop. The performances gave rise to deep reflection and discussions centering on the effectiveness of poetic elements and music/movement skills.

CONCLUSION

In all TAPS workshops, as with students in classrooms, time must be allotted for reflective thought before poems are written or extensions of completed poems are created. Interspersed within the framework of the TAPS workshop are moments of group brainstorming, individual shared insights, facilitator-modeled examples, and fine-tuning of work through editing. This may involve using masterwork or facilitator examples, or excerpts from TAPS poems can be displayed on an overhead projector for interactive application of line break, enjambment, removal of extraneous words, tightening, and finalizing language choices.

Often in larger workshops, TAPS are invited to turn to a neighbor and share their creative effort. We believe that sharing completes the creative process by allowing interpretation and thus enlarging the meaning and significance of the work. Time constraints are a consideration in TAPS workshops just as they are in student classrooms and do not allow for each person to have his or her whole poem considered by the group, but no participant should be denied the connection that results from sharing feelings through the sculpting of poems.

Why Field Trips?

The rationale for using field trips as departure points in Section III is that almost every school has field trips. A field trip is a many-faceted experience that requires planning, and dialogue among departments (e.g., art, music, and physical education). This could provide an impetus for the integration of the experience throughout the curricula. Field trips lead to varied sites of interest, such as sculpture gardens, zoos, planetariums, museums, aquariums, and botanical gardens, to name a few, and in the process, they expose students to potent, new sources of intellectual and imaginative stimuli. Specifically, we have chosen to highlight field trips in this section because we have found that the most frequent request is to adapt a workshop around a planned, school-related trip.

Why Time-Sensitive Issues?

Today's time-sensitive issue is tomorrow's history lesson. The rationale for teaching current events is that they define and very often change the world. From a learning perspective, time-sensitive issues are works in progress, challenging each person both intellectually and emotionally and inviting him or her to become active creative participants.

Such events are topically referenced and discussed, but they need to be inventively scoured as well in order to expose deeper levels. Through the application of language extension skills, we can slow these events down to a speed where students are able to better process and learn from them. Applying sensitized energy allows them to become one with the experience as responsive observers. By giving expression to each person's need for a viable language, whether in the form of poetry, music, or movement, these activities allow students to assimilate the event more intensely and thus make it their own. Finally, this book embraces a philosophy of seamless learning, in which a consistent harmony between disciplines triumphs.

EXPLORING WATER WORLDS
Without, Within, With Wonder

A "water world" field trip can be an exciting, eye-opening, extended adventure in learning. Our planet, primarily covered by water, offers a kaleidoscope of possibilities for exploration:

- Natural habitats

- Playgrounds

- Dwindling, compromised resources

Presenting students with an intimate insight into water worlds through field trips, whether oceanic, brackish river, local swimming hole, or natural pond, establishes a connection that is real, informative, and emotionally pertinent.

The teachers of the Vista Academy for the Visual and Performing Arts, a public magnet school,[1] requested a field trip workshop exploring tidal pools. A field trip to a tidal pool environment along the coast of San Diego, California, at the Orange County Marine Institute was used to develop the requested theme. The teachers wanted to be able to use the field trip as inspiration for the creation of original poetry and extension through music and movement. Following their experiences, they intended to take their classes on the same trip, which was then to be followed by student-written and layered applications. This chapter describes the experiences and creations of the group of Teachers as Participants (TAPS).

PREPARATION AND PLANNING

The day began with an introduction to tidal pool life. Having come prepared with clipboards, pencil, and paper to save and savor, the authors and TAPS were guided by a naturalist through a hands-on exploration of native sea creatures living in tanks in the Orange County Marine Center.[2] Through a slide presentation, we learned

---

[1]A *magnet school* is a public school that has been chosen to receive a particular focus (e.g., arts, sciences). It accepts students of all ethnicities who exhibit an interest in or talent for the school's active focus.

[2]For more information about the Orange County Marine Center, contact the Director of Communications, P.O. Box 68, Dana Point, California 92629. For more general information, contact your local Department of Natural Resources.

Marilyn Cauthen and Rodney Goldenberg,
two workshop participants, on site, witness tidal pool wonders.

names of tidal pool inhabitants (e.g., periwinkles, sea lettuce, anemones, limpets, barnacles, sea stars) and discovered visual characteristics, specific habitats, and survival needs. (The appendix to this chapter contains a brief guide to tidal pool inhabitants.) We were then invited by our guide to explore, with all of our senses, the actual tidal pool environment, consisting of an expansive landscape of miniature, self-contained communities of plant and animal sea life.

This natural world was a living canvas that delighted the senses. There were textures, colors, sounds, scents, and flavors that could be translated later into creative images. We began word collecting and were elevated beyond the ordinary. Individual words and word combinations—prickly, slippery, spongy, slimy, dense, damp, humid—spoke poignantly of a new reality, a harmony of life and death: "gull shattered shells," "lacey sand textures," "crab skeletons."

We began thinking as poets: *The air was dense with the insinuation of discovery. We fantasized that we could hold it, palpating with life, in our hands. We imagined the feel of it: rough/smooth, warm/chilled, heavy/light. We exchanged words like gifts, inspiring one another to look deeper within. The need to explore was compelling. Wandering alone or in small groups, we kicked off our shoes and got down on hands and knees to better become one with the environment. Damp sand oozed between our toes and fingers, and we were truly launched on journeys of disclosure.*

Our guide encouraged us to investigate by touch the vast array of living things the tides had deposited at our feet. Creatures that were examined needed to be replaced in exactly the spot we had found them, as their survival depended on staying within microscopic parameters. Our intellect was overwhelmed with facts; our senses burgeoned with inspiration. In so heady a place, we had to remind ourselves to take notes. Hastily scribbled words recorded changing shapes and undulations of anemones, the tenacity of barnacles, and the languid body movement of the limpet. We observed as poets shadows shifting as clouds moved across the sun, deepening the colors of the tidal pools from blue to green. Gulls shrieked raucously in the distance. Somewhere, beyond our sight, we sensed that the tide was quietly, inexorably inching back to reclaim the life it sustained.

WITHOUT: COMING TO THE TIDAL POOL ENVIRONMENT AS OBSERVERS

We were onlookers, seeking to give language to this time and place: patterns of sea shells, broken and scattered across the sand; remnants of seaweed; water-patterns; sunlit colors of tide-polished stones. Instinctively we sought to personalize the experience, to find our own words, metaphors, similes, and images that voiced their own meaning, giving substance to our essential selves, thus enabling us to share.

Our imaginations stirred to the need for artistic expression. We reassembled in a conference room of a nearby hotel where the workshop continued. Encircled by chairs, a spacious area had been created for movement. An assortment of Orff instruments, small percussion, and "found" sounds (e.g., paper clip boxes, rulers to tap together) were available for later use in extension enhancements. An overhead projector was in place to facilitate brainstorming and editing.

This second stage of the "Tidal Pool" workshop opened with TAPS being invited to spend some time going over their notes, and adding to or expanding on any additional impressions while the experience was still fresh. (An earlier workshop had provided the basic skills needed to turn random images into poetry and extensions.)

The following poem, written in response (on site) to the field trip by the poet/facilitator, was offered as a model, using a wide array of poetry techniques. The lines of the poem were annotated and presented on an overhead projector for more in-depth instruction.

WITHOUT

We witnessed with wonder
worlds within worlds
tongues tasting and trying
the flavor of words:

Sea lettuce and limpets
rock pricklebacks, kelp,
goose barnacles, sea palms,
anemones, snails,

Silently singing their
song of the sea
hypnotic, compelling
eternally free.

—SUSAN A. KATZ

The music facilitator provided TAPS with small percussion instruments, and also invited them to explore vocal sounds, thus creating a background soundscape as a mood enhancer based on the words and images. The rhythmical surf was mimicked

Anne Fennell, teacher and coordinator of tidal exploration
workshops, experiences rhythms and textures of the Pacific.

by drumheads being lightly stroked; shrill vocal inserts became gull sounds, the strident scrape of the guiro became the scurrying of crabs and behind the poem's
words, the group created an aleatoric vocal sound by everyone choosing a pitch and
sustaining it on "oo."

WITHOUT (POEM WITH ANALYSIS AND EXTENSIONS)

(Group sang aleatoric swath of multipitched, steady tones behind reader.)

We witnessed with wonder	[observation, alliteration and emotional investment]
worlds within worlds	[alliteration, imagery]
tongues tasting and trying	[alliteration, sensory perception]
the flavor of words:	[sensory perception, imagery]

(At the beginning of the slowly read poem and throughout were random gull sounds
and the drum/surf—the poet-reader paused in between stanzas to let the soundscape move into the foreground.)

Sea lettuce and limpets	[observation, alliteration]
rock pricklebacks, kelp,	[observation]
goose barnacles, sea palms	[observation]
anemones, snails,	[observation]

(Random, short punctuations from wood blocks, guiro, ripples of the mark trees added to the drum/surf.)

silently singing their	[alliteration, sensory perception, and personification]
song of the sea	[imagery, alliteration, sensory perception]

(The poet-reader paused to allow the soundscape to be heard, then all vocal sounds and small percussion stopped, leaving only the sounds of the drum/surf.)

hypnotic,	[emotion]
compelling	[emotion]
eternally free.	[emotion, internal rhyme]

[Aleatoric swath of sounds resumed, and the random vocal birds and isolated small percussion faded at the end.]

The focus of this initial experience was simply to enjoy the flavor of words and to work with a variety of basic poetry skills. Words and names of water-world creatures were the starting points for poetic exploration. Building vocabulary and playing with words until they became familiar was essential to the process. The extension experience was one of creating an enhanced soundscape, unmeasured rhythmically and based on a composer's instinct: discovering available vocal and instrumental sounds and then honing artistic skills in order to effectively apply them to the piece.

Creating Word Collections

Sea, shore, foam, spray, wind, rocks, purple, shore, crabs, abalone, periwinkles, sea palms, rock pricklebacks. These words collected by TAPS became the main beams on which were built reactions, notated observations, poetry, and extensions. The words allowed us to branch out into the following extensions, which are explained in the rest of the chapter:

- Rhythm word chains

- Annotated poem with extensions

- Layered speech pieces

- Textures created through canonic treatment

- Instrumental pieces

- Rhythm patterns

- Increased expressiveness through interpretation

- Melodies

- Tonal percussion

- Movement

- Synthesis of musical techniques

Creating Complementary Rhythm Word Chains Through Ostinati

In re-reading the collected words and redesigning their order and the ways in which they were spoken, repeated combinations of words (ostinati) made into word chains became an accompaniment that was whispered randomly beneath fragments of the TAPS' images.

SINGING THE SEA

Sea sweeps
To shore, foam
Leaps to spray
Wind whips
The ragged rocks and purple
Shore crabs creep
To snuggle deep in sand:
Abalone, periwinkle, sea palm
Rock prickleback: creatures
In a tidal pool compose
A rhythm set
Against a song
Of sweeping sea

—SUSAN A. KATZ, in response to the tidal pool observation/experience

Principal Rodney Golenberg
examining tidal pool treasures.

During the following poem, the group randomly whispered patterned words beneath the reading of the poem. The beat and word pattern was as follows:

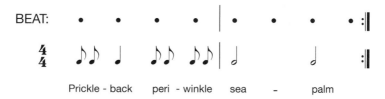

The rhythm was created by music facilitator Judith Thomas, in response to the tidal pool observation experience.

POEM WITH ANNOTATIONS AND EXTENSION

Sea sweeps	[alliteration]
To shore, foam	[alliteration continues from previous line]
Leaps to spray	[animation]
Wind whips	[alliteration, animation]
The ragged rocks and purple	[alliteration]
Shore crabs creep	[alliteration, enjambment]
To snuggle deep in sand:	[personification/internal rhyme]
Abalone, periwinkle, sea palm,	[alliteration]
Rock prickleback; creatures	[alliteration continues from previous line]
In a tidal pool compose	[visual image]
A rhythm set	[image]
Against a song	[image]
Of sweeping sea	[three lines of alliteration and metaphor]

This whispered pattern was effective because of the variety of rhythm possibilities. Notice that the whispered word pattern "prickleback" (with a plosive sound) has three syllables and is positioned next to "periwinkle," which has a smoother sound with four syllables. This word pattern ended with the sustained vowels, "eee" of *sea*, and "ah" of *palms* in two one-syllable words.

Creating Layered Speech Pieces
Through Combinations of Contrasting Patterns

The following two examples were intentionally created by the author to afford the greatest rhythmic contrast between patterns as well as within themselves. Thus when performed at the same time by three different groups, rhythmic and word clarity became possible.

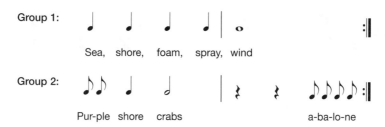

Creating Textures Through Canonic Treatment

Rhythmic texture was also created using the canon technique by overlapping patterns that had rhythmic and/or tonal contrast. Here, one group spoke the pattern repeatedly, and a second group entered when the first group was on the word "sea":

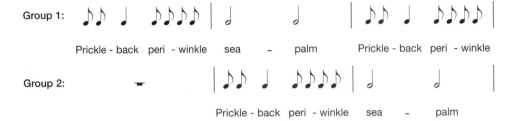

Group 1:
Prickle - back peri - winkle   sea   –   palm   Prickle - back peri - winkle

Group 2:
Prickle - back peri - winkle   sea   –   palm

Like layered rhythms, canons also depend on contrast for their musical well-being, and in this example, the contrast was healthy. While one group had the peppery, alliterative words of "prickleback" and "periwinkle," the other group had the languid vowel sounds contained within the words "sea" and "palms," affording the desirable contrast.

Heather Papandrea
examining tidal plant life.

Sharing tidal pool treasures.

Creating Instrumental Pieces
Through the Transference of Word Rhythms to Body or Small Percussion

Exploring textures further, we transferred word rhythms to small percussion instruments (e.g., guiro, woodblock, hand drum, triangle), which echoed the onomatopoetic qualities of the word sounds. For example, "prickleback" in one instance became three scratches on a guiro, "periwinkle" became four light taps on a triangle, and "sea palms" became the luxurious sounds of bell chimes. In order to determine whether the patterns to be played were physically possible, word rhythms were explored using various instruments (e.g., a person would have a problem negotiating the rhythm of "prickleback" on a bell tree because of the indefinite characteristic of its tones.)

Creating Rhythm Patterns
Through the Inspiration of Creature Characteristics

The unique appearance of various sea creatures served as inspiration for rhythm chains. The five legs of the bat star became an interesting metrical challenge when performed beneath a vocal reading of its characteristics. The task also became one of speaking the descriptive words above the rhythm chains in a way that did not distort their natural syllabic accents.

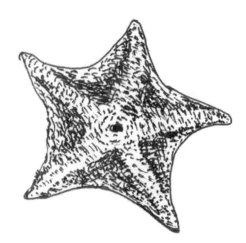

   Preparing for the 5-beat meter to be used in the "Bat Star" group poem, the performance of "Five-Armed Bat Star" was explored using the body, as well as small percussion.

1	2	3	4	5		1	2	3	4	5
stamp,	clap,	clap,	click,	click	OR	drum,	scrape,	scrape,	tap,	tap

Creating More Expressive Work

We spoke of which phrases or words would benefit from expressive considerations: choosing particular inflections, using loud/soft dynamics such as accent, crescendo, deciding where accents might occur, and determining whether the words were to be spoken by the group or by a solo voice. The following is a list of vocabulary for talking about these considerations:

Forte (*f*): Loud

Piano (*p*): Soft

Crescendo: Gradually louder

Diminuendo: Gradually softer

Ritardando: Slow down

Accelerando: Speed up

Accent: Speak a particular syllable or make a particular sound louder than the rest

Subito: Suddenly loud or soft

Presto: Fast

Lento: Slow

Using this list, we created a group poem using expressive elements.

Bat Star Group Poem Using Expressive Elements in 5/4 Meter
(Each dot indicates one of the 5 beats per line.)

	1	2	3	4	5
Group (forte)	BAT	STAR	•	•	•
Solo 1	Ten	cent-i	meters	•	a-cross
Solo 2	Webs	•	•	be-tween	arms
Solo 3 (inflection)	S c a l e y			•	•
Group	BAT	STAR	•	•	•
Solo 4 (inflection)	Mottled	red,	orange,	brown,	yellow
Solo 4	Green,	purple	•	•	eats
Solo 5 (cres.)	Sea	stars	•	and al-	gae
Group (diminish)	Tidal	•	sub - tidal	five-	armed
	BAT	STAR	•	•	•
	BAT	STAR	•	•	•
	BAT	STAR	•	•	•
(subito forte)	BAT	STAR!	All instruments played on the third beat with an accent and stopped.		

Creating Melodies Through Rhythm Transfer

Here is a drawing of a brittle star.

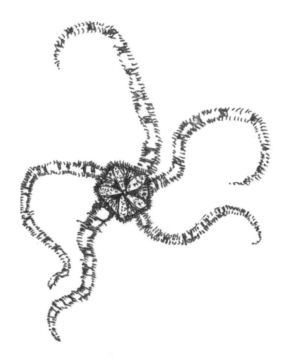

An ostinato based on pitches was created using the five beats offered by the number of the brittle star's arms. Do pentatonic was used in C (C D E G A). This mode was created by removing the F and B bars from the xylophones. The ostinato was played throughout, by a TAPS under the entire group's improvised melody using the brittle star's characteristics as text:

Vocal Improvisation (varied with individual interpretation)

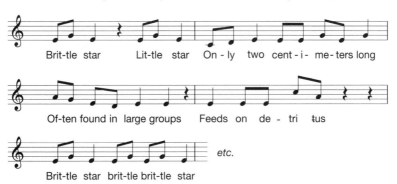

Brit-tle star   Lit-tle star   On - ly   two cent - i - me- ters long

Of-ten found in large groups   Feeds on   de - tri   tus

etc.

Brit-tle star brit-tle brit-tle star

A vocal ostinato group was added, singing one fact about the brittle star on one tone as the solo improviser created a melody for other characteristics on the do pentatonic.

Small-est brit - tle star on this coast

Creating Tonal Percussion Using the Eleven-Armed Sun Star

The participants agreed that for older students, the eleven-beat arm pattern of the sun star's eleven arms would be intriguing.

We explored how the eleven beats might be broken up into a variety of two-, three-, and four-beat groupings indicated by accents:

$$
\begin{array}{llllllllllll}
 & \overset{>}{} & & & \overset{>}{} & & \overset{>}{} & & & \overset{>}{} & & \\
1: & 1 & 2 & 3 & 4 & 1 & 2 & 1 & 2 & 3 & 1 & 2 \quad (4+2+3+2 \text{ beats} = 11 \text{ beats})
\end{array}
$$

$$
\begin{array}{llllllllllll}
 & \overset{>}{} & & \overset{>}{} & & & \overset{>}{} & & \overset{>}{} & & & \\
2: & 1 & 2 & 1 & 2 & 3 & 1 & 2 & 1 & 2 & 3 & 4 \quad (2+3+2+4 \text{ beats} = 11 \text{ beats})
\end{array}
$$

Setting up an alto and a soprano xylophone in do pentatonic on C (C, D, E, G, A), we experimented, sharing the patterns in the second example between the two instruments, always playing C on the first beat. The second example was transferred to tones and made into an ostinato:

Alto xylophone   Soprano xylophone

The accented notes played on "C" were punctuated by small percussion: wood blocks, triangles, and so forth as various participants sang the creature's characteristics in recitative style in do pentatonic.

Creating Movement as Extensions

While studying TAPS poems for extension possibilities, which had been edited earlier in the workshop through facilitated instruction and group dialogue, we discovered that words that suggested movement offered themselves for experimentation. Some poems gave compelling invitations to movement interpretations, such as the following piece, again using the "Brittle Star."

> BRITTLE STAR
>
> Brittle star
> Wildly waving weaving arms
> Slowly moving
> Alone
> Under rock and holdfast
> Hidden from prying eyes
> Home.

An introduction to the poem became an improvised, random, undulating melody on a metallophone set up in the minor la pentatonic, E G A B D.

Creating a Synthesis of Musical Techniques

Drawing on all of the amassed musical possibilities, the group set a poem about a keyhole limpet, also known as the diodora aspera, to a melody, using movement as well. A small group sang the following vocal ostinato composed of the creature's name, supported by a gently played drone (bordun) on a metallophone.

> DIODORA ASPERA
>
> Keyhole limpet, linked to land, exposed
> by turning tides, gray, brown
> and white, caught
> by the light, a small
> volcano, radiating ribs
> like waving fans beneath
> the water's cradling hands.
> Diodora Aspera

Poem line	Movement possibilities	Solo/group possibilities	Instruments
Introduction			Played as slow metallophone continuing under the next three lines
Brittle star	Moved by three people joined at the creature's "body"	Sung randomly by group twice	Brief interlude created by insertion of little sounds (e.g., guiro, woodblock)
Wildly waving	Movement went faster	Solo voice	Metallophone quickened
Weaving arms	Movement slowed	Solo voice	Metallophone stopped
Slowly moving			
Alone	Arms imploded subito	Solo voice	Triangle struck after "alone" to signal the creature to pull arms in
Under rock and holdfast		"Creature" sang line on random pitches as it slowly moved down	Metallophone played sparsely
Hidden from prying eye		Solo voice	
Home		Solo voice	Metallophone played a cluster once after "home" (a cluster is played by using three mallets and striking three close notes at the same time)
Home (repeated)		"Creature" sang "home" on random pitches	Metallophone played a final soft cluster

Coda: Slow metallophone with small sounds of guiro and woodblock fading.

The poem's reading was passed between speaking group, solo voice, and dancers, and it was read freely over the instrumental ostinato. The movement group explored both the "turning tides" and the "water's cradling hands" around the limpet phrases, as well as the volcanic-shaped limpet itself with its waving fans. The sung ostinato served both as an introduction and coda and thus gave the poem greater impact.

Extended poems were shared as examples of ways in which to play with poetry using movement, melody, tempo, form, and combinations. These excursions into *divergent thinking*,[3] facilitated by the leader, represented developing steps in the application of imagination through the arts. It was also the impetus for allowing the boundaries of formal thinking to expand in a limitless way so that scents became sounds, sounds became colors, action words became body movements and rhythms, and in turn, these became choreographies. The experiences were of absorption of stimuli, creative processing, and reinvention.

WITHIN: MOVING, THROUGH
IMAGINATION, INTO THE TIDAL POOL ENVIRONMENT

Moving from observation to investment through the process of *anthropomorphism*,[4] we indulged ourselves by becoming one with the environment. Traveling "within" to reach a deeper, more intimate level, we became the anemone. And it became us, echoing flower-like undulations, rhythms of surf translated to arm movements, sensitivity of tentacles, paralyzing prey with savage, explosive contractions. We imagined our senses perceiving what their senses perceive—water temperature, water movement, the taste and feel of sand or rock, the interplay of relationships (symbiotic or antagonistic)—we were ultimately immersed within this tidal pool community.

Imagining the world from within the anemone inspired the facilitator/poet's feelings and resulted in the poem, "I Am Anemone," which was used as a model for the within portion of the workshop.

I AM ANEMONE

I am anemone
graceful as willows that
wave in the wind
caressed by the current
swelled by the sea

I am anemone
In blossoming gardens
rooted in sand
fragile but deadly
as darts dealing death

I am anemone.

—SUSAN A. KATZ

---

[3]According to Mel Levine, *divergent thinking* is "a willingness and ability to free associate, to emancipate your mind to go off in interesting and original tangents, often not knowing where exactly you're likely to end up. Divergent thinking is the opposite of convergent thinking. In the latter, thoughts are highly specific and directed at finding a narrowly defined fact or solution to a problem" (2002, p. 209).

[4]*Anthropomorphism* is the process of using human traits or qualities to describe something that is not human (e.g., an embarrassed cat).

Brainstorming Possible Extensions

In brainstorming how this poem might have been extended, participants observed that the reiterated line, repeated at the beginning and end of the poem, gave an opportunity for some sort of special treatment, such as the group singing it as a chordal announcement.

The middle of the poem might have been sung in D minor pentatonic mode (D F G A C) in a free, recitative style, with the singer improvising over a simple drone played on a resonant instrument, such as a metallophone:

The middle section might also have been simply read, with the instrument playing a drone to support the reading throughout. It was agreed that the poem was suitable for movement possibilities as well.

Evocative Questioning and Information Seeding

Another way in which we helped TAPS to begin thinking about the within theme as poets was to ask them pertinent questions:

- What does it feel like as you move along the sand?
- What does the water feel like as it washes over you?
- What are the tastes of the things you eat, such as seaweed?
- What is the texture?
- What does the food smell like—salty, sour, sweet?
- How deep and dark are the crevices you live within?
- What do you fear?
- Whom do you embrace in friendship? In anger?
- What do you like about your world?

Information was provided that gave in-depth understanding about the anemone and would enhance the writer's ability to identify with the creature.

Brainstormed Group Poems

The following are examples of brainstormed group poems, with editing by the poet/facilitator. These poems represent a synthesis of learned poetic skills and invite the reader to annotate them poetically and to consider and apply music/movement extension possibilities.

TAPS POEMS

BROODING ANEMONE

Kept safe, like secrets
in soft sand or mud
deep diver down 10,000 feet
imploding inward, needle stings
decide the fate of prey and yet
you let selected fish and shrimp
stay safe, unharmed
by trembling tentacles:
Anemone. Anemone, you seed
yourself or simply break
in two. Anemone, you glide
like light or race
a captive to the current
and survive.

THE CRAB

Hermit crab
safe in the shelter
of someone's borrowed
home; two fierce black
eyes size up the world
and tiny claws
give pause
defying giant hands
from plucking them
like flowers
from the sea.

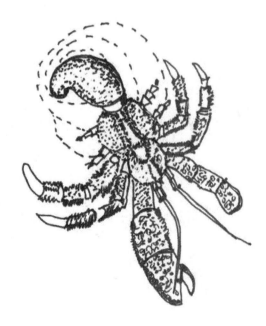

TIDAL POOL

The sand has shifted
with a gentle shrug,
leaving a valley
filled with life; a scene
of such soft wonder
fragile as the echo
of a sigh; time holds
in that uncertain scene
life, death
and all that comes between.

LEATHER STAR

Behold me,
leather star!
I am a
soft and slippery
patchwork fellow
speckled red, brown, purple
skin of leaden gray;
behold me as I spend
my days munching
on passing feasts
of urchin, sponge,
anemone; I travel
nowhere far.
I am
the leather star!

IMAGES

Frisky fragments of spray
caught by the wind
flash like bits of broken
glass against the rocks.

Waves whisper secrets
to the sand and call
a cadence to the circling
gulls or hurl themselves

like hammers at the shore
until the final, tiniest remnant
of foam fades
and is no more.

WALKING THE TIDAL POOLS

Mindful of where my feet fall,
crashing like boulders
into crumbling
craters of sand;
awed by the multitudes that
live and die within these
unnamed worlds, feeling
the enormity
of time in this timeless place
where nothing ever changes
and nothing ever
stays the same.

TIDAL POOLS, SEA MIST, AND ME

Salty sea mists lift
    wisps of smoke
        above waves that glide
to rocky shores, like tree-slung swings
that sway in summer breezes.

Waves reach
    retreat in indecision, rocks
        like soldiers guard
the innocent shore.

Tides pull small, rounded
    rocks and they collide, composing
        songs, clicks, trickles, laughter
        rhythms
tumbling in the water's draw.

Salty sea spray lifts
    like wisps of smoke
        above the lapping
        of the waves.

WITH WONDER: PROCESSING THE EXPERIENCE IN ITS ENTIRETY

As observers of tidal life, initially we discovered from without, watchful from a distance. Cultivating the senses by taking the time to deal emotionally with the world, we moved within the experience and attempted to go to a place of unconventional reverence. We eliminated boundaries in order to travel to a deeper empathy and sensory commitment and thus took a journey beyond ourselves.

This experience in its entirety awakened us to a sense of wonder about the variety and abundance of life and the interaction of a complete world within the confines of a single tidal pool. We were astounded. The tenacity of that life—the will to survive—served up lessons to be learned. They were many and profound; from the starfish, we learned the ability to regenerate our losses and become whole again, to revitalize ourselves. From the anemone, we learned of survival, adaptation, and the symbiosis of interdependence. From the abalone, we absorbed perhaps the most important lesson of all: that life is fragile and that we as caretakers need to do our part to ensure survival.

As our tidal pool workshop approached its conclusion, we pulled together strands of possibilities into a culminating piece about the brown buckshot barnacle. The characteristics of the brown buckshot barnacle offered compelling qualities:

- Brown and nubby

- Glued tenaciously to rocks, ships, pilings, abalones, and whales

- Waiting for food to wash by and taking advantage

- Feathery, barbed legs

- Youth spent swimming

- Adolescence spent molting

- Sedentary adulthood spent bonded by strong natural adhesive

- Enemies: worms, snails, sea stars, fish, shorebirds, and oil spills

These characteristics, the alliterative name of this small, unpretentious fellow, and his light-hearted, whimsical qualities lured us to explore in rhyme. Although this text adheres to the merits of free verse poetry, "The Brown Buckshot Barnacle" is the one digression. This subject seemed to demand the familiar symmetrical rhythms and rhythmical speed found in childhood rhymes.

The rationale for not rhyming, as stated in Chapter 1, is twofold: first, it is not the primary language of contemporary American poetry, and second, it tends to overpower the creative process, demanding that attention be given to the rhyme instead of the imagery. (It is particularly difficult for students who are beginning poets to attend to rhyme and imagery at the same time. One almost always suffers.) Despite the movement toward rhyme in "The Brown Buckshot Barnacle," the process of creating a framework for the barnacle was based on the solid footing of learned skills. Ultimately, there was a certain heady delight in allowing this tidal pool survivor to dictate direction and lead the group in a final celebration.

Poetically and from a music/movement standpoint, the poem kept faith with the philosophy of free verse. There are metaphors, similes, internal rhymes, slant rhymes, personification, alliteration, and so forth; musically, there are choral interludes, orchestrations, repetition, and the opportunity to melodically improvise the words.

The Brown Buckshot Barnacle

(words and setting by Susan A. Katz and Judith A. Thomas)

INTERLUDE (3 GROUPS):

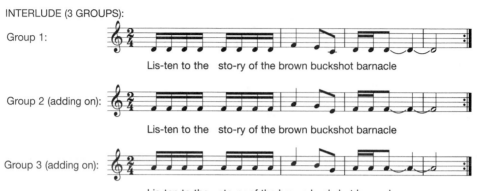

Group 1:

Lis-ten to the   sto-ry of the brown buckshot barnacle

Group 2 (adding on):

Lis-ten to the   sto-ry of the brown buckshot barnacle

Group 3 (adding on):

Lis-ten to the   sto-ry of the brown buckshot barnacle

INTERLUDE ACCOMPANIMENT (2 MALLETS IN RIGHT HAND):

Alto and soprano xylophone:

Bass xylophone:

Alto Glockenspiel:

Guiro:

Temple blocks:

Rachet:

Singers improvise verses on la pentatonic: D F G A C

ACCOMPANIMENT FOR VERSES:

Soprano metallophone:

Alto metallophone:

Bass metallophone:

THE BROWN BUCKSHOT BARNACLE

Listen to the story of the brown buckshot barnacle:
In a ragged rush of eggs, I found my freedom
Took to the sea like a bird to the sky.
As a restless youth I swam with abandon
And revoltingly molted as the years washed by.

Listen to the story of the brown buckshot barnacle:
I eluded all the shore birds, sea stars, oil spills
Worms I outwitted using wisdom and wiles, caught a
Ride on a whale's back, dinner as it washed by
First class passenger, traveling in style.

Listen to the story of the brown buckshot barnacle:
Weary of wandering, I settled on a rock like a
Tree in a forest with its roots held fast, and I
Staked a claim in my watery world, reaching
Out with my legs as the plankton swam past.

Listen to the story of the brown buckshot barnacle:
I've made my peace with sedentary ways, and
Discovered that our world doesn't always tilt right,
Learn a lesson from a barnacle: intractable tenacity
Another way of saying it is, "hold on tight."

SUMMARY: TIDAL POOL EXPERIENCE

The tidal pool field trip experience encouraged vivid and substantial trust in the power of imagination. Although not all schools have the luxury of nearby tidal pools, all do have environments that can be explored from without, within, and with wonder through the imagination. Whether walking city streets, visiting local farms, or simply meandering along a short path adjacent to a school, teachers can adapt the concepts of this tidal pool lesson into pertinent and creatively expansive exercises.

The TAPS who participated in the San Diego Tidal Pool Exploration workshop, brought their experiences back to their classrooms and initiated field trips for their own students. These students were then expertly guided by teachers who had themselves viewed the experience from the vantage point of student, into the miniscule world of tidal pools. New discoveries were made, and a heightened excitement and creative force found its way back into the classroom and into student poems and extensions.

The kind of teaching energy that is open to the wonder of chance discovery by both teacher and student and that encourages risk-taking leads to uncharted territory: a "learn by going where you have to go" experience. It is the perception of new worlds. It is faith in the journey without knowing the exact destination. Like the tidal pool environment, it is the essential ebb and flow of the "now," as well as the future currents of creativity, that awaken, nourish, and sustain.

The ocean reclaiming the shore.

A BRIEF GUIDE TO TIDAL POOL INHABITANTS

In order for the lesson to be more effective, students should learn more about the inhabitants of the tidal pool. Following is a brief guide to the animals that are commonly found in tidal pools and discussed in this chapter.

Abalone

Abalones are mollusks closely related to limpets, but larger. In 13 years, an abalone will grow to be about 10 centimeters long and have a muscular foot able to exert a grip of about 180 kg. With its rasping tongue (radula), it scrapes and eats seaweed that it finds by smell and the sensitive black tentacles protruding from under its shell. Water passing under the shell supplies oxygen to well hidden gills and carries off wastes (also eggs or sperm in late spring and summer) through holes near the shell's edge. Abalone blood contains properties that are useful against penicillin-resistant bacteria, but it lacks a blood-clotting mechanism. Abalones may bleed to death when cut by a careless diver or other enemy.

Abalones require and thrive in water that is well oxygenated by strong waves and currents. They're often in deep crevices or under ledges. Once an abalone population declines, algae-eating urchins, who graze more efficiently, tend to crowd out abalones and prevent their reestablishment. Abalones are regularly eaten by cabezon fish, moray eels, crabs, octopuses, sea stars, and sea otters. The current abalone scarcity is caused, however, by pollution, competing for food with urchins, and human collectors, not by natural predators. Harvesting should be controlled by temporarily closing off sections of the coast to divers to allow for abalone recovery.

Anemone

Anemones are coelenterates. They attach themselves to rocks, pilings, and even kelp. They occur intertidally at depths of up to 10,000 meters. Needle-like stinging cells on their tentacles inject paralyzing compounds into their prey. Certain fish live among the tentacles unharmed and protected from predators in a symbiotic relationship.

Bat Star

The bat star is webbed between its arms, and it is scaly. Its color varies: solid or mottled red, orange, brown, yellow, green or purple. The bat star eats sea stars, tunicates, and algae. Worms live in its arm grooves.

Brittle Star

The brittle star is black and white, often nearly all-white. It does not drop its arms easily. Often found in large groups under rocks for protection and to avoid suffocating, the brittle star is fast moving.

Brooding Anemone

The brooding anemone is typically brown to greenish brown, although some specimens are red, pink, or dull green. White lines radiate near its base and on the oral disc. Its tentacles are the same color as its body. Young brooding anemones develop around the base of the column. When five meters tall, they move away from adults to locate their own space.

Keyhole Limpet

The keyhole limpet is also known as the diodora aspera. Limpets have spiral shells as larvae but soon settle down and grow flattened, conical shells. Most limpets prefer the cooler waters of the Atlantic and Pacific oceans. Most grow attached to rocks.

Leather Star

The texture of the leather star is soft and slippery. It is generally lead gray with patches of red, brown, or purple. The leather star often has a garlic or sulfur odor. It eats urchins, sponges, bryozoans, and sea stars. Leather stars live in open, rocky pools but are more abundant in sheltered places.

Sun Star

A sun star's texture is gritty. The color of the sun star is orange or rose with streaks of gray, blue, or purple from its center to its arm tips. The arms of the sun star taper uniformly. It is one of the most beautiful intertidal stars in the low-tide zone.

SEEDING THE
GARDEN OF LANGUAGE

*From the Word to the
Narrative to the Poem and Beyond*

Classroom teachers and students in San Diego and Poway, California, requested a series of workshops with a spring theme (gardens, seeds, and growing). These workshops were geared to explore the word through narrative and move from narrative to poems. This writing sequence ultimately lent itself to initial selection of the theme "Words as Seeds," the process through which creative language evolves. Narratives, like poems, are written a single word at a time, yet they provide the luxury of a more leisurely pace through the maze of language possibilities and choices. In the narrative, we are permitted repetition, connective words and phrases, an abundance of adjectives, and a variety of multiple images and descriptions. From this resulting lush language garden, we are able to harvest the most tempting "fruit" for our poems. Following is a narrative example, "Spring is a Rainbow," by Susan A. Katz:

> The colors of spring are many and varied, and I watch excitedly as spring bursts forth from winter's cold grasp. It seems to me to be much like the cramped, untried wings of a weary butterfly, slowing unfolding and stretching, and exercising. I am enveloped by the scene and feel a sense of anticipation as I observe small shoots of green grass poking proudly out of the soil, and leaves fattening on trees, and a yellow hint of daffodils opening to morning.
>
> I think of spring as a Robin, sitting on the fence between the seasons of its birth and full blossoming. It is, I think, fragile, and perhaps even a bit fearful but tempted to emerge by warming breezes, longer days, and softer nights. Spring delights me by brightening the scene, creating a canvas of colors beyond my winter dreams. I am light-hearted and eager to accept spring's invitation, to look, to seek, to play, to enjoy, this season garbed in the robes of rainbow.

From this narrative exercise, which reveals the author's personal perspective of the nuances of spring, those words, word combinations, and images that will most powerfully and economically capture the essence, the meaning, and the emotional energy of the theme can be creatively gleaned and crafted into the poem. The words of the narrative may inspire us to select new words or new images as well.

EDITED NARRATIVE TO POEM: "SPRING IS A RAINBOW"

Spring unwinds like weary
wings of butterflies from winter's
cold cocoon; slender shoots,
pale grass, leaves round to red,
yellow yawn of daffodil
greets the dawn.

Arching between seasons
of birth and blossoming; fragile
as mauve mist softening
soil, sun tempts seeds
and breezes pirouette amidst
flexing fingers of flowers.

Tulip-pink, violet-purple,
apple-blossom white,
poppy-orange, iris-blue:
spring is

a carousel,
a magic show,
a picnic in the park
moon-glow, sun-spark
rainbow!

—SUSAN A. KATZ

This "translation" of narrative to poem is another way of beginning the "word in play" process. It may, in fact, offer a comfortable approach to the poem because students and teachers are more familiar and have more experience with the structure of prose. However, when approaching the poem from this direction, it is important to emphasize that one is not limited to what has been created within the narrative. The narrative can serve as inspiration but should not limit the parameters of the poetic process.

PREPARATION AND PLANNING

Prior to creating the workshops, we discovered that TAPS would be involving their students in the planting of spring school gardens. The host schools gave us some details about the physical set up of the gardens and they said that classes would be observing the metamorphosis of butterflies at approximately the same time. This helped us plan workshops that would fit comfortably inside those requirements.

In the planning phase, we began by focusing on the themes (gardens, seeds, and growing) and the view of spring as a time for new life. We asked ourselves questions that would elicit adjectives that might serve as inspiration for images and ultimately student- and teacher-written poetry: Using self-generated lists, we went on to ask questions that were pertinent to the extension process. We also collected some masterwork poems as a resource for seeding the garden of language. In addition, we compiled a list of garden terms and their definitions

- Cultivate: To prepare or to prepare and use; to raise or foster the growth of; to civilize or refine; to devote time or thought to

- Flower: To come into the finest or fairest condition

- Garden: To lay out, cultivate, or labor in

- Germinate: To begin to grow or develop

- Grow: To spring up and mature; to be developed or produced naturally

- Hoe: To weed or cultivate

- Plant: To put or set in the ground for growth; to attach or fix in place; to introduce or establish

- Seed: That from which anything springs; to sow or plant; overripeness

- Sow: To scatter, as seed, on the earth for growth; to plant by strewing; to spread abroad or disperse

- Sprout: To germinate, as a seed; to push out new shoots

- Weed: Unruly plant growth in ground that has been cultivated; growth that threatens cultivated crops; to remove offensive plants from cultivated gardens

PREPARING THE SOIL

We began by conducting student-demonstration workshops for staff observation. These classes consisted of the poetry and music facilitators interacting with a group of students while classroom teachers (and all teaching staff participating in follow-up teacher workshops) acted as observers. It was thought that these sessions would highlight and delineate the process of evoking relevant creative responses from children, paralleling work that would be addressed in the subsequent TAPS workshop. As well, the process provided insights into the following:

1. Introducing poetry through colors, feelings, and the spring theme

2. Initiating the writing experience through narrative

3. Investigating the poetic possibilities within narrative

4. Applying elementary editing skills to student poetry

5. Extending original student poetry through body/small percussion, Orff instrument orchestrations, found sounds, and movement

6. Celebrating by sharing student works and developing them into "theater pieces" for presentation

PLANTING THE SEEDS

In their reversed roles as students, TAPS were invited to delight in creative flowering and explore the possibilities for seeding the garden of language. We began with questions that address emotions and senses, intending to evoke lists of words that were rich in potential and pertinent to the theme. Throughout this introspective procedure of word compilation, we were involved in an active exchange of ideas and emotional responses, thus deepening and intensifying the experience.

- What are the colors of spring?
  Yellow, green, blue, white, purple, red, pink, violet

- What are the textures of spring?
  Soft, sticky, moist, smooth, rough, velvety, warm, cool, prickly

- What are the sounds of spring?
  Chirping, peeping, singing, blowing, rustling, croaking, whispering, thundering, raining

- What are the fragrances of spring?
  Sweet, perfumed, damp, new, fresh, grassy, floral, earthy, sunshiny, rainy

- What are the tastes of spring?
  Lemony, sweet, sour, creamy, chocolaty, minty

- What emotions does spring evoke?
  Joy, nostalgia, exuberance, happiness, wistfulness, wonder, awe, pride, peace, well-being, anticipation, euphoria

ENRICHING THE SOIL

Immediately following the brainstorming session, we began thinking of ways in which to generate extensions into music and movement by asking the following questions:

- What movement does the sound of a particular color inspire? Can you say the color in your own time and move it as you speak (e.g., *pink* might become a flick, *blue* a sustained motion, *yellow* a cheerful leap)?

- How might spring textures be moved? What is the speed of the movement for the word *soft?* What part of the body could initiate the word? Which texture word would be moved in a way similar to *soft* (e.g., *velvety*)? Which texture would contrast the soft movement? Can you make a movement form out of two contrasting textures? Try an ABA form (e.g., velvety/rough/velvety). Can you turn the form into a movement rondo (e.g., rough/sticky/rough/velvety/rough)? How many different ways can you initiate the movements (with arms, fingers, shoulders, head, back, thigh, ankle, foot, leg, elbow)?

- Can you initiate a spring sound and combine it with a movement that coordinates those two elements (e.g., for a windy sound, make a sweeping motion of arms and body moving around the room)? Can you be conscious of all of the places in your body that might start such a motion as you do them (e.g., "chirping" with shoulder or elbow dabs, "thundering" with arm or leg slashes)?

- Can you make a word rhythm chain by selecting some of the fragrances of spring to later chant behind a poem line?

Hypothetical poem line

Scent ostinato

- Try combining some of the tastes of spring and see how they might sound using this do pentatonic scale: C, D, E, G, A. Can you sing it as an accompaniment for a short song about fragrances?

Poem fragment about spring tastes

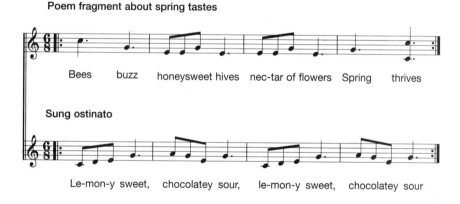

Sung ostinato

- From the list of emotions you created, using a volunteer to point to the words, can the group chant a familiar rhyme in the way the word suggests (e.g., when the word *joy* is pointed to by the leader, it is spoken joyfully)?

HOW DOES YOUR GARDEN GROW?

Taking selected words, TAPS were invited to extend them into images through the use of metaphor and simile and the five senses. They were invited as well to draw on poetic skills demonstrated for them earlier in the student workshops (e.g., alliteration, onomatopoeia). The selected words extended into images became the composition of a group poem:

> Springtime is the **violet** of sunset
> a **red** bird singing
> sun-**warm** tongue of pussy willows
> **sighing** wind
> **exuberance** of children popping soap bubbles
> **damp** scent of **earthy soil**
> stained black by rain
> **velvety** embrace of softening breezes
> **minty** taste of **green**
> grass, leaves, gardens
> spring is a **floral** bouquet.

At this point, TAPS were given time to develop personal narrative, and then, using group dynamics, invited to select and offer to the group words from the list or self-created images. Using the springtime garden theme as inspiration for a group narrative (in order to ultimately provide nourishment for individual culminating poems) the process began.

The following example of a TAPS narrative is a synthesis of multiple offerings:

SPRINGTIME IS VIOLET (narrative)

> Springtime to me is the color violet, and violet is as fragrant as sweet peas growing in the garden behind the house. It is the color of a sunset, viewed in the company of family and friends. Spring lifts my spirits as no other season and invites me to putter about in the garden and follow the paths of butterflies.

To begin to think in terms of the poem, the process involved the group traveling through the narrative and collecting those words and images that spoke to the core of the intent and the emotional impact. The following highlighted words and phrases demonstrate the course the narrative took on its way to becoming a poem:

> **Springtime** to me is the color **violet,** and violet is as **fragrant** as **sweet peas growing in the garden** behind the house. It is the color of a **sunset,** viewed in the company of family and friends. Spring lifts my spirits as no other season and **invites** me to putter about in the **garden** and **follow** the **paths of butterflies.**

SPRINGTIME IS VIOLET (POEM)

> The violet fragrant fringe
> of flower petals, sweet
> peas growing in the garden
> sunset deepening to the song
> of evening, spring invites
> bees to the flower and dreams
> to follow paths
> of butterflies.

Gentle sounds from small percussion instruments enhanced this airy poem, with a soft triangle struck at the poem's beginning and after the following words: petals, garden, evening, flower. butterflies. TAPS found other timbres that added colors to the words, such as playing the mark tree on the words "flower petals," playing a glissando on a barred instrument after the word "sunset," improvising a melody as a coda after the word " butterflies."

RED BIRD SINGING (narrative)

As I sit on the **porch swing** watching the **sunset behind the mountains,** I feel the **breeze** of **early evening, soft against my cheek.** The **night calls** from a **distance,** as **crickets** chirp, **frogs** croak in the pond, and the soft **rustle** of leaves announces birds settling **deep within** the **branches** of **lollipop-shaped trees.** A moment of color catches my eye against the **sky, not quite deepened to purple.** I am **startled** by the **exclamation** to this spring day of a **red bird singing.**

RED BIRD SINGING (POEM)

The porch swing squeaks
as the sun
sets behind the mountains, early
evening breezes tease
soft against my cheek.

Night calls in distant cries
of crickets and frogs
and the rustling
deep within branches
of lollipop-shaped trees.

The sky
not quite deepened
to purple, is startled
by the exclamation of one
red bird singing.

As one idea for an extension using do pentatonic (see Section I), we chose lines from the poem to set melodically that juxtaposed in a musical and interesting way.

Spring   is   like   one   red   bird   sing-ing   soft   a - gainst   my   cheek

This line might then become a repeated interlude occurring at the beginning of the poem as an introduction and at the end as a coda or perhaps interspersed between verses.

THE HARVEST

After interactive group brainstorming and extension, it was time for individual contemplation and creation. TAPS were given time to harvest and refine their narrative
ideas and cull individual poems from these personal narratives. At the conclusion of
their writing, TAPS were invited to share with one another and then with the group
as a whole for those who were so inclined. These poems were used as models for the
application of final editing.

Even though the TAPS poems had been thoughtfully extracted from the narrative, they often still retained much of their prose-like quality. This retention of
narrative form is common because everyone tends to write as he or she speaks and
can be reluctant to let go of connective words that seem to complete thoughts. Editing demands the fewest words in the best possible order, thus attaining the most
powerful and effective use of language.

UNEDITED POEM

Pink and brown are the fuzzy
Whiskers popping out of those
Stick-like arms reaching skyward
For the hot streaks of bright light
That encourage more than the black
Earth induced breath of warmth,
the pussy willow bursts forth.

EDITED POEM

Pink, brown, fuzzy
whiskers popping out
of stick-like arms reaching
skyward for hot streaks
of bright light encouraging
more than black
earth induced
breath of warmth
the pussy willow bursts
forth.

The active verbs in this edited version lent themselves to movement interpretation.
The group explored such words and phrases as "popping out," "stick-like arms reaching skyward," "breath of warmth," and "bursts forth." Then three TAPS (one for each
word) were assigned to speak and move the words "pink, brown, fuzzy," freezing
after each word and holding their pose until just before the last line of the poem. A
selected group spoke and moved the line, "whiskers popping out / of stick-like arms
reaching / skyward," and at the signal of a cymbal sound, a solo speaker darted
among the first group speaking "hot streaks / of bright light." The whole group
moved to a downward sway, saying the words, "encouraging / more than black /
earth," remaining in this low position. The cymbal softly accompanied for a few moments, mingling with vocal wind sounds, and one person spoke, "induced / breath of
warmth." The cymbal then played a final crescendo, moving from very softly to force-
ful, as the entire group trembled with anticipation as "the pussy willow burst / forth."

This final performance embraced the cornucopia of ideas and provided a verbal, melodic, orchestrated group-conceived theater piece. All TAPS were involved in the preparation and the presentation, and the performance (with the performers acting as their own audience) became a joyous celebration of the self and the group.

Scattering Seeds

(Words by Susan A Katz. Melody and skeletal orchestration by Judith A. Thomas)

SCATTERING SEEDS

We came to scatter
    seeds in your garden, word-
    seeds dispersed upon
    the fertile soil
    of your imagination

CHORUS (see above)

We planted what we know
    with all the wild,
    unbridled hope that bursts
    out of the soul
    of every spring-rich earth, soft sun
    flower bud, monarch wing.

CHORUS (see above)

We go knowing
    with lines and time.
With patient care, lush
and lovely
will your garden grow.

(three players softly accompany the verses)

SUMMARY

The purpose of this lesson was to enter and extend the poem through the narrative and explore a particular theme, gardens. Themes enhanced and presented through the arts should result in increased individual and group awareness and development of heightened sensibility toward details of the environment and one's place in it. We believe that it is the work of teachers to alert children to the endless and fascinating aspects of themselves and their place in the world and to provide them with a voice with which to celebrate. This workshop for TAPS intended to nourish the soil of *their* creative lives so that they as teachers might share with their students the joy of the metaphorical journey.

Mozart in Motion
Integrating "Eine Kleine Nachtmusik" into the Curriculum

At the invitation of the Westchester Philharmonic Education and Community Outreach Program, the authors planned a poetry/music/movement workshop based on the inspiration provided by the music of Mozart. The first movement of "Eine Kleine Nachtmusik" was chosen as a representative selection by the authors, from the compact disc recorded by the Westchester Philharmonic. The overall rationale for the project (of which the author's workshop was a part) was to help TAPS prepare their students:

- To fully experience the music of Mozart through the application of layering the arts

- To understand and make connections between music and the broader curriculum-wide implications (e.g., history class, social studies class, art class)

- To interpret and translate personal music-inspired feelings through poetry (using imagery, the five senses, emotion, and other elements) and physical movement

- To anticipate attending a Westchester Philharmonic concert featuring Mozart's music, planned for later in the year

- To be able to deeply immerse into many levels of understanding and appreciation for the artistic expansiveness of the experience

The workshop was held at Pace University in White Plains, New York, and about 65 TAPS from the Westchester area attended. TAPS represented all curricula disciplines from school librarians, to music and art teachers, regular classroom teachers, administrators, and interested parents. The two consecutive workshops were each 2.5 hours long.

PREPARATION AND PLANNING

The authors began by reviewing materials presented to them by the coordinators of the outreach program of the Westchester Philharmonic. The information was designed to lead TAPS in threading the theme of Mozart throughout the curriculum. Included was a compact disc of the planned concert and a workbook.

In listening to the compact disc, the authors chose "Eine Kleine Nacht Musik" as a suitable piece for study, as it fit well into the allotted workshop time frame. It was also chosen for its contrasts: passion and tenderness, loud and soft dynamics, fast and slow tempi, and dramatic accents. We prepared a handout for the TAPS that included a *listening map* to be used as a visual aid for discovering the form and depth of the music. It was also used as a departure for movement exploration. Also provided to the TAPS was a list of Rudolph Laban movement qualities (slash, press, punch, glide, wring, float, flick, dab) and a chart that demonstrated the basics of poetry and poetic techniques.

EDGING INTO THE EXPERIENCE

The workshop was begun by handing out a graphic map of "Eine Kleine Nacht Musik," prepared by Judith A. Thomas. It was designed to direct the TAPS to imaginative places that would help them to fully focus on the music as the main mental event. TAPS were asked to note the following:

- Theme One and its recurrence on the lines A, E, and the end of F

- The visual repetition of musical themes through repeated graphic lines (Theme One can be seen on lines A, E, and the end of F; Theme Two appears at the end of line A and F; a large development that crescendos can be seen on lines B and G.)

- Theme Three appears on line C and again on line H.

- Theme Four can be seen at the end of line C, the beginning of line D, and variations of it in the middle of line E.

- Unique designs appear as a coda on lines I and J.

First, we asked the TAPS to study the map for form, inviting them to find parallel visual patterns, thus discovering Mozart's musical architecture. They also studied it in order to extrapolate from the heavy and light graphic lines where dynamic contrasts might appear. Then the music was played as TAPS followed the work on the graphic map from beginning to end. This exercise revealed a number of ideas:

- Music has more than one theme.

- Themes reappear, thus creating forms.

- Dynamics are used to ignite passion as well as offer zones of comfort.

- Music can be translated into lines, dots, and squiggles, and these can be translated into movement, thus providing an additional way to process the music.

- Music can be mapped; thus TAPS could use this lesson generically to assist their students in creating additional music maps of any composition.

The movement qualities of Rudolph Laban were then introduced to demonstrate a vocabulary for gestures that allowed TAPS to completely "live" the sound

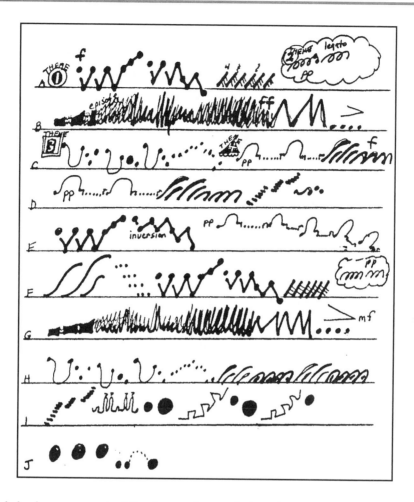

through body movement while the music was being played. For example, Theme One used the movement qualities of slash and punch at the beginning of the disjunct main theme and dabs at the end of Theme One. Theme Two involved glides, floats, and presses for the ligato theme, leading to the crescendo, which used punch and slashes again in line B. Following Laban movement work with the map, TAPS were again invited to listen to the music, this time thinking about sound as color. Brainstorming colors, TAPS then explored, as a group, movement potential in the sounds the color words inspired: flicks for "pink," press for "brown," slash for "red," and so forth. This activity demonstrated the circular motion of the total experience: sound to movement to sound to color words to movement.

MOZART AND METAPHOR

TAPS were introduced to the basics of poetry through visual handouts and detailed discussion of poetic techniques.

The Poetry Recipe	The Sensory View	The Metaphor and Simile
How ⟨ 1. Images: Word pictures 2. Feelings: Emotions, memories, and experiences What — 3. Subject	1. See: How things *look* 2. Hear: How things *sound* 3. Taste: How things *taste* 4. Touch: How things *feel* 5. Smell: How things *smell* 6. Emotions: How things make us feel *inside*	1. Metaphor: Out of the pale moon of her face 2. Simile: Her eyes shone like stars.

We asked them to embrace the multiple poetic possibilities (e.g., alliteration, onomatopoeia, simile, metaphor, the senses) inherent in the experience, as they listened for the third time to the music and jotted down words and phrases that best described feelings and emotions, visual memories, and experiences. These were then shared in the group setting, revealing inner reactions such as "dying sunsets," "elegant marble ballrooms," "still, liquid lakes in summer," "passionately playful," "carefree wandering," and "turbulent clouds twirling and tumbling." During the discussion that followed, interactive sparks ignited mutual inspiration, with TAPS listening to the music by hearing others' responses to it. This, in fact, became yet another way to listen to the music of Mozart.

THE HEART OF THE
MATTER OF MOZART: INDIVIDUAL POETRY BY TAPS

Mozart Music Is

Commanding, confident, coy
starry skies dancing playfully,
brightening innocently
with youthful wanderings

—Michael Gelfer

Mozart Music Is

Royal, energetic
vibrant conversing
joyfully gliding

Mozart music is
wind whirling, wandering

playfully, twirling and spilling
like champagne

Mozart music is
a joyful, jumpy journey;
triumphantly prancing
majestic ballroom.

—Timothy C. Brown

Mozart Music Is

to lift, strike and stroke,
to worry, question and resolve.
high heels tiptoe on a
wood plateau.

—Judy Scheck

MOZART MUSIC IS

Intense, vibrant firecrackers
boasting triumphantly in
the vast night sky,
fading into darkness

to strike forcefully,
fearlessly again
for a fiery phenomenal
finale!

—KATHLEEN COYNE

THE HEART AND SOUL OF THE
MATTER OF MOZART: CULMINATING PIECE

TAPS first shared these poems in groups of two or three, and then individual volunteers were asked to offer their work to the entire group. The authors and the group then analyzed the poems for successful use of poetic techniques and for music and movement potential. TAPS suggested and tried several ideas for layering movement and music, and the group selected the best choice. The resulting decisions enhanced and transformed individual words, lines, and poems into little "theater pieces" that were presented by and to the group. As a culminating piece intended to draw the individual "creative brush strokes" of the workshop into a "finished canvas," we offered a poem we created with musical Mozart extensions as a refrain that would include, in presentation form, the original shared TAPS poems. The following is a transcript of that presentation.

MUSIC TAKES ME

makes me feel
words
words

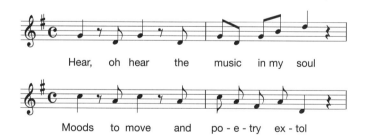

But, the word all alone is as flat
as an unturned page,
still as a song
unsung

(FOLLOWING POEM READ BY TAPS POET LAURA OLIVIERI-REYES)

MOZART

Butterflies
on blue skies flowing
joy of moving

waves on the rise.
Exhilarating in excitement
joy of energy released from
the soul.

(AUTHORS' POEM CONTINUED)

Metaphorically speaking
the word
is a bird taking flight
on the wings
of the wind
while the simile plays
the word as bright
as lights of stars
on ebony nights

(MAIN THEME SUNG)

(POEM READ BY TAPS POET ELLEN LEDERER)

MOZART

Music is
    Sound and sight of pebbles
    skating across water
    a silent sound
    standing up, sitting down
    pirouettes across a room

Music is
    daydreaming
    waking
    and hiding
    like clouds on a sunny day.

(AUTHORS' POEM CONTINUED)

Alliteration wonders
whether words should wave
wandering the wind
like flags on poles

Onomatopoeia speaks itself
a hissing snake
a creaking door
a screech, a bleat, a snore

(MAIN THEME SUNG)

(POEM READ BY TAPS POET YUN SHIM KIM)

MOZART MUSIC IS

Carefully planned
ideas
wistful journeys shared
through growth, search, toil
lead triumphantly
where?

(AUTHORS' POEM CONTINUES)

A word is a word
'til embraced by another
sparks glow
and grow into flame
words come together
like children at play
and imagery blossoms
like laughter
out of words joining hands
in warmth and acceptance
the fragile beginnings
of poems.

(MAIN THEME SUNG)

SUMMARY

The significant goal of this type of workshop is to provide insight into masterworks, often an integral part of planned lessons and curriculum formats, such as:

- Picasso's painting "Guernica" used in a history lesson to study the Spanish uprising

- Lewis Carroll's poem "Lobster Quadrille" interpreted through movement in a physical education class

- T.S. Eliot's poem "The Hollow Men" studied in the context of the human condition in a social studies lesson

- Alvin Ailey's dance composition "Revelations" used to study black history in a social studies class

- Paul Winter's sound recording "Ocean's Child" studied as part of an ecology or environmental science lesson

- Second movement of Prokovieff's "Flute Sonata" used in a language arts class to explore emotions through writing

This type of workshop gives TAPS the tools to help their students enter and absorb the artistic energies of diverse creative worlds. Listening to music is a natural place to begin because music is a part of our everyday lives, available to everyone through radio, videotapes, compact discs, digital videodiscs, and live performances. This workshop demonstrates from many personal perspectives, the power that can be generated by interpreting the dynamics of a single artistic genre. In fact, the arts can and should be used to take us deeper and more intensely into the vast terrain of the learning experience.

THE CIRCLE OF MY WORLD
Personalizing
Commitment to the Poem and Beyond

Dr. Rosemary Omniewski of Edinboro University requested a TAPS workshop with the theme "The Circle of My World" for her graduate students. We faced unique challenges and abundant possibilities: The theme was designed to inspire introspective journeys and considerable exploration of individual feelings and relationships. We hoped that this intense focus would promote not only creative responses but personally meaningful ones as well. One of the many possible rewards of sharing these self-revelatory perceptions was the strengthening of the group dynamic. The workshop involved several challenges:

- This workshop would require consciously placing oneself in the center of the poem and its extensions through emotional commitment (i.e., the substance of self: "I need. I think. I feel.")

- It would require being able to explore and process the intimate emotional identity in creative form.

- It would require inspiring (through imagery) responses that would evoke understanding, empathy, and connection.

In addition to these challenges, the workshop offered overwhelming possibilities:

- It would invite intimate self- and group revelation.

- It would encourage turning vulnerability into strength through recognition of shared experiences and common denominators.

- It would encourage releasing the voice within, saying the ineffable, and covering the gamut of human emotions and experiences.

- It would allow for emotional catharsis.

This type of writing requires self-definition and reaching even deeper within to that protected well of all that identifies each person as a unique individual. It dares the writer to honestly confront him- or herself, and it becomes the landscape of self-portrait. This exercise allows time for each TAPS to wonder and dare. The initial revelation may ripple outward like a rock-disturbed pond, changing, growing, and reverberating. As it is with adults in workshops, so it is, as well, with children in classrooms.

PREPARATION AND PLANNING

When preparing this workshop, we recalled personal events to use as models, thinking about a particular sunset, a moment in time, another sunset, another place, another moment. These poignant memories became a shared experience and illustrated the combustible power of this three-pronged happening: observing, remembering, sharing. In his poem "Let Me Tell You How," Miller Williams exhorts us to first notice everything. We extolled the workshop TAPS to first remember everything they had noticed just as they would instruct their students to do when adapting this workshop for their classes.

We also prepared by analyzing and editing poems created by Dr. Omniewski's graduate education students (who used the first edition of this book as a model). These poems provided us with the opportunity to offer feedback prior to the actual TAPS workshop. The subject of these initial poems was colors, and this abstract starting place allowed us to emphasize the powerful nature of imagery as a means of self-expression without fear of possibly treading on sensibilities. With imagery as the focus, we were able to highlight those aspects of the poems that were most revealing, most potent, and most persuasive, and these would ultimately be the "maps" that TAPS would follow into their "The Circle of My World" poems. Several poetry skills are evident in samples from this graduate work.

Alliteration	From TWO CRYSTAL GOBLETS by Rosemary Omniewski
	    Ringing, resonating voice
	    now forever silent

	From WHITE IS BRIGHT by Charmene Check
	    It is a squinty, sunny,
	    crisp, snowy day

	From PINK by Joni Brown
	    Cotton candy
	    at the county fair

Onomatopoeia	From WHITE by Rosemary Hanson
	    Owl screeching
	    bleached white sheets flapping

	From ROLLER SKATES by Jodi Brown
	    Flying clickety clack,
	    clickety clack,
	    over the rough sidewalk cracks

Sensory image	From GREEN by Dick Burlingame
	    The taste of wild mint, a tart apple waiting
	    to ripen, fresh beans snapped from the vine,
	    a hay-stem chewed while
	    walking the pasture

Enjambment	From GREEN by Dick Burlingame
	    A breeze across the lake
	    whispering through woodland leaves

Emotion	From ORANGE by Linda Burroughs
	  I am tall poppies
	  dancing in the summer sun.
	  My mother is red,
	  My father yellow.
	  I am the best of both,
	  Glorious orange.

	From METAL DEATH by Deanna Wilhelm
	  Aim
	  Click
	  Bang

	From RHAPSODY RUNNING DOWN by Scott Blume
	  The hot sound
	  on the radio sinking into
	  my soul running
	  down my spine

Metaphor	From RHAPSODY RUNNING DOWN by Scott Blume Blue is a rushing stream.

Simile	From ORANGE by Rhonda Thompson
	  A brilliant sun is setting like
	  dancing campfire flames

	From MY WIFE'S DRESS by Jeffrey Passaro
	  My wife's dress is the color that looks like
	  streets and streets and blocks and blocks
	  of the bowels of the urban jungle

Personification	From RED by Kitty Morse
	  A shiny, shimmering
	  fire engine
	  screaming its shrill sound

Memorable imagery	From WHAT IS PURPLE by Karen Tremblay
	  Moist, lumpy spread of grape
	  jam adorns
	  freshly baked bread

Five senses	From NATURE IS WORKING by Susan Cronmiller
	  The sound of a tractor, John Deere,
	  plowing a field, finding low gear

	From WHITE by Lorrie Mineweaser
	  A sweet marshmallow
	  roasting in the glow of a
	  campfire flame
	  sticky, ooey, gooey as it's
	  pulled from the roasting rod
	  and placed in my mouth for a
	  sugary, lip-smacking taste

(continued)

(continued)

From WHAT IS PURPLE? by Karen Tremblay
  Bluish violet radiant shine and
  glimmer of the amethyst stone

From BLACK by Laurie West
  Ripe earth
  leaves
  decomposing
  into dirt

From BROWN by Christina Chase
  Rough bark of a tree
  under your fingers,
  soft hair
  of a brown-eyed girl,
  and gritty sand
  under your toes at the beach

EDITING AND RATIONALE PROCESS

The following poem was written in a class conducted by Dr. Rosemary Omniewski at Edinboro University and submitted to the authors prior to the TAPS workshop. This provided ample time for consideration of the poems for editing analysis and detailed explanations of the rationale behind editing suggestions. (This type of in-depth critiquing could not have been accomplished within the time constraints of the TAPS workshop.)

"Green" by Deanna Wilhelm offered clearly delineated opportunities for applying editing techniques intended to embrace and enhance the feel, intent, and spirit of the lines.

GREEN (ORIGINAL VERSION)

Field
Pine tree
Garden
Whispering in the wind
Sliding through my toes
With every step I take
Freshly mowed grass on a
Warm summer's day
Crisp garden salad
Welcomes a new day

—DEANNA WILHELM

This poem had a lovely, crisp feel that suggested early spring. By choosing to start the poem with a single word on its own line and follow with another image, the poem entices the reader to move swiftly, in a slightly breathless manner. Changing "whispering" to "whispers" and the word "in" to the word "to" gives life and persona to the wind and makes the event more intimate. Following the invitation of this mood, we changed "sliding" to "slides" and removed the line "with every step I take." (This word combination tends to be overused, as well as having already been stated in the previous line, "slides through my toes.")

"Freshly mowed grass" brought the reader naturally to a "warm summer's day" and so we removed the words "on a." Taking out these two words changed the rhythm of the poem and echoed back to the poet's beginning rhythm, "Field / pine tree / garden." Changing the next line from "crisp garden salad" to "garden salad crisply" elongated the line, rather than ending it with a hard consonant, and created a fluid slide to the final line of the poem. In the last line of the poem we changed "a" to "the" in order to make it a singular day. The editing sought to enhance the spirit and energy of the poem by tightening and changing the tenses.

GREEN (EDITED VERSION)

Field
Pine tree
Garden
Whispers to the wind
Slides through my toes
Freshly mowed grass
Warms to summer
Garden salad crisply
Welcomes the new day.

—DEANNA WILHELM

EDITING "THE CIRCLE OF MY WORLD" POEMS

The poems that TAPS created in the "The Circle of My World" workshop illustrated a new depth of self-revelation and demonstrated newly acquired poetry techniques. The poet/facilitator critiqued the TAPS work in the course of the workshop, with an emphasis on poetry skills and how to turn the corner of prose into poetry. This is a pertinent exercise that leads to better understanding and greater ability for application in the classroom.

TAPS were encouraged to let the theme "The Circle of My World" lead them to places and faces framed in memory. The theme was a key that unlocked memories and revealed the intricacies of feelings and the infinite wonder of one's own emotional life. In fitting words to feelings and creating lines that ignited the flame of human emotional experience in others when shared, it was hoped poetry, music and movement would become partners in the powerful and purposeful dance of self expression.

Editing of "The Circle of My World" by Treena L. Holmes

THE CIRCLE OF MY WORLD (ORIGINAL VERSION)

The circle of my world
isn't really a circle at all but
an unnamed shape with
dark little caves and
large bright fields.
The circle of my world is
an adventurous hike up
trying mountain sides with
emotions flowing like streams
until they puddle below so
I may bask in
the victory or defeat,
a never-ending search for
the knowledge to recognize
what is honest and true.

—TREENA L. HOLMES

THE CIRCLE OF MY WORLD (EDITED VERSION)

My world is

The shape of dark
closed-in caves, light
cradling sun bright fields   [metaphor for "my world," alliteration]
menacing mountains, passion   [alliteration, onomatopoeia]
plays in me like a restless   [simile]
stream snaking its way   [personification, animation, alliteration]
to ponds of extremes:

   victory defeat
   success failure   [this could be eliminated but may be impor-
                                 tant to the poet]

scanning horizons
of my soul to know   [alliteration]
who I am
what to do   [slant rhyme, internal rhyme]
what is real   [conclusive rhyme ending with finality]
what is true

—TREENA L. HOLMES

Editing Explained

This poem offered the opportunity to use a poetic "scalpel" to carve out the essence from an abundance of words, thoughts, and images. This is the most common form editing takes. Beginning writers are prone to write in prose rather than poetry, particularly in this first creative stage. The impulse is to use too many words, which dilutes the poem, and editing techniques leads to more compelling expression through imagery and the emphatic voice of the poet.

We have chosen to echo the title of the poem by opening with the line "My world is," turning the rest of the poem into a metaphor for the poet's world. Prose allows for explanation: "The circle of my world / isn't really a circle at all but." Poetry does not, and so the poet has to give the reader something tangible to see, taste, touch, hear, smell, or emotionally experience so that he or she will be able to fully experience what the poem expresses. One way to do this is to take out extraneous words, collapse wordy phrases, and use more potent descriptions. For example, with some editing and recasting, "and unnamed shape with / dark little caves and / large bright fields" becomes "the shape of dark / closed-in caves, light / cradling sun bright fields." Both sets of lines gesture toward the same content, but the second set is more evocative.

Rather then tell the reader "with emotions flowing like streams / until they puddle below so / I may bask in / the victory or defeat," which resembles prose, the poet can extend the stream image into an active ongoing experience with hints of personification and animation and an emphasis on alliteration and internal rhyme: "plays in me like a restless / stream snaking its way / to ponds of extremes." The four words "victory, defeat, success, failure" could have easily been eliminated from the poem without detracting from the message or the impact of the poet's intent. We chose to leave the words because they might warrant inclusion for the poet. The poem could have seamlessly moved from "ponds of extremes" to "scanning horizons," and the meaning would not have been changed or diminished in our opinion. Ultimately, however, each poet must choose for him- or herself. This lesson embraces suggestions but must limit itself to offering suggestions and not imposing changes. That point is equally as applicable to TAPS as to students.

"A never-ending search for / the knowledge to recognize / what is honest and true" is the final message the poet wants to leave with the reader; however, the intent is weighed down by too many words and too much telling. "A never ending search / for the knowledge." could have easily been translated into "scanning horizons / of my soul." ("Soul" could have been "heart" or "mind.") This creates a visual image and broadens the poet's purpose. "The knowledge to recognize / what is honest and true" is also wordy and commonplace. We included the issues the poet was probably thinking of in the poem: "of my soul to know / who I am / what to do / what is real / what is true." We chose to end with a conclusive rhyme to help the poem feel finished.

Editing is the real working part of the creative process, and the individual must contend with it as it relates to his or her work. Suggestions are merely that and do not imply that there is one right way of editing. Poems are written for different reasons and with different audiences in mind. The poet is responsible for taking all factors into consideration and applying appropriate skills and techniques that will enrich and complete the poem.

Extension Explained

Because the first stanza referred to shapes, it lent itself to creating "closed-in caves" and other images with movement. The repetitive, dark sound of a drum beat could

TAPS developing and performing extensions of original poetry.

accompany and softly hold the first stanza together. The sound of the triangle and a wine glass being rubbed at the edge could herald the change of image for "light / cradling sun." The drum could resume on "menacing mountains," perhaps louder. From the word "passion" on, the tempo of the poem increases, so thickening sounds of other small percussion instruments could be woven in along with the drum beat, thus creating the "restless stream / snaking its way / to ponds of extremes."

In the second stanza, static movement and vocal sounds complement the four exposed words "victory defeat / success failure." Locomotive movements could resume in the final stanza. For a more dramatic effect, some of the words could be echo-spoken and some echo-sung by one person or a group. The title could become a repeated, sung melody, while the whole group forms circles as a visual coda.

Editing of "My Life" by Susie Pirillo

My Life (original version)

The circle of my world is tall and strong.
Black and white
Moving in different ways and different directions.

The circle of my world is

TAPS developing and performing extensions of original poetry.

Copy machines, paper shredders, phones ringing,
Keyboards clacking, whines and barks, licks and laps,
Crying and laughing, singing and dancing,
And hugs and kisses.

The circle of my world is comforting like an afghan made
With love,
Warm like a new puppy,
Safe yet ever changing like a crisis in a cocoon.

The circle of my world is Maggie, Murphy,
And David.

—SUSIE PIRILLO

MY LIFE (EDITED VERSION)

—*to Maggie, Murphy, and David*

The circle of my world is wide
And strong
Black and white   [animation]
Moving to the music of   [alliteration]

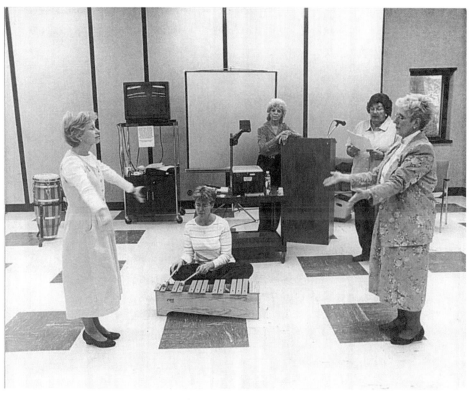

TAPS developing and performing extensions of original poetry.

Copy machines, paper shredders, ringing
Phones, keyboards clacking, whines, barks,   [alliteration]
Licks, laps,   [alliteration]
Tears and laughter
Song and dance
Round hugs and soft
As summer   [simile]
Kisses.   [metaphor]

My world is an Afghan quilt woven   [metaphor]
From threads of love, warm   [enjambment]
Wet-tongued puppies.   [alliteration, sensory image]

Safe, yet changing,
Clamorous,
Calamitous, an "abracadabra"   [alliteration]
Crisis
In a cocoon.   [metaphor]

My world is you.   [slant rhyme]

—SUSIE PIRILLO

TAPS developing and performing extensions of original poetry.

Editing Explained

This poem offered some exciting rhythms and moved rapidly from one thought to another. This quality needed to be preserved, yet its flow needed to be adapted to a poetic pulse and poetic language. We therefore suggested changing "moving in different ways and different directions," which is wordy and prose-like, to "moving to the music of." At this point, the line "the circle of my world" interferes with where the previous line intends to take the reader.

The next stanza contains a great staccato beat of sounds and emotions and then ends with images "round hugs / and soft / as summer / kisses" that purposely slows down the pace of the poem as though all of the machinery were grinding to a halt. This slowing pace directs the reader toward a new course, one of soft and sentimental circles of life.

We changed the lines about the afghan into a metaphor and removed some of the words, which helped maintain a loving quality without being overly sentimental. "Wet-tongued puppies" provides the reader with a sensory image that "new puppy," a redundant, prosaic phrase, did not. Poetry demands precision.

The image "crisis in a cocoon" is very fine and thought-provoking, and we moved it to the next stanza in order to frame it in a way that both highlighted and incorporated it: "safe yet changing / clamorous, / calamitous, an 'abracadabra' / crisis in a cocoon." We knew the crisis was one of change, growth, and expansion beyond the limits of one's world. With that in mind, our editing strove to emulate the

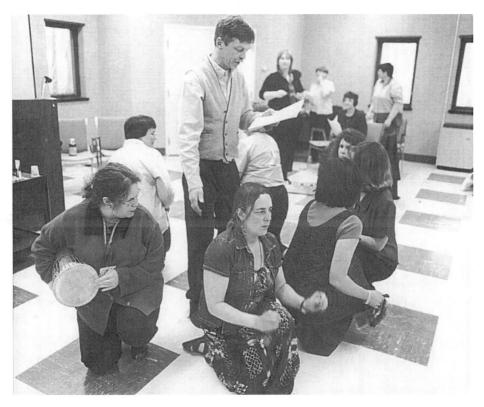

Group theatre piece presented as culminating work for TAPS.

soul-shaking significance of the metamorphosis by choosing words that ascend to a crescendo and even suggest a magical outcome. To add anything beyond that line, in the same stanza, would have diminished the drama of the image, and so we chose to end the stanza there.

The poem itself could have ended there as well, but we added the line "my world is you" because it is the final message the poet wants to leave with the reader. In this particular instance, even more serious thought should be given to the poem's ending, as the last lines of a poem are often the ones readers remember and reflect upon.

Extension Explained

The first stanza invites movement and music, while the slow spacing of words create time for tall, strong gestures, literally extending in different directions. Sounds can punctuate the spaces between the words. Some interesting choices are a cymbal crash, a short drum pattern, or an interspersed wood block percussion.

The second stanza is rhythmical. TAPS could create machine-like movements through repetitive motions, emphasizing mechanical interactions. The reading of the poem could vary in tempo and volume. Small, appropriate percussion instruments could be played to accentuate certain words and at times, the silences between them. The magical sound of a mark tree could be used to end the stanza.

TAPS accompany extensions on an Orff instrument.

In the third stanza, TAPS could interpret the woven image of the afghan by moving in and out among each other, and the "threads of love" could overlap canonically and create a blend of word-sound along with the movement. The last stanza seems to call for punctuating sounds of a variety of small percussion instruments to emphasize the movements on such words as "clamorous / calamitous." "My world is you" could be elevated by repeating the line from solo to group and by singing it. At the final word, the group could break into many drumming layers, along with improvisatory movement, and the resulting driving rhythm could initiate a celebration of the poem's energy.

SUMMARY

The types of exercises presented in this chapter are of special importance, for they helped TAPS:

- Dissect the process, thus defining the function of the teacher as creative conductor

- Reveal the building blocks of the poem in progress, establishing the realization of language as a living entity

- Reaffirm that creative expression is dependent on application of learned skills and techniques

- Realize the joy of serendipitous inspiration as well as the successful finesse of crafting work

This introspective chapter covers material that is particularly significant because it lays the groundwork for addressing emotionally charged experiences, such as the terrorist attacks of September 11, 2001. These become, by necessity, a part of the school curriculum and need to be handled in a timely manner with sensitivity and confidence. Language and the arts provide a bridge connecting the experience to understanding and, hopefully, healing.

REACT:
REACHING EMOTION THROUGH ARTS-BASED CREATIVE TEACHING

WILDPEACE

Not the peace of a cease-fire,
not even the vision of the wolf and the lamb,
but rather
as in the heart when the excitement is over
and you can talk only about a great weariness.
I know that I know how to kill,
that makes me an adult.
And my son plays with a toy gun that knows
how to open and close its eyes and say Mama.
A peace
without the big noise of beating swords into ploughshares,
without words, without
the thud of the heavy rubber stamp: let it be
light, floating, like lazy white foam.
A little rest for the wounds –
who speaks of healing?
(And the howl of the orphans is passed from one generation
to the next, as in a relay race:
the baton never falls.)

Let it come
like wildflowers,
Suddenly, because the field
must have it: wildpeace.

—YEHUDA AMICHAI[1]

From *Selected Poems of Yehuda Amichai* (1996, p. 88). Berkley: University of California Press.

In response to youth violence that "claims nearly as many years of potential life as heart disease or cancer, and many more than AIDS," the Yale Prevention Research Center felt compelled to address the issue of violence and its inherent consequences through intervention. In the wake of the tragedy of September 11, 2001, the Center recognized that the volatile climate and overload of media messages increased risk factors for the emotional well-being of the youth of this nation and this world. The Center studied issues such as suppressed rage, deteriorating attitudes toward ethnic groups and religions, hostility, frustration, fear, and a troubling inability to find acceptable outlets of expression. Dr. David L. Katz, Director of the Yale Prevention Research Center, confirmed that

> Current efforts in health promotion and disease prevention require a broad definition of health that must include emotional well-being. The Yale Center is pleased to be working in cooperation with area schools in addressing issues resulting from the disastrous events of September 11, 2001. The REACT (Reaching Emotions through Arts-Based Creative Teaching) response is designed to reflect the increasing evidence suggesting that the arts serve as a viable and effective vehicle in interventions, fundamental to good health.

We were invited to become a part of a study designed to address violence-related implications of the terrorist attacks of September 11 at Mead Elementary School in Ansonia, Connecticut.

The initial step in the proposal was for teachers to talk to students and organize group dialogues addressing the possible chaos imposed on their inner lives by world events. Next, an intervention approach was adopted that used language arts and music/movement as vehicles for empowering students to become active partners in self-discovery. The intention was to expose and temper negative thoughts and feelings—which often result in depression, anxiety, impaired functioning, or socially unacceptable behavior—by having students share their experiences and reactions in written and verbal forms.

This second step provided ways for students to give voice to their feelings and emotions through the introduction and refinement of writing techniques. By learning the elements of poetry and ways to extend written work through music and movement, students would encounter new vocabularies and develop new proficiencies. By honing these skills, students would be able to give shape to their thoughts and articulate their feelings in meaningful and comprehensive ways.

Our goal was for the students to produce work, in the form of poetry, prose, or extensions, that would ultimately be sent to an Arab "sister school" in order to initiate a pen-pal correspondence. The creative invitation to students was to be broad, and drawings, videotapes, audiotapes, extensions, and photos would be considered for inclusion in the package.

The concomitant advantage would be the ease with which this type of program invites curriculum inclusion: from the history lesson on conflicts, to the art classroom revelatory visual example. Furthermore, a cohesive and adaptive school environment would be nurtured, and curriculum lines blurred. Students would be made aware of the connections that exist in their lives and in the relationships between them and their immediate and expansive world.

Should the energy of the project overflow and students express a desire to share their feelings and their works beyond the scope of their own classroom, then room-to-room presentations might result. This, in turn, could lead to an assembly

Group leaders define
the parameters of the experience.

format for wider sharing. These concentric circles of communication within the school would endorse the original concept of the intervention by reinforcing the value of self-expression as a means of dealing with shattering events. The students' work would be made even more powerful by the immediacy of its impact on fellow schoolmates.

The ultimate goals and rewards of the project are many, not the least of which is the provision of cathartic, artistic tools that might foster the healthful processing of negative emotions. Simultaneously, developing relationships with Arab children could empower these American students to become ambassadors of understanding and healing and initiators of constructive change.

PREPARATION AND PLANNING

Teachers First

In keeping with our philosophy of teachers going first where they would lead their students, these workshops began with a 3-hour TAPS session paralleling what would occur in the classroom. The music/movement facilitator began by initially asking for TAPS to create a list of general emotions, which would then be explored through speech, inflection, tempo, and movement games. Specific emotion words were listed on the board: joy, anger, boredom, fear, anguish, amazement, terror, excitement, delight, and so forth. TAPS were invited to recall and suggest familiar nursery rhymes, lines from poems, proverbs, or quotes to speak in the style of a specific emotion:

Sad: If at first you don't succeed.

Angry: Try, try again.

Delighted: If at first you don't succeed.

Terror: Try, try again!

One TAPS was selected to point to an emotion listed on the board for the group's speech response and speak the chosen poem in the mood, nuance, and tempo of the emotion:

Angry: Humpty Dumpty sat on a wall,

Confused: Humpty Dumpty had a great fall,

Joyous: All the kings horses and all the kings men,

Sad: Couldn't put humpty together again..

TAPS created forms in movement, using contrasting emotions and adding small percussion instruments.

A	B	A
JOY	boredom	JOY
cymbal crashes	one tone plays repeatedly on a barred instrument	cymbal crashes

A	B	A	C	A
anger	sadness	anger	fear	anger
random cymbal	mark tree	random cymbal	woodblock	random cymbal

These somewhat lighthearted activities introduced an overview of emotions that allowed for the beginnings of introspection. The focus then became specific to those emotions that were relevant to the events of September 11, such as terror, anxiety, fear, disbelief, shock, anger, hatred, and grief.

The music facilitator harvests words.

Poetry Skills Highlighted through Color/Emotion Poetry

Using the listed emotions as the stimulus, we began to teach poetry techniques. We asked TAPS to choose a specific emotion and assign a color to it. Using that color, they had to expand it into an image using metaphor, simile, alliteration, or another poetry technique.

Emotion	Color	Image
Terror	Red	Terror is a red flame.
Grief	Gray	Gray is the empty space your smile filled.

These images were shared and discussed by the group, and deeper, more intense reflection became necessary. Questions were asked, such as "Where were you on the morning of September 11? How did you hear about the events? What was your first thought?" The mood of the session shifted toward remembrance and self. At this point, TAPS were instructed to take their original color/emotion images and extend them into lines using the skills and techniques that had been presented and discussed.

TAPS POEM

RED TERROR

Terror is red
flame, the screech
of sirens, the settling
of silence, thick
as ashes.

Gray is the empty space your smile
filled, fog clouding
laughter, tears
falling as relentless as
rain.

—GROUP POEM

CULMINATING POETRY AND EXTENSIONS

Having experienced the release of emotions through imagery with colors as the framework, TAPS were now ready to move deeper into their own emotional landscapes. They were instructed to liberate through language the passions and pathos generated by the events of September 11. The following works reflect that deep emotional journey. These remarkable introspective examples extended an invitation to empathy.

TAPS POEMS

SEPTEMBER 11 MADE ME FEEL

broken like the jagged fragile
edge of an eggshell
unsure
like a stranger not knowing
what to do next
speechless like a broken television
with no volume

children's voices asking questions
why?
frozen in horror, disbelief
wordless
wanting to comfort
yet feeling unsettled

—LYNDA FRATTALONE

SEPTEMBER 11 MADE ME FEEL

The screeching roar of a saw slicing
through metal
the smoke
the ashes
hovering over the city
like sawdust that covers the floor
suffocating us
as we try to scream.

—JOANNE WIACEK

SEPTEMBER 11 MADE ME FEEL

A pushing, beating through
my chest
pulse in my neck
throbbing pain on my temples
fleeting rush through my
fingertips

A bumpy, coldness of my skin
dampness from my tears
a million hairs standing
straight
hands clenching
and tight.

—MARISA PORTERA

SEPTEMBER 11 MADE ME FEEL

Panicked hands touch
my belly, swollen to
a full nine months.
I speak to you in a
soothing voice that
betrays my true and deepest
fears.

What kind of world are
you about to enter?

Worried hands touch
my belly, feeling you
move unaware.

I want to leave.
I want to run.
I want to keep you safe.

—SHANNEN SHARKEY

SEPTEMBER 11 MADE ME FEEL

Smokey as a choking deer
In a forest fire.
Masks of soot, dust, death
Brave as a phobic child
Chasing his frightening fears
Caring, Loving, Feeling
Lost as a mortal with no soul
Afraid, Foul, Frightened.

—PAMELA M. MUDRY

SEPTEMBER 11 MADE ME HEAR

Crying, howling, sadness, sobbing
as loud as sirens
silence
smoke, smoldering, somber faces
people running like scared children,
crumbling buildings

—JENNIFER HALLINAN

PLANE-ENORMOUS MONSTER

Slicing like a knife
Yellow, orange, red
Explosion
Black dust rising falling spreading
People fleeing
Running for their lives.

Fear—ever present
Where do we go from here?
Waiting, worrying, wondering
Pulsing through my being
Why?

—SHEILA KOZEROWITZ

SEPTEMBER 11 MADE ME FEEL MORTAL

I feel as naked as an abandoned
    newborn
hopelessly searching for answers to
the scandals that erupted in the
aftermath

I see burning buildings waiting
to collapse in a big city
as I search for solace in my sleep.

Charred structures and bones seep into
the souls of all
smoke rises and clouds thoughts
of those hoping and praying for a
    better
reality

Broken memories of the crushed,
    heaping
rubble are embedded in our history.

—ELIZABETH NIMONS

SEPTEMBER 11 MADE ME FEEL

like a large comforting blanket
wrapped around my classroom
protecting all that was inside.

Feel the panic swell inside me
and run up to my face reddened
with disbelief

fight back and push down the
uneasiness for fear my students
would sense danger

If our time on Earth was near
the end, comfort and
calmness was needed

—AMY O'BRIEN

Extensions for Movement

The images in Amy O'Brien's September 11 poem emerged slowly, and there were several cues for movement. A small group created a circular blanket, with arms working in tandem to indicate the weave. Then as they read the first stanza aloud, the group lowered their arms gently as if to cover three seated people. "Panic" gives the movement cue for the second stanza. The "blanket" group tightened the movement and pressed upward and outward into the room while the people in the center reacted to the word with jabs and thrusts. In the third stanza, the word "push" generates the movement idea, which is then resolved in the last stanza. The group returned to the "blanket" position, swaying from side to side in a circular, comforting movement.

SEPTEMBER 11 MADE ME FEEL

as patriotic as an American flag
flying on a windy spring day.
as sad and sorrowful as a tearful
daughter at her dying mother's bedside.

The commemoratory of a mourning nation,
together,
as one.

Not a sound to be heard but the
feel of a deep, piercing silence.

—MARY ANN MUROLO

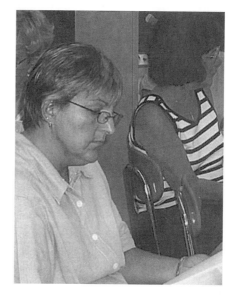

TAPS explore movement ideas.   TAPS begin committing
                                     their words and images to paper.

Extension for Movement and Music

Mary Ann Murolo's opening line is visual and rhythmical. A parade-like steady drum beat could accompany the group as they march in place in single file, waving mimed flags and speaking the two lines randomly, rhythmically, and repeatedly.

BEAT: •   •   •   •   •   •

As patriOtic as an aMERican   FLAG   FLYing on a WINdy spring DAY

The marching accompanied by speech could fade as a glissando is played on a resonant instrument, such as a metallophone. When the group's motion is quiet, the next line could slide under the music sounds leading to the "sorrowful" mood. The drum could then resume its steady beat, quietly at first, causing the group to begin to crescendo in movement, finally returning to a march, chanting the "commemoratory" line and coming together in one, arm-raised circle on "as one." A sudden cymbal crash could cause the group to freeze and a solo speaker/mover could say the last lines in wonderment, moving in and out of the frozen dancers.

SEPTEMBER 11 MADE ME FEEL

A single tear dropping from
an unwiped face—as the sorrow
of an individual waiting for
a loved one who will never
come.

—LINDA BETH BRONN

Extension with Melody

Linda Beth Bronn's poem could call for a beautiful ringing sound representing the "single tear," such as a triangle, a glockenspiel key, or a classroom bell played once after the word "tear." A melody sung in a minor pentatonic (such as E, G, A, B, D) would enhance the words, probably ending in an unresolved way (on B if the beginning tone is E, on A if the beginning tone is D) to correspond with the unresolved word meaning.

In order to encompass all of the contributions in an artistic and musical way, we taught the TAPS a song that we wrote (which could have been written by the TAPS) with Orff instrument accompaniment, and they rehearsed it. This then became the musical glue that held the entire class's rondo presentation together. In a rondo form, the main theme is always reiterated, with contrasting sections placed in between. Using this structure, the accompanied song became the A, or main theme, and the TAPS poems were read in series of four and became the contrasting sections.

J.A. Thomas/S.A. Katz

TAPS begin to experience
the language of movement.

SUMMARY

The TAPS workshop clearly revealed how vulnerable a person can feel when sharing his or her inner consciousness, but we hope that this TAPS catharsis allowed for the formation of connections and an awareness of common bonds. This sense that all people are connected suggests a burgeoning strength and offers the possibility of viable ways of coping together with shattering events that previously made us feel hapless. By experiencing this process, TAPS begin to visualize how they will adapt their own revelations for classroom application, guiding their students through the harsh landscape created by the terrorist attacks of September 11.

TAPS may then share the perception with their students that there is release through language as it unlocks the silence of static fear and anxiety. By speaking, through the forms of poetry, music, and movement, a person can conceptualize a nameless, shapeless thing, thus making it more emotionally manageable. This generic

Author/music facilitator demonstrates
an ostinato within extension piece.

way of healing, and the qualities inherent in self-expression through the arts, can be applied to any negative events.

Unhappily, violence in general has always filtered into the lives of children through media, in their neighborhoods, and even on their school playgrounds. The consequences of violent behavior, thoughts, and events must be confronted and defused. We hope that the silent, fearful words that gather behind the eyes of children can be released through the skillful hands of experienced teachers, and perhaps these words will lead us all to a place where we discover that which makes us unique and that which ultimately may unite us.

APPENDIX A: LESSONS

The purpose of an appendix is to offer pertinent, supplemental materials at the end of a chapter or book. It can also provide information that extrapolates concepts from the body of the work and transpose them into succinct, easily accessible applications. With this in mind, seven sample lessons are offered using a format that reveals adaptable, theme-transferable teacher templates with the first concept (adjectives) serving as the model for subsequent lessons. Under each goal, the scripted lesson shows the teacher asking questions, modeling skills, and guiding students. Possible answers, extensions, and notes to teachers appear in italics.

These lessons examine what the authors consider to be the foundations of poetry and extension. The goal is to reinforce student understanding and proficiency and to fortify teacher confidence in refining writing and communication skills and discovering extension possibilities. The lessons cover seven areas, each with a randomly chosen theme for illustration purposes:

1. Adjectives: "The Things I Love Best"

2. The Five Senses: "Holidays"

3. Metaphor: "Poetry Is"

4. Simile: "Before I Was Born"

5. Alliteration: "Guessing"

6. Onomatopoeia: "Storm/Weather"

7. Line Breaks: "The Places I Live"

It is important to note that in any of the lessons, teachers can supplant the theme with one that is pertinent to a particular curriculum need of their own.

Lesson I

ADJECTIVES: "THE THINGS I LOVE BEST"

GOALS

- Reinforce the importance of adjectives as part of effective imagery.
- Experiment with the use of adjectives through word collection.
- Study adjective model and extension.
- Create adjective-rich images and poetry.
- Apply layering through music and movement.

MOTIVATION AND ACTIVITIES

Reinforce

What is the definition of an adjective?

An adjective is a word that describes another.

What is the importance of adjectives in imagery?

Adjectives enrich the quality of images and provide clearer sensory word pictures.

In what ways do the following adjectives elucidate the imagery?

To see: The air shimmered like Aspen leaves in a mountain ravine.

To feel: The scalding sand seared bare feet.

To hear: Whimpering, the sad wind died off in the distance.

To smell: Flaring nostrils adored the scent of baking bread.

To taste: Hot apple pies and melting vanilla ice cream exclaim the end of a holiday dinner.

Emotion: Playful laughter tumbled about us like gold coins as the marionettes comically twirled for the children.

Where in the following lines could you add modifiers?

Seagulls are flying in the sky at the beach.

Black *and* **white** *seagulls are flying* **high** *in the* **cloud-speckled** *sky at the beach.*

The snow fell hard and heavy.

Fat, fluffy *snowflakes fell* **hard** *and* **heavy** *on our* **frosted** *mittens.*

The mountains rose in the distance like fingers reaching to embrace the clouds.

The **craggy** *mountains rose in the* **misty** *distance like* **ancient** *fingers reaching to embrace* **hovering** *clouds.*

In what way have we created brighter, more vivid word pictures by adding adjectives? Do they make the moment and the scene described in the lines easier to imagine and to visualize?

Do they deepen the meanings of the images? Can you give examples?

Can you see how, by adding adjectives, language is elevated to new levels, revealing not only the meanings of words, but the sounds of words and how they interact with one another?

Misty distance   *(alliteration)*
Comically twirled   *(animation)*
Whimpering wind   *(personification, alliteration)*

Experiment

Our topic today is "The Things I Love Best," so let's begin by suggesting subjects that reveal things that you love best and collecting adjectives that describe them.

Subjects	Adjectives
Beach	*Hot, sunny, soft, itchy, magical*
Puppies	*Soft, furry, adventurous, loving, cuddly*
Summer	*Fun, colorful, water-filled, fragrant, delicious*
Friends	*Caring, fun, special, loyal, sensitive, happy*
Wolves	*Elegant, faithful, secretive, playful, noble*

Now that we have collected our subject and adjective lists, let's take the subject and create imagery by adding selected adjectives.

Hypothetical Lines

1. *The hot, sunny beach is filled with magical, itchy sand.*
2. *Puppies are loving as kisses and soft, cuddly, fur-balls.*
3. *Colorful summer is fragrant flowers, delicious ice cream, and long, fun, water-filled days.*
4. *Special friends are caring nurses, loyal soldiers, and happy parties.*
5. *Elegant, secretive, noble wolves can be playful as kittens.*

Study

Before writing our own poems today, let's look at a model poem that uses adjectives to create images and explores the subject, "The Things I Love Best." *(Note: Present the poem as a handout, on the overhead projector, or on the board.)*

THE THINGS I LOVE BEST

I love sweet
morning breezes teasing
solemn trees, I love rounded
rainbows, purple, green, white,
red, blue, orange, flowering
wild wind, billowing
ballerinas in fragrant gardens
of roses; trees playing
their leaves like clear flutes and
clarinets.

I love half suns, red and restful
soft, quiet sunsets
stretching in slow
retreat to Asia, the serene
sound of Mother whispering
in my ear.

I love the satin of you
and the denim
of me.

—FIFTH GRADE

As we begin to look at this poem for extension, we need to discover its music and movement possibilities. What is the general mood of the poem?

Gentle, wistful, reflective, happy, contented

If you were to offer a sound that demonstrated the mood of the poem, would it be loud or soft?

> *Soft*

Do you feel the words of the poem would best be spoken or sung?

> *Either*

If spoken, how might we bring music into the poem?

> *As background*

Of the possible instruments available to you, which would you choose that could most effectively serve as a gentle, soft, unobtrusive backdrop to this poem?

> *Glockenspiels, metallophones, voice*

Extension Possibilities for the Model

This poem seems like it could simply ride over a short, soft melody, played as an enhancement to the words. It would be the challenge for the class to find those sets of sounds (key instrumental or vocal) that would best capture the soft and nostalgic quality of the poem.

Create

Using what we have discussed, and remembering that this particular poem needs to concern itself with the importance of adjectives in creating imagery, write a "The Things I Love Best' poem." *(Note: Following the writing and sharing of student poetry, have the group select one poem that they would like to extend.)*

Apply (Extension of Student-Selected Poem)

Let's analyze as a group this selected poem for music and movement possibilities considering mood; word rhythm; lines that might be repeated, spoken or sung in solo or group format; lines that might be moved; and in what ways. Might we use percussion instruments for an accompaniment (e.g., found sounds, body or small percussion), Orff instruments, or vocal song? Should there be an introduction or coda? When we have a final piece shaped and refined by your suggestions, shall we present it to another class or in assembly?

Lesson 2

The Five Senses: "Holidays"

GOALS

- Reinforce the importance of sensory imagery as part of creative writing.
- Experiment with the use of sensory imagery.
- Study sensory imagery models and extension.
- Create sensory-rich images and poetry.
- Apply layering through music and movement.

MOTIVATION AND ACTIVITIES

Reinforce

What are the five senses?

To see, to hear, to taste, to touch, and to smell

What is the importance of the senses in poetry?

The senses provide ways to present experiences, events, places, details, and visions, using all perceptive faculties in a universally understood, familiar language.

Does the use of one or more of the five senses help us become part of what is being described?

> *By appealing to the senses, we make connections that are familiar and also allow for the reader to exchange personal images, and thus become more a part of the experience. For example, in "the flavorful feast filled the air with sumptuous scents," the reader can personalize "flavorful feast" so that it becomes honeyed ham and yams, turkey and mashed potatoes, or pumpkin pie with whipped cream. "Sumptuous scents" can be the smell of chicken on the barbeque, bread baking in the oven, or a campfire cookout.*

How can we incorporate one or more of the senses in the following lines?

> I like holidays because they are fun.

> *I like the **home-baked taste** of holidays, **the sound of laughter,** and the **feel of hugs on doorsteps.***

> I like snow days when you wake to a white world.

> *I like the **snow-startling sight** of days when you wake to the **sound of shoveling** and the **scent of a lazy pancake breakfast, hot and maple-syrup sticky.***

> The Fourth of July is a festival of colors and sounds and celebrations.

> *The **firecracker** Fourth of July is a **rainbow festival of colors—red, white, and blue—sounds exploding in star-lit skies, fragrance of lingering smoke,** and the **fading tastes of picnic offerings.***

In what ways have we enriched the language of our images by adding the senses?

> *We have personalized, exposed details, sharpened the clarity, and made it possible to discover the common denominators that allow for greater empathy and understanding.*

Can you find examples in the above lines of sensory images that you related to? Can you create an image of your own using sensory imagery?

In what way have we created brighter, more vivid word pictures by adding adjectives? Do they make the moment and the scene described in the lines easier to imagine and to visualize?

Do they deepen the meanings of the images? Can you give examples?

Can you see how, by adding adjectives, language is elevated to new levels, revealing not only the meanings of words but also the sounds of words and how they interact with one another?

Experiment

Our topic today explores the senses, so let's begin by creating a list of sensory words that speak about our holiday memories and experiences. Ultimately, we will use these words to create a poem that incorporates the five senses.

Brief Hypothetical List of Sensory Words

1. *Fragrant (smell)*

2. *Warm (feel)*

3. *Scrumptious (taste)*

4. *Loud (hear)*

5. *Bright (see)*

Using these sensory words, let's create some images.

1. *Holidays are fragrant as cinnamon and cider.*

2. *Holidays are warm as fireside hugs.*

3. *Holidays are scrumptious as walnut banana bread.*

4. *Holidays are loud bells and laughter.*

5. *Holidays are bright as wind-blown confetti.*

Study

Before writing our own poems today, let's look at a model poem that uses the five senses to enrich images and subject matter. Today's subject is holidays. *(Note: Present the poem as a handout, on the overhead projector, or on the board.)*

HOLIDAYS

The fourth of July is raucous
as thunder, bright as swarms
of fireflies.

Thanksgiving is pumpkin-bread baking
pecan pie warmed with
melting ice cream puddling
on my plate.

Christmas is white
as snow cones, prickly
as pine cones, and soft
as brand new woolen mittens.

Holidays are home, fireside
friends, loud, luscious,
laughter.

—FIFTH GRADE

As we begin to look at this poem for extension, we need to discover its music and movement possibilities as it relates to sensory images. Going through each stanza, tell me which images are key to the verse.

First stanza: sound and sight

Second stanza: taste, smell, and sight

Third stanza: sight and touch

Fourth stanza: sound, taste, and emotion

Returning to the stanzas, select the sensory words that best lend themselves to movement, and then decide what quality of movement would seem most appropriate, such as slash, press, punch, glide, float, flick, or dab.

In the first stanza, punch and slash for "raucous / as thunder," flick and dab for "bright as swarms / of fireflies"

What instrumental sounds might support these phrases?

For thunder, drum and stamping. For fireflies, the triangle, finger bells, and sleigh bells

Do you envision a few or many people moving these phrases?

Could be either or a variety

Now we can explore the rest of the poem by asking ourselves these same questions for each of the other stanzas.

Extention Possibilities for the Model

Pace the reading of the poem to make time for the music and movement happening. Look for additional words that might inspire new movements (e.g., prickly, soft) and invite students to suggest other instruments to accompany these adjectives and verbs while moving the remainder of the poem.

Create

Based on class discussions and remembering that this particular poem is concerned with the importance of sensory imagery, write a holiday poem that draws from your own personal memories and experiences. *(Note: Following the writing and sharing of student poetry, have the group select one poem that they would like to extend.)*

Apply (Extension of Student-Selected Poem)

Let's analyze this selected poem for music and movement possibilities, considering mood, word rhythm, and whether it can be spoken or sung in solo or group format. Might percussion instruments, found sounds, body or small percussion, or Orff instruments be used for an accompaniment? Are there any lines especially worthy of repetition that might be used as an introduction or a coda? Might these lines also be set with a simple melody and sung? When we have a final piece shaped and refined by your suggestions, shall we present it to another class or in assembly?

Lesson 3

METAPHOR: "POETRY IS"

GOALS

- Reinforce the importance of metaphor as part of effective imagery.
- Experiment with the use of metaphor by creating word combinations.
- Study a metaphor model and extension.
- Create metaphor-rich images in poetry.
- Apply layering through music and movement.

MOTIVATION AND ACTIVITIES

Reinforce

What is the definition of a metaphor?

A metaphor is language that suggests a relationship between two distinctive identities without using the words "like" or "as."

What is the importance of metaphor in imagery?

Metaphors enrich language and offer unique views into individual perceptions.

In what ways do metaphors illustrate our ability to see resemblances between diverse things?

> *Making the connections between seemingly unrelated things sharpens our creative acuity and allows us to expand our imaginations to believe in the unbelievable. For example:*
>
> *The **ocean** was an undulating **scarf.***
>
> *The **river**, a sinewy **snake**, twisted and writhed through the countryside.*
>
> *The **tree** was a solid and stoic **soldier.***

How could you change the following lines to include or make a metaphor?

Poetry reminds me of bees buzzing in the petals of flowers.

> *Poetry **is** a bee buzzing in the petals of flowers.*

Poetry is like the music the wind plays to the trees.

> *Poetry **is** the music the wind plays to the trees.*

Poetry is like the startling colors of a sun setting behind a summer sea.

> *Poetry **is** the startling colors of a sun setting behind a summer sea.*

How does the addition of metaphor to the image strengthen it?

> *By making us aware of the connections between unlike things*

Using the examples, can you form new metaphors?

> *Poetry is a summer sea, painted red by the startling colors of a setting sun.*

Can you now create your own metaphors for poetry?

Experiment

Our topic today is "Poetry Is," so let's begin by creating a list of words to which we can compare poetry and ultimately create our own metaphors.

> *Brief Hypothetical List*
> 1. *Flowers*
> 2. *Tears*
> 3. *Love*
> 4. *Storms*
> 5. *Rainbows*
> 6. *Ice cream*

Let's experiment with these words and see if we can create metaphors.

> 1. *Poetry is a field of fragrant flowers.*
> 2. *Poetry is the salty taste of joyful tears.*

3. *Poetry is the loving, wet tongue of a puppy.*

4. *Poetry is the fist of a storm.*

5. *Poetry is a double grosgrain ribbon rainbow.*

6. *Poetry is a chocolate, strawberry, vanilla, hot-fudge sundae.*

Study

Before writing our own poems today, let's look at a model poem that will help us understand the role of metaphors in poetry. *(Note: Present the poem as a handout, on the overhead projector, or on the board.)*

POETRY IS

Poetry is
a meadow of fragrant flowers—
daisies, daffodils, dandelions
buttercups—joyful
and lively.

Poetry is
silk robes, satin sheets,
the wind whistling
like a gypsy rover.

Poetry is
sweet cider, hayrides,
and leaves spinning
in the mischievous wind.

Poetry is
quiet conversation,
a hand holding mine.

—6TH GRADE

As we begin to look at this poem for extension, we need to discover its form and music and movement potential. Do you notice similar beginnings in the stanzas?

Poetry is

How might we highlight these repetitions in a musical way?

Speak the first line two or three times or sing the line with a group-created or solo improvisatory melody.

In the first stanza, what is the predominant characteristic in the rhythms created by the words?

The rhythms are lively, dance-like, and leaping.

Can you speak the stanza in such a way that we feel a heartbeat?

     •   •   •   •

a MEADow of FRAGrant FLOWers (rest)

     •   •   •   •   •   •

DAIsies, DAffodils, DANdelions, BUTtercups, JOYful (rest)

     •

and LIVEly.

Can two groups speak this stanza in canon, the second beginning after the first, while a third group dances it?

Extension Possibilities for the Model

Beginning each stanza with some form of repetition, spoken or sung, focus on the word qualities and verbs for movement cues. For example, use glide, float, or press for "silk" and "satin" in the second stanza. Use glide for "wind whistling." In the second stanza, use slash, dab, or glide for "leaves spinning," and use changes of tempo, flick, or glide for "mischievous wind." On the final stanza, explore ways of bringing the group to a visual close, circular or otherwise, with the "quiet" of the stanza pervading, along with "hand holding mine." End with the repetition of "poetry is," spoken or sung.

Create

Using what we have discussed and keeping in mind that this particular poem emphasizes the metaphor for achieving powerful images, write a "Poetry Is" poem. *(Note: Following the writing and sharing of student poetry, have the group select one poem that they would like to extend.)*

Apply (Extension of Student-Selected Poem)

Let's view a selected poem as a group and look for music and movement possibilities. Taking into account the mood of the poem, its rhythms created by words and word combinations, lines that call for repetition (spoken or sung, in solo or group format), and words that inspire movement, how can we best bring this poem to life through extension? Let's consider also how to use accompaniment through musical instrumentation, body percussion, or found sounds as well as introductions and codas. When we have a final piece, shaped and refined by your suggestions, shall we present it to another class or in assembly?

Lesson 4

SIMILE: "BEFORE I WAS BORN"

GOALS

- Reinforce the importance of similes as part of effective imagery.
- Experiment with the use of similes through word collection and combinations.
- Study a simile model and extension.
- Create simile-rich images in poetry.
- Apply layering through music and movement.

MOTIVATION AND ACTIVITIES

Reinforce

What is the definition of a simile?

A simile is a poetic technique that draws a comparison between two things using the words "like" or "as."

What is the importance of simile in imagery?

Similes, like metaphors, create word pictures and make language memorable.

How could you change the following lines to include a simile?

Before I was born, the world was black.

*Before I was born, the world was **as black as an underground cave.***

The cat slept in the corner, curled in a ball.

*The cat slept in the corner, curled **like a ball of yarn.***

The parade came down the street, noisy and colorful.

*The parade came cascading down the street **like bright confetti, as noisy as a thunderstorm and as colorful as a box of crayons.***

How does the addition of a simile to an image make it more vivid?

It provides visual cues that grant us access to the scene.

How do similes turn everyday language into poetry?

By creating unique word pictures that make language memorable

Can you now create your own metaphors for poetry?

Experiment

Our topic today is "Before I Was Born," so let's begin by creating a list of words that can be used as the beginning of our similes.

Brief Hypothetical List
1. *Weary*
2. *Fresh*
3. *Cold*
4. *Crying*
5. *Falling*

Let's experiment with these words and create similes.

1. *Before I was born, I was as weary as a racehorse after a race.*
2. *Before I was born, my dreams were as fresh as dewdrops.*
3. *Before I was born, the world was a cold as a stone in a mountain stream.*
4. *Before I was born, wolves were crying like babies at the full moon.*
5. *Before I was born, the world was falling like rain through space.*

Study

Before writing our own poems, let's look at a model poem that is rich in simile. *(Note: Present the poem as a handout, on the overhead projector, or on the board.)*

BEFORE I WAS BORN

I was like a pony
sleeping in green fields,
quiet as an old, gray owl perched
on the beam of a falling-down barn.

I filled the air with the scent
of perfume and sounded like waves
crashing on white sandy beaches.

I was the taste of fresh
blueberry muffins and sticky
butterscotch candy.

I felt like the inside
of a glossy, wet
sea shell in a green
glass jar, smooth as a blade
of meadow grass, lucky
as a four-leaf clover.

—FOURTH GRADE

The pensive nature of this poem provides a good basis for musical reflection, such as when you make up or improvise a song. Listen to these five sounds: E, G, A, B, D. Using them, can the class make up a melody for the words in the first stanza, trying it at the same time?

Would one person volunteer to sing their musical ideas alone while another group plays an accompaniment of E and B on an instrument? Whoever sings this improvisation will do it differently each time.

Can we as a group decide on a melody for the title, "Before I Was Born," and sing this in between the verses?

Extension Possibilities for the Model

Look to expressive words that might call for accompanying sounds, instrumental or vocal, and add them over the words throughout the poem. Here are some examples:

- *Soft whinnies or barn owl hoots in the first stanza*
- *A rainstick or ocean drum sound effect in the second stanza*
- *A mark tree, bell tree, or metallophone improvisation in the third stanza*

Create

Using what we have discovered about similes and their importance in creating vivid and powerful imagery, write a "Before I Was Born" poem. *(Note: Following the writ-*

*ing and sharing of student poetry, have the group select one poem that they would like
to extend.)*

Apply (Extension of Student-Selected Poem)

Let's view a selected poem as a group and look for music and movement possibilities. Taking into account the mood of the poem, its rhythms created by words and
word combinations, lines that call for repetition (spoken or sung, in solo or group
format), and words that inspire movement, how can we best bring this poem to life
through extension? Let's consider also how to use accompaniment through musical
instrumentation, body percussion, or found sounds. Should there be an introduction
or a coda? When we have a final piece, shaped and refined by your suggestions,
shall we present it to another class or in assembly?

Lesson 5

ALLITERATION: "GUESSING"

GOALS

- Reinforce the significance of alliteration as part of effective poetry.
- Experiment with the use of alliteration.
- Study an alliteration model and extension.
- Create alliteration-rich images in poetry.
- Apply layering through music and movement.

MOTIVATION AND ACTIVITIES

Reinforce

What is the definition of alliteration?

Alliteration is the repetition of initial consonent sounds.

What is the importance of alliteration in a poem?

Alliteration provides rhythm and pleasant sound patterns that are fun to write, read, hear, and speak aloud.

In what ways does alliteration help create a mood in poetry?

The repetition of soft consonant sounds (e.g., w, s, l) creates a gentler mood, while the repetition of hard consonant sounds (e.g., t, p, k) creates a more intense, harsh mood.

How does alliteration create form in poetry?

> *When alliteration is consciously inserted into a poem in repetitive patterns, it can create a sense of form by bringing us back to reiterative sounds.*

What can you add to the following lines to make them sound alliterative?

The sky was dark.

> *The **silent, sullen sky** was filled with **dark, drab** clouds.*

The meadow was filled with flowers.

> *The **morning meadow**, awash in sunlight, revealed a **fiery field of flowers**.*

A sad face stood out among the happy crowd.

> *A **single silent** face among the happy crowd **screamed sadness**.*

Experiment

Our topic today is "Guessing," so let's collect some words that will lend themselves to alliteration and can be used as inspiration for the imagery in our poems.

> *Brief Hypothetical List*
> 1. *Whine*
> 2. *Deadly*
> 3. *Rumble*
> 4. *Glisten*
> 5. *Scamper*

Let's experiment with these words and create similes.

> 1. *A whine, a wheeze, a whimper (an old car's engine)*
> 2. *A dark and deadly silver shape darts beneath the waves (shark)*
> 3. *Raging thunder rumbled off into the distance of rain-drenched hills (a thunderstorm)*
> 4. *Gold-soaked, glistening, sun sips at drops of dew (a garden)*
> 5. *Scattered by wind, they scamper on air and settle in heaps (leaves)*

Study

Before writing our own poems, let's look at a model poem that presents a wealth of alliteration and offers us an opportunity to guess at its subject. *(Note: Present the poem as a handout, on the overhead projector, or on the board.)*

GUESSING

I am silent and salty,
a bully, a babe
smooth and rough I rumble
and rage. I scream
like an eagle, sing
sorrowful songs to seagulls. Let
the sun sink behind me
and welcome a rush
of wind-whipped
spray,
a new day.

—SUSAN A. KATZ

How many rhythmical ways can we read this ebullient poem? *(Suggest places to stop and keep a common heartbeat going under the various student rhythmical interpretations.)*

Having decided on one way to read it, can we vary vocal timbres by choosing certain people to read certain lines?

> *For example, "I am silent and salty" could be spoken as a solo by one student. Another student could do a solo for "a bully, a babe," and then the group could speak "smooth and rough I rumble / and rage."*

How shall we accompany this poem? Where do words stop and the accompaniment continue?

> *Patterns (ostinati) that are different than rhythms created by the words (complementary patterns) can be explored using body percussion and small instruments.*

Are there any lines in this poem that could serve as a complementary rhythm?

Extension Possibilities for the Model

Decide on instruments to play (body percussion, found sounds, or small percussion instruments) the group-selected word pattern that is serving as the accompaniment. Invent an introduction using this and other created patterns, and repeat this at the poem's conclusion as a coda.

Use a solo, a group, or a variety of solo voices for the reading to make a good vocal timbre contrast.

Explore places to pause in the reading, such as after "seagulls," where four heartbeats can be felt before the poem's resumption.

On a second reading, consider taking isolated alliterative words from the poem and use them as vocal ostinati (e.g., rough, rumble, rage [rest]).

Create

Remembering that we are exploring the lively nature of alliteration and how much it adds to poetry, write a "Guessing" poem that generously uses alliterative words and word combinations. *(Note: Following the writing and sharing of student poetry, have the group select one poem that they would like to extend.)*

Apply (Extension of Student-Selected Poem)

Let us analyze the selected poem for music and movement possibilities, considering alliterative qualities of the lines; mood; word rhythm; lines that might be repeated, spoken, or sung in group or solo format; or moved. Might we use percussion instruments for an accompaniment (found sounds, body percussion, or small percussion instruments), Orff instruments, or vocal song? Should there be an introduction or coda? When we have a final piece shaped and refined by your suggestions, shall we present it to another class or in assembly?

Lesson 6

ONOMATOPOEIA: "STORM/WEATHER"

GOALS

- Reinforce the special qualities that onomatopoeia brings to poetry.
- Experiment with the onomatopoetic characteristics of words and word combinations.
- Study an onomatopoeia model and extension.
- Create rich images and poetry using onomatopoeia.
- Apply layering through music and movement.

MOTIVATION AND ACTIVITIES

Reinforce

What is the definition of onomatopoeia?

Onomatopoeia describes words that sound like the thing or action they are describing, such as buzz or splatter.

What role does onomatopoeia play in poetry?

Words that sound like the thing or action they are representing, give greater definition to the meaning of the poem, add verbal energy, and provide lively extension possibilities.

In what ways does onomatopoeia make poetry more colorful and interesting to read?

> *It provides a sonic insight into the word and its meaning.*

What words with onomatopoetic qualities can you add to the following line?

Frosty snow fell through the long, slumbering night.

> *Frosty snow **tapped and scratched** at the window as it fell through the long, slumbering night.*

As night stalked into the forest, creatures foraged.

> *As night stalked **hissing** into the forest, creatures foraged, **screeched, and slithered.***

Fear filled the small room.

> *Fear, like **crackling** ice beneath one's feet, filled the small room as a rat **skittered** beneath the table.*

Experiment

Our topic today is "Storm/Weather," so begin by listing words that have onomatopoetic qualities that we can use in a poem we will write about a storm or some type of weather.

> *Brief Hypothetical List*
> 1. *Growl*
> 2. *Splatter*
> 3. *Crunch*
> 4. *Zoom*
> 5. *Screech*

Let's experiment with these words and see if we can create lines that might become part of a group poem.

> 1. *The storm growled like a leopard as it crept down the mountain.*
> 2. *Raindrops splattered and plopped in puddles on the muddy ground.*
> 3. *Yesterday's snow crunched like broken glass beneath my warm rubber boots.*
> 4. *Lightning zoomed across the black, velvet sky.*
> 5. *The wind was an owl screeching through the groaning, snow-weighted branches of the old apple tree.*

Study

Before writing our own poems, let's look at a model poem that illustrates the creative use of onomatopoeia. *(Note: Present the poem as a hand-out, on the overhead projector, or on the board.)*

STORMY WEATHER

Storms growl like leopards as they creep
down mountains, prowling
fields and meadows. Raindrops
splatter, plopping
in muddy puddles. Winter storms bring
whirling snow that crunches like broken
glass beneath warm, rubber boots.
Lightning zooms across black, velvet
skies and wild, wicked winds screech
through the snow-weighted, creaking,
groaning branches of the old apple tree.

—FIFTH GRADE

Let's discover ways in which we can extend the poem that will highlight and reinforce our use of onomatopoeia. Consider the images in the poem that invite movement, such as the leopards that "creep down mountains, prowling," for slow movements. Find other words that call for different movement, such as "splatter" and "plopping."

Discuss among yourselves how you want the words to be read. Might they be read by one reader or should some words be spoken by a group? Should there be pauses anywhere? Could instruments accompany the movements? Which ones?

Extension Possibilities for the Model

From an extension perspective, the onomatopoeic words in "Stormy Weather" add a richness of language and suggest movement. A group of "leopard dancers" could creep and prowl, using slow, pensive beginning movements and tempo, perhaps accompanied by a low drum roll and occasional cymbal tremolos. The drum might continue throughout the poem, varying its dynamics and tempi along with the pacing of the reading. As the "leopard dancers" freeze their action, another, more bumptious group of dancers might come from a contrasting direction using the words "splatter" and "plopping" as their movement impetus, accompanied by rain noises created by mouth sounds, claps, slaps on legs, and rattled paper. They might then also freeze. A third group depicting "winter storms" might emerge from the center to disperse and "whirl' throughout the leopard and raindrop groups, to the sound of a cymbal, freezing at the line "wicked winds screech." At that point, the reading of the poem might become slower, as all groups move in slow motion into shapes of gnarled, swaying, apple trees, punctuated by cymbal crescendo tremolos and ending in a freeze-frame tableau of trees, as the drum and cymbal fade. The poem could be read by one reader, with key words taken up by the groups and spoken randomly as they moved, or their movements could be done in between the words, accompanied by a drum and cymbal.

Create

Emphasizing words that have onomatopoetic qualities, write a poem using "Storm/Weather" as the subject. *(Note: Following the writing and sharing of student poetry, have the group select one poem that they would like to extend.)*

Apply (Extension of Student-Selected Poem)

In order to extend the selected poem, let's analyze it for music and movement possibilities. Let us consider mood; word rhythm; lines that might be repeated, spoken, or sung in solo or group format; or moved in various ways as we extend and enrich this poem. Might we use percussion instruments for an accompaniment (found sounds, body percussion, or small percussion instruments), Orff instruments, or vocal song? Should there be an introduction or coda? When we have a final piece shaped and refined by your suggestions, shall we present it to another class, or in assembly?

Lesson 7

LINE BREAKS: "THE PLACES I LIVE"

GOALS

- Reinforce the importance of line breaks as features of poetry.

- Experiment with the use of line breaks.

- Study line breaks in model and extension forms.

- Create line breaks that enrich the imagery and the poem.

- Apply layering through music and movement.

MOTIVATION AND ACTIVITIES

Reinforce

What is the definition of a line break?

A line break is the end of a line of poetry.

What purpose does the line break serve in poetry?

The line break helps to develop the poem's rhythm and dramatic intent. It often leaves an invisible question mark—an unanswered question—that the following lines address.

How does the line break affect the poem's meaning?

Where a line of poetry ends affects conceptual and dramatic pauses and influences the interpretation and understanding of a poem's intention.

Are there other ways in which line breaks influence the interpretation of a poem?

The placement of line breaks can emphasize or de-emphasize a word or word combination by placing it on a line of its own, breaking it in a distinctive or unusual way, or burying it within a long line. For example, the sentence "How silent the night seemed before it disappeared into the cacophony of dreams" could be broken in several ways:

> *How silent the night*
> *seemed before*
> *it disappeared into*
> *the cacophony of dreams.*

> *How silent*
> *the night*
> *seemed before it disappeared*
> *into the cacophony*
> *of dreams.*

> *How silent the night seemed before*
> *it disappeared*
> *into the cacophony of dreams.*

Where might we break the following lines in order to heighten dramatic impact and leave an unanswered question?

The city skyline stretched across the horizon like mountain peaks.

> *The city skyline stretched*
> *across the horizon*
> *like mountain peaks.*

> *The city*
> *skyline stretched across*
> *the horizon like mountain*
> *peaks.*

Captive cliffs embedded in ocean depths, worn, weary, disintegrating beneath rhythms of time and tempest.

> *Captive cliffs*
> *embedded in ocean depths,*
> *worn, weary, disintegrating beneath*
> *rhythms of time*
> *and tempest.*

> *Captive cliffs embedded*
> *in ocean depths, worn, weary, disintegrating*
> *beneath rhythms*
> *of time and tempest.*

Captive
cliffs embedded in ocean
depths, worn, weary,
disintegrating
beneath rhythms
of time
and tempest.

Experiment

Our topic today is "The Places I Live," so begin by listing words that might describe or relate to the places we live.

Brief Hypothetical List

1. *Busy*
2. *Crowded*
3. *Quiet*
4. *Lonely*
5. *Noisy*

Let's experiment with these words by creating lines of poetry, keeping the line break in mind.

1. *The busy city streets*   *(How did they look?)*
   looked like bustling   *(Like bustling what?)*
   beehives.

2. *People hurrying down*   *(Down what?)*
   crowded streets look like   *(Looked like what?)*
   rivers running to the sea.

3. *The farm at night is as quiet as*   *(Quiet as what?)*
   a secret.

4. *My hilltop house is*   *(What is it?)*
   lonely as a flower blossoming   *(Blossoming where?)*
   among a field of weeds.

5. *Taxis' horns hoot like*   *(What are they like?)*
   hunting owls, buses bark, and   *(What else?)*
   voices blend into a noisy   *(Noisy what?)*
   chorus of sound.

Study

Before writing, let's look at a poem that illustrates the creative use of line breaks. *(Note: Present the poem as a handout, on the overhead projector, or on the board.)*

THE PLACES I LIVE

I live in a busy town that buzzes
with people hurrying
down crowded streets, they look
like rivers running
to the sea.

I live in country quiet where
birds chirp and wind sings
secrets to the trees.

I live high on a hill where
the clouds sit
on my lonely roof and the sky
is brighter than blue.

I live in the city where
taxi horns hoot like
hunting owls, buses bark, and
voices blend into a noisy
chorus of sound.

—FOURTH GRADE

Let's try different readings of this poem, adding spaces of silence at the line's end to emphasize the breaks and using the created time to consider how the poem might make us move.

If we were going to use only voices and movement for the poem, how would we explore ways of solo and group movement and spoken word?

Let's experiment with some soundscapes that appear in the poem, such as "crowded streets." Can you think about what a city sounds like at rush hour and create a sound picture for this?

Extension Possibilities for the Model

This is a poem that lends itself to the effect of only movement, narration, and vocal sound effects without instrumentation. Students might start standing expressionless, equidistant from each other around the movement area. They might all speak "I live in a busy town that buzzes," and at the word "buzzes," begin to mechanically walk quickly in many directions, accompanied by busy vocal conversations and sounds, while the narrator speaks the other lines in the stanza over the melee. The group might resume the beginning shape and again speak as a group, "I live in country quiet where." At the word "where," each individual might move quickly into the shape and activity of either a bird, the wind, or a tree, as the narrator slowly reads the rest of the second stanza. Freezing at the stanza's end, one person might wander to the front to say, "I live high on a hill where / the clouds." At the word "clouds," the group might move in slow motion behind the mover/reader as the stanza is completed. Changing the gentle mood to strident, the whole group might then again loudly decry, "I live in the city where / taxi horns hoot like / hunting owls" and proceed to move in disjunctive, quick ways, accompanied by appropriate loud vocal honks and other urban sounds, as the narrator completes the final stanza. The group noise level on the stage might crescendo with city sounds and end with a strong movement gesture, signaling immediate quiet and a freeze pose.

Create

Thinking carefully about line breaks, write a poem about "The Places I Live." *(Note: Following the writing and sharing of student poetry, have the group select one poem that they would like to extend.)*

Apply (Extension of Student-Selected Poem)

In order to extend the selected poem, let's analyze it for music and movement possibilities. Let us consider line breaks; mood; word rhythm; lines that might be repeated, spoken, or sung in solo or group format or moved in various ways as we extend and enrich this poem. Might we use percussion instruments for an accompaniment (found sounds, body percussion, or small percussion instruments), Orff instruments, or vocal song? Should there be an introduction or coda? When we have a final piece shaped and refined by your suggestions, shall we present it to another class, or in assembly?

Conclusion

These germane lessons are the rainfall that feed the streams of reader imagination, flowing into swelling rivers of ideas and concepts that will ultimately become part of the "curriculum sea." The authors' intentions are that these compact lesson models will

- Provide outlines for ease of lesson application

- Reinforce essential concepts of poetry and extension through repetition

- Provide varied and unique perspectives for lesson planning

- Spark new and additional teacher/student ideas

- Illuminate new directions

The possibilities for idea development are endless, and it is implausible to provide a finite list. We tried several ideas and avenues of development that were successful but could not be included because of space limitations. Here are brief descriptions of some of these ideas.

COMPUTERS AS INDIVIDUAL TOOLS

We have used or seen other teachers successfully use computers in the following ways:

1. Word collecting using the thesaurus and dictionary

2. Creating imagery by finding word comparisons and collecting appropriate adjectives

3. Using existing or teacher-generated interactive programs to develop and enrich language skills

4.   Formatting and finalizing creative products

5.   Formatting music writing through existing programs such as *Coda* and *Finale,* when available

6.   Formatting movement ideas through icons and sketches in drawing programs

Although we embrace the concept of computers as essential teaching and learning tools, general classroom access to computers is often limited to no more than two or three stations. The necessity of students waiting their turn causes time lapse that can inhibit spontaneity, an essential part of the creative process. The impersonal nature of computers, as well, can place constraints on the joy that comes from ideas shared and reinvented through interpersonal dialogues. The most palpable creative experiences are emotionally charged exchanges, providing human validation, fundamentals that are absent from person-to-computer relationships.

Certainly some teachers have thorough knowledge of computers and skills that lead them to write interactive programs, use existing programs, and incorporate computer-generated lessons into their classrooms. We hope that some of those future lessons will be inspired by ideas found in this text.

MASTERWORKS AS INSPIRATION

We have often used masterworks in a variety of ways:

1.   Masterwork rhymed poem recreated by students into free verse poetry and then extended into music and movement

2.   Masterwork free verse poetry recreated into prose

3.   Masterwork prose recreated into free verse poetry and then extended into music and movement

4.   Masterwork art translated into narrative or free verse poetry and then extended into music and movement

5.   Masterwork music translated into free verse poetry and then extended into music and movement

The translation from masterwork creations to poetry is fairly straightforward and uses all of the skills students have learned about poetry writing and editing. In our experience, when using music as the impetus for writing poetry, it can be helpful to find selections with one predominant mood, such as in New Age music, which is composed primarily as background mood music. Choosing works with a single disposition helps focus student efforts and makes it easier for them to elucidate their ideas. When selected music presents a variety of tempi and dynamics, students need time to listen and process before writing and then listen a second time while word collecting (i.e., jotting down single words or brief word combinations) and documenting the kaleidoscope of personally perceived images, reactions, and emotional responses.

Another imaginative classroom challenge to listening/writing skills is to play nature environment sounds, such as bird calls, whale songs, waterfalls, jungle soundscapes, or wolf songs, and have students respond through poetry while actively listening.

ADDITIONAL THEMES FOR CONSIDERATION

1. "I" oriented poems, such as:

    "I Am"

    "I Was"

    "I Am Becoming"

    "I Seem to Be, But Really I Am"

    "I Used to Be, But Now I Am"

2. ABC Poem: Begin each line of the poem with a consecutive letter of the alphabet.

3. "The Things I Do and the Places I Go"

4. Simile Poem: Create a poem in which each line contains a simile.

5. Metaphor Poem: Create a poem in which each line contains a metaphor.

6. Alliteration Poem: Choose words for each line that have the same beginning consonant sounds to create imagery.

7. Nonsense Poem: Create poems that emphasize the imagery over the subject.

8. Personification Poem: Create a poem that gives human qualities to something.

9. Animation Poem: Create a poem that gives living qualities to a nonliving thing.

10. Onomatopoeia Poem: Create a poem using words in each line that sound like what they are in order to craft imagery.

APPENDIX B: GLOSSARY

Aeolian mode	From ancient Greek times, a minor mode arrangement named after the city of Aeolis around 1100 BCE. It ranges from A through A': A, B, C, D, E, F, G, A.
Accent	Emphasis of a particular syllable in speech or note in music.
Adjective	A word that describes a noun or pronoun (e.g., The *tall, stately* trees stood like *silent* soldiers).
Alliteration	The reiteration of initial consonant sounds (e.g., *T*owering *t*rees *t*rembled in the storm's fury).
Anacrusis	An upbeat.
Animation	To attribute living qualities to inanimate objects (e.g., The sword slept by his side). See also *personification.*
Artistic bonding	The bringing together of a variety of artistic elements—such as sculpture, painting, music, movement, and poetry—into a creative whole.
Beat	Equally spaced repetitive pulses.
Bloom's taxonomy	A theory of cognitive development in which knowledge and comprehension are thought to require the least amount of brain activity, and subsequent levels (application, analysis, synthesis and evaluation) are thought to demand commensurately more cognitive activity.
Body percussion	The act of creating rhythms using the body as drum (e.g., hand claps, finger clicks, leg slaps, foot stamps).
Bongo drum	Waist-high drum with a skin head. Of African origin and characterized by a deep tone. Part of the Orff instrumentarium.
Bordun	A simple harmony created by the root and 5th tones. C played with the left hand and G played with the right together is an example of a simple bordun.

Brainstorming	A process that encourages vocalization and lively dialogue between students and teacher, in a sharing of ideas and information.
Cabasa	A cylindrical instrument that is bead-covered and has a handle. It is played by twisting the palm of the hand around the instrument, creating a scraping sound. Part of the Orff instrumentarium.
Cacophony	A combination of many strident and discordant sounds happening simultaneously.
Cadence	Pertaining to rhythm, much like musical phrasing in that it provides shape and symmetry in the place of metrical patterns.
Canon	A musical application in which instruments, voices, rhythms, or movements perform the same sequence of notes, sounds, or movements one after the other.
Chant	A repeated phrase spoken rhythmically, usually by a large number of participants, sometimes using a simple singsong intonation.
Choreograph	In movement, to plan a series of steps or moves to always be repeated as agreed; in the creative classroom, the placement of various elements into a cohesive unit, such as accompanying a poem with music and movement.
Claves	A pair of wooden sticks. When played, one stick rests lightly in the left hand on top of curved fingers; the second is held in the right hand and used to strike the first, creating a sharp wooden sound.
Coda	In music, a concluding section that adds dramatic energy to the piece.
Complementary	In music, the enhancement of a rhythmic pattern or melody through contrast.
Compound meter	More than one group of beats within one meter: for example, 6/8 equals two groups of three beats (for a feeling of two) or three groups of two beats (for a feeling of three).
Contemporary poetry	Poetry that is of modern time and voice, specifically poetry written in the 1940s to the present time.
Contrast	The creation of something unexpected or different with sound, rhythm, texture, or imagery.
Crescendo	Italian word meaning to gradually get louder.
Cross-curricular teaching	A desirable approach to teaching that allows for the blurring of curriculum lines and suggests the relevance between subject matters.
Diminuendo	Italian word meaning to gradually get softer.

Do pentatonic	A major 5-toned mode built on the first step of a scale with a major 3rf as the third tone. For example, built on C, it would be C, D, E, G, A. Built on G, it would be G, A, B, D, E.
Dorian mode	Named after Doric, a dialect of ancient Greece, a minor mode with the characteristic of a raised 6th tone, giving it a sweet sound and spanning D to D': D, E, F, G, A, B, C, D.
Double bell	A large and small bell joined vertically by a handle that produces a loud, metallic clanging sound. Often leads ensembles.
Downbeat	The first and heaviest beat of a measure.
Disjunct melody	A melody with an irregular and radical contour, containing sudden ups and downs.
Duple meter	Comprising two beats to a bar or measure.
Dynamics	In music, loudness or softness. *Forte (f)* is loud. *Piano (p)* is soft. *Pianissimo (pp)* is very soft. *Fortissimo (ff)* is very loud. *Mezzo (m)* is medium.
Echoing	A rote technique of teaching in which students copy the facilitator.
Editing	The application to one's poem of learned poetic techniques and skills in order to improve the quality of the creative effort.
End rhyme	Traditional rhyme patterns that appear at the end of lines, in any structured pattern.
Enjambment	The breaking of a line in the middle of a phrase or thought to enhance or change the meaning (e.g., Her mind sang / in harmony with the breeze // Her mind sang / angrily accompanied by the wind)
Evocative teaching	In the creative classroom, a format with equally weighted, creative interaction between teacher and students.
Extension	In poetry, enlargement of the image through the use of detail and poetic skills; multiple layering of written work, music, movement, performance.
Facilitator (teacher as)	Taking poetic, musical, or movement ideas offered by students and directing them toward completion.
Feeling words	Words that suggest or imply emotional connections.
Fermata	A musical symbol represented by an arch with a dot under it that tells one to hold a note, chord, or pause longer than the note it is over indicates.
Finger cymbals	Small cymbals that make a pleasant ringing sound when the edges are struck lightly together.

Five senses	Awareness of anything through the use of visual, auditory, tactile, olfactory, and taste perception.
Fixing the poem	The point at which a student poet claims permanent responsibility for their creative work through sharing, extension, or performance.
Form	The structure, design, or arrangement of a piece of music. In poetry, the composition or organization of a poem through line, stanza, and metrical considerations. The application of definitive shape and emotional vitality through the use of poetic techniques and skills.
Found sounds	The use of random objects as musical instruments to create sounds, such as a ruler tapping on a desk or paper clips rattling in a plastic container.
Free verse	A form of poetry that does not adhere to the rules of metrical or classical verse. It depends on a sensitivity to cadence (for writer and reader).
Geode	A rough, sphere-shaped rock with crystal formations lining a hollow center.
Gestalt	A German word meaning various elements that compose a whole, amounting to more than the sum of its parts.
Glockenspiel (student model)	Tuned metal bars (C–A') set over a resonator box, which, when struck by a mallet, produce resonating tones that decay quickly. Part of the Orff instrumentarium and available in two ranges: alto and soprano.
Graphics	Any art design, particularly contemporary, that can easily be translated to sound or movement.
Hand drum	A frame drum held in the hand, with a plastic or skin head.
Harmony	In music, any notes that are sung or played at the same time; also the supporting musical chords of a piece.
Image	The intimate and evocative description of a particular thing; an appeal to the senses through the use of descriptive language, metaphor, or simile.
Improvisation	Spontaneous creation in music, movement, and speech.
Inflection	In music, a change in the pitch or tone of voice. In poetry, the subtle change of meaning through emphasis or tense.
Interlude	A connective space (spoken, musical, or movement) between larger sections of music/poetry/movement.
Internal rhyme	A rhyme that appears within the body of the poem (e.g., She moved like *light* across / the ebony landscape of the *night* // She moved like *light* across / the *night,* ethereal as a song).

Introduction	In music and movement, that which begins the piece.
La pentatonic	The minor 5-tone scale, related to the major do on C and beginning with a minor third: A, C, D, E, G.
Layering	To apply one texture on top of another as with voice or instrumentation.
Line	A delineated arrangement of words.
Line break	The end of a line of poetry, often containing a dramatic implication or an unanswered question that the next line addresses (e.g., Dreams as big as laughter / spilled off the page and ran / like a river around the room). Line breaks can also be based on visual considerations (how the poem looks on a page) or determined by the natural pause taken for breath when read aloud.
Lydian mode	Relating to ancient Lydia in Greece, this major mode is characterized by its raised fourth tone, giving it a magical quality: F, G, A, **B,** C, D, E, F.
Major third	An interval made up of four half steps that determine it as a major mode when appearing at the beginning of a scale.
Maraca	A gourd-shaped, hollow, handheld instrument filled with seeds or gravel that makes a coarse scratching sound when shaken.
Mark tree (chime tree)	Seventeen or more 1/8" tubes or keys suspended on a frame that make nontonal, "magical" sounds when stroked. Part of the Orff instrumentarium.
Melody	A unit of notes that form a phrase, usually possessing a distinct rhythm.
Melodic ostinato	A short melody idea that is repeated over and over.
Melodic shape	The contour of a melody, and the rise and fall perceived when the note heads are connected by a line.
Metallophone	Tuned metal bars (C–A') set over a resonator box. When struck by a mallet, the bars produce a resonating tone that is sustained. Part of the Orff instrumentarium and available in three ranges: soprano, alto, and bass.
Metaphor	Language that suggests a relationship between two distinctive identities without using the words *like* or *as* (e.g., The *trees* were silent *soldiers* guarding the gate).
Meter	In poetry, a regular rhythm created by stressed and unstressed syllables, duration of line, and possible rhyme application. The relationship between the imposed scheme and the rhythms of natural speech. In music, beat patterns that combine to create rhythms.

Minor third	An interval made up of three half-steps that determines it as a minor mode when appearing at the beginning of a scale.
Modeling	In education, demonstrating a skill or a task with the hope of inspiring creative imitation.
Narrative poem	A poem that tells a story or gives an account of an event.
Nonmetered speech	Free speech with no metrical considerations.
Nuance	The infinite and varied differences of inference, feeling, color, and tone, implying subtle shades of meaning.
Octave	An interval between two notes comprising 8 tones (inclusive), such as from low C to high C.
Onomatopoeia	Words that sound like the thing or action they are representing, such as *buzz* and *splatter.*
Orff instrumentarium	Set of instruments developed by Carl Orff for use with young children and based on world instruments; see entries for *cabasa, congo drum, double bell, glockenspiel, hand drum, maraca, metallophone, recorder, triangle,* and *xylophone*
Ostinato	In music, a pattern that can be rhythmical, melodic, or harmonic. The plural form is *ostinati.*
Pacing	The quality of acuity in teaching that understands the importance of flow (speeding up a lesson or allowing it to move slowly) in order to achieve the greatest degree of creative and educational potential.
Patsch	German word for to slap, as on one's legs with hands to create a sound.
Pattern	Any repetitive order.
Personification	To attribute human qualities to something that is not human (e.g., the sun stretched out its arms across the horizon before sinking from sight).
Phrase	In music, a series of notes that form a unit of melody within a piece of music. In poetry, words that combine to create meaning, rhythms, and form.
Pitch	The level of a sound in a scale, defined by its frequency.
Prose	The natural flow of the spoken language in written form.
Pulse	A regular beat, as with the heart.
Rap	A form of popular music characterized by spoken or chanted lyrics accompanied by syncopated, rhythmic beats.
Recitative	Dialogue that is sung, as in operatic form.

Recorder	A wind instrument requiring no embouchure to play with a two-octave range (C–CC) (The alto recorder is an instrument with a transposed range of F–FF). Use of the recorder dates to the 13th century. Part of the Orff instrumentarium.
Repertoire	The collective material with which one is familiar in a specific body of arts; that which one is prepared to perform.
Rest	In music, a pause or silence.
Revision	A draft of a poem derived from the application of editing techniques and skills.
Rhythm	In music, the pattern of beats or pulse; in poetry, stressed and unstressed syllables; also the word flow created by a line break.
Rondo	A musical form wherein the first part reoccurs throughout, with contrasting sections interspersed in between: A, B, A, C, A.
Round	A song sung by two or more groups wherein each person sings a different part of the song at the same time.
Sensory perception	An awareness of one's surroundings through the five senses.
Simile	A poetic technique that draws a comparison between two things using the word *like* or *as* (e.g., The trees were *like* silent soldiers guarding the gate).
Slant rhyme	A rhyme suggested by two words that do not, in fact, rhyme exactly (e.g., Silent and *chill* / the snow *fell*).
Solo	Going it alone.
Sound duration	How long a tone lasts before it decays. For example, xylophones have a short sound duration, metallophones a long duration.
Soundscape	A vocal or instrumental backdrop created to enhance the spoken word.
Stanza	The division of a poem through the grouping of lines.
Synthesis	The compatible joining of multiple ideas and forms.
Tempo	Speed.
Texture	The layering of different musical components to create a variety of thick and thin effects.
Timbre	The quality and color of a vocal or instrumental sound. For example, the tuba's timbre is brown or black, the flute's pink or yellow.
Triangle	Metal, triangle-shaped instrument that produces a ringing sound when struck by a metal rod.

Trouble shooting	Detecting problems that are likely to occur in the classroom and planning affirmative and constructive strategies.
Upbeat	An unaccented beat, especially the last one in a measure bar.
Vocal sounds	Sounds created in the mouth: plosive *(p, b)*, affricate *(ch)*, continuant *(m, n)*, lip pops, tongue rolling, and glottal *(h)* sounds.
Xylophone (student model)	Tuned wooden bars (C–A") over a resonator box that produce a nonresonating tone when struck by a mallet. Part of the Orff instrumentarium and available in three ranges: soprano, alto, and bass.

APPENDIX C:
ADDITIONAL RESOURCES

Following is a list of books representing a variety of classroom possibilities for poetry, music, and movement enrichment that the authors have used and found inspirational over the years.

THE RATIONALE FOR CREATIVE TEACHING AND LEARNING

Eisner, E.W. (1972). *Educating artistic vision.* New York: Macmillan.
Eisner, E.W. (1994). *Cognition and curriculum reconsidered* (2nd ed.). New York: Teachers College Press.
Eisner, E.W. (1995). *The enlightened eye: Qualitative inquiry and the enhancement of educational practice.* Upper Saddle River, NJ: Merrill.
Eisner, E.W. (1998). *The kind of schools we need: Personal essays.* Portsmouth, NH: Heinemann.
Levine, M. (2002). *A mind at a time.* New York: Simon and Schuster.
Singer, D.G. (1993). *Playing for their lives: Helping troubled children through play therapy.* New York: The Free Press.
Singer, D.G., & Singer, J.L. (2001). *Make believe: Games and activities for imaginative play. A book for parents, teachers, and the young children in their lives.* Washington, DC: Magination Press.

PERCEPTIVE POSSIBILITIES

These are good reference books for teachers who want to introduce new ideas and possibilities into the classroom in terms of creative curriculum expansion and who want to encourage students to look at the familiar in new ways.

Applegate, M. (1965). *When the teacher says, "Write a poem."* New York: Harper & Row.
Bagley, M.T., & Hess, K.K. (1984). *200 ways of using imagery in the classroom.* New York: Trillium Press.
Gensler, K., & Nyhart, N. (1978). *The poetry connection: An anthology of contemporary poems with ideas to stimulate children's writing.* New York: Teachers and Writers Collaborative.
Leff, H.L. (1985). *Playful perception: Choosing how to experience your world.* Burlington, VT: Waterfront Books.

Murphy, R. (1974). *Imaginary worlds: Notes on a new curriculum.* New York: Teachers and Writers Collaborative.

Wallace, R. (1982). *Writing poems.* Boston: Little, Brown and Co.

Walsh, C. (1962). *Doors into poetry.* Englewood Cliffs, NJ: Prentice-Hall.

Wendt, I. (1983). *Starting with little things: A guide to writing poetry in the classroom.* Salem: Oregon Arts Foundation.

Zavatsky, B., & Padgett, R. (Eds.). *The whole word catalogue II.* New York: McGraw-Hill Paperbacks, Teachers and Writers Collaborative.

MOVEMENT

The following books give the teacher excellent movement vocabulary for evoking interesting, expressive, and varied movements from students. They deal with words that prompt movement and with movement qualities, time, weight, and space.

Gray, V., & Percival, R. (1962). *Music, movement, and mime for children.* London: Oxford University Press.

Laban, R. (1963). *Modern educational dance.* London: MacDonald & Evans.

Mettler, B. (1960). *Materials of dance as a creative art activity.* Tucson, AZ: Mettler Studios.

ORFF-SCHULWERK PHILOSOPHY AND HISTORY

The following autobiography by Carl Orff covers those years in which the Schulwerk was developed.

Orff, C. (1970). *Das Schulwerk.* New York: Associated Music Publishers.

CHILDREN'S ORIGINAL WORK

These books may be helpful in providing teacher focus on expansion themes and may provide valuable examples from which students may be able to depart.

Benig, I. (Ed.). (1971). *The children: Poems and prose from Bedford-Stuyvesant.* New York: Grove Press.

Community School District 6. (1977). *It is time for the trees to get big in spring* (project). New York: Author, The Arts in General Education Program. Available from the Bureau of Curriculum Development, 665 West 182nd Street, New York, NY 10033

Community School District 6. (1978). *I caught a snowflake in my hand: Poems and prose by the children of District 6.* New York: Author, with The Academically Gifted Child Program. Available from the Bureau of Curriculum Development, 665 West 182nd Street, New York, NY 10033

Forever is a carousel: An anthology of children's poetry from the Gateway District 22. (1979). New York: Author. Available through the Community Superintendent, 2525 Haring Street, Brooklyn, NY 11235

Koch, K., & students of Public School 61. (1970). *Wishes, lies and dreams: Teaching children to write poetry.* New York: Vintage Books.

Rose, where did you get that red? Teaching great poetry to children. (1974). New York: Vintage Books.

EVOCATIVE TEACHING

This section offers books that present teaching registers and ideas for innovative interpretation through drama and improvisation.

Boal, A. (2001). *Games for actors and nonactors* (8th ed., A. Jackson, trans.) London: Routledge.

Bolton, G., & Heathcote, D. (1999). *So you want to use role play? A new approach on how to plan.* London: Trentham Books.

Johnson, L., & O'Neill, C. (Eds.). (1984). *Dorothy Heathcote: Collected writings on education and drama.* London: Hutchinson & Co.

Johnstone, K. (1992). *Improv: Improvisation and the theatre.* New York: Routledge.

REFLECTING ON MASTERWORK POETRY

The following books may prove helpful in providing threads from masterwork poetry that might be woven into the fabric of teaching. These books also familiarize teachers with the kinds of contemporary writing they hope to elicit from students.

Altenbernd, L., & Lewis, L.L. (1975). *Introduction to literature: Poems* (3rd ed.). New York: Macmillan.

Ellmann, R., & O'Clair, R. (Eds.). (1973). *Modern poems: An introduction to poetry.* New York: W.W. Norton.

Kostelanetz, R. (Ed.). (1970). *Possibilities of poetry: An anthology of American contemporaries.* New York: Dell Publishing.

Littell, J. (Ed.). (1979). *Poetry lives.* Evanston, IL: McDougall, Littell and Co.

Moffi, L. (Ed.). (1982). *Intro 13.* Norfolk, VA: The Associated Writing Programs.

van den Heuvel, C. (Ed.). (1974). *The haiku anthology: English language haiku by contemporary American and Canadian poets.* Garden City, NY: Anchor Books.

Williams, M. (Ed.). (1973). *Contemporary poetry in America.* New York: Random House.

GESTALT

The following books cross lines: Some use classical works, some use contemporary works, and some use a combination of the two. Some offer ideas and suggestions for how to interpret and use poetry, and some discuss masterwork poets, analyzing their works and contributions.

Hunter, J.P., Booth, A., & Mays, K.J. (Eds.). (2002). *The Norton introduction to poetry* (8th ed.). New York: W.W. Norton.

Kennedy, X.J. (1974). *An introduction to poetry* (3rd ed.). Boston: Little, Brown and Co.

Packard, W. (Ed.). (1987). *The poet's craft: Interviews from the "New York Quarterly."* New York: Paragon House Publishers.

Poulin, A. (Ed.). (1996). *Contemporary American poetry.* Boston: Houghton Mifflin.

Riding, L., & Graves, R. (1971). *A survey of modernist poetry.* Folcroft, PA: Folcroft Library Editions.

Shawcross, J.T., & Lapidas, F.R. (1972). *Poetry and its conventions: An anthology examining poetic forms and themes.* New York: The Free Press.

REFERENCE BOOKS

These books help to standardize the definitions of poetic form. They also deal with vocabulary, grammar, punctuation, poetic terms, elements of literature, and writing techniques.

Bernstein, T.M. (1965). *The careful writer: A modern guide to English usage.* New York: Atheneum.

Brittain, R. (1981). *A pocket guide to correct punctuation.* Woodbury, NY: Barrons Educational Series.

Deutsch, B. (1974). *Poetry handbook: A dictionary of terms* (4th ed.). New York: Barnes and Noble Books.

Foley, S.M., & Gordon, J.W. (1986). *Conventions and choices: A brief book of style and usage.* Lexington, MA: D.C. Heath and Co.

Freeman, M.S. (1983). *A treasury for word lovers.* Philadelphia: Institute for Scientific Information Press.

Garner, B.A. (1998). *A dictionary of modern American usage.* New York: Oxford University Press.

Hacker, D. (2002). *A writer's reference* (5th ed.). New York: St. Martin's Press.

Johnson, E.D. (1982). *The handbook of good English.* New York: Facts on File Publications.

Lewis, N. (1975). *Word power made easy.* New York: Pocketbooks.

Scholas, R., Klaus, C.H., & Silverman, M. (1978). *Elements of literature.* New York: Oxford University Press.

Sisson, A.F. (1966). *Word and expression locater.* West Nyack, NY: Parker Publishing.

Turco, L. (2000). *The new book of forms: A handbook of poetics* (3rd ed.). Lebanon, NH: University Press of New England.

Williams, M. (1986). *Patterns of poetry: An encyclopedia of forms.* Baton Rouge: Louisiana State University Press.

Zinsser, W. (1985). *On writing well: An informal guide to writing nonfiction* (3rd ed.). New York: Harper & Row.

SOUND SOURCES

The following compact discs are useful classroom tools for building imagery through aural stimuli and enriching the classroom experience through sound examples that may be used as points of departure. This brief list reflects successful "listening" lessons used by the authors and can be richly augmented by and searching any online book or music seller for the following categories: nature songs/sounds, whale songs, bird songs, New Age music, environmental and ecological sounds, Native American music, and so forth.

Baldwin, R.W. (1993). *Jazz wolf* [CD]. Chanhassen, MN: NorthWord Press.

Creation's Journey: Native American Music [CD]. (1994). Washington, DC: Smithsonian Folkways.

Hempton, G. (1989). *Ebb and flow* [CD]. New York: Miramar.

Hempton, G. (1990). *Tennessee nightwalk* [CD]. New York: Miramar.

Taliesin Orchestra. (1996). *Orinoko flow: The music of Enya* [CD]. New York: Intersound Records.

Winter, P. (1991). *Canyon* [CD]. Litchfield, CT: Living Music.

Winter, P. (2001). *Canyon lullaby* [CD]. Litchfield, CT: Living Music.

Winter, P. (1989). *Common ground* [CD]. Litchfield, CT: Living Music.

Winter, P. (1989). *Icarus* [CD]. New York: Sony.

Winter, P. (1989). *Journey with the sun* [CD]. New York: Sony.

Payne, R. (1992). *Songs of the humpback whale* [CD]. Litchfield, CT: Living Music.

INDEX